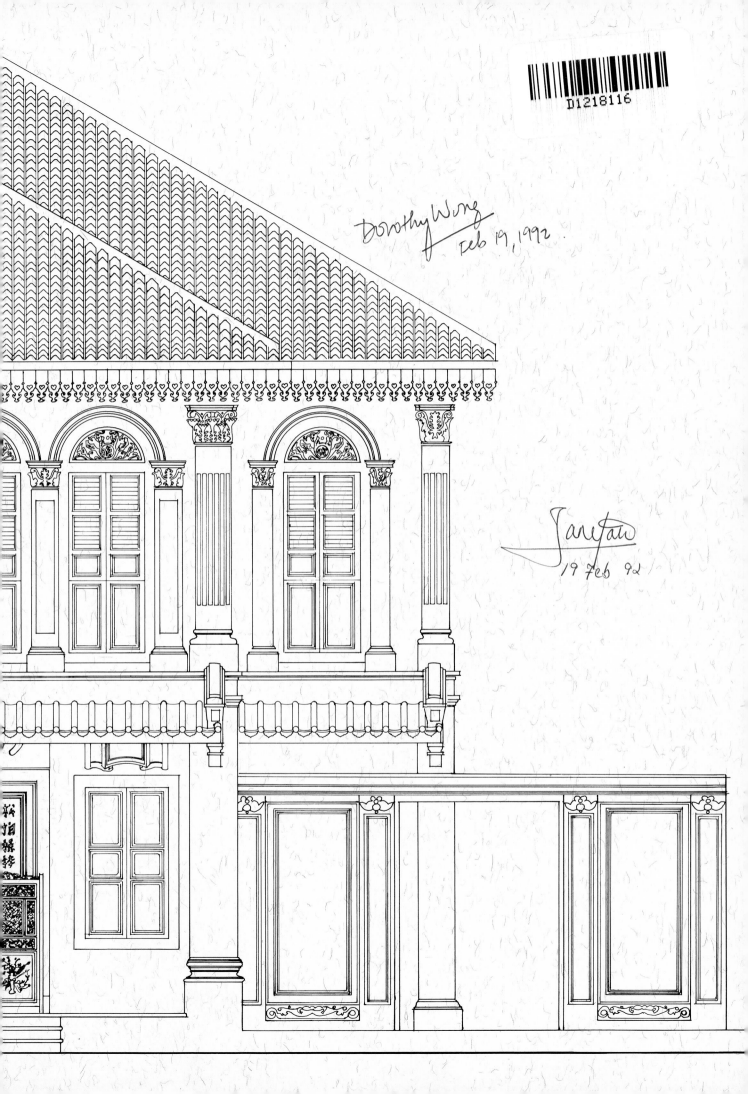

Dorothy Wong
Feb 19, 1992.

Jane Fan
19 Feb 92

THE SINGAPORE HOUSE

1819~1942

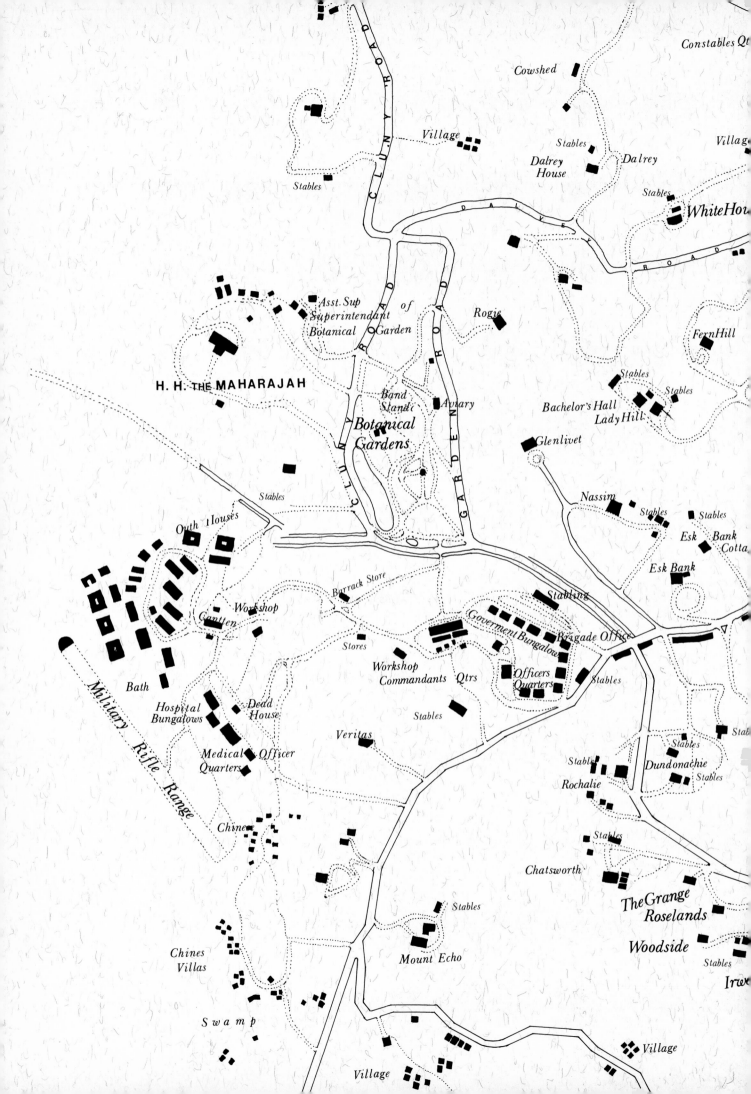

THE SINGAPORE HOUSE

H·O·U·S·E

1819~1942

by

Lee Kip Lin

Edited by Gretchen Liu

Designed by Kathleen Lau

TIMES EDITIONS

PRESERVATION OF MONUMENTS BOARD

To Peng Hui, Pek Yen and the younger generation.

A Note to the Reader
Because all of the houses discussed in this book were built
prior to the use of the metric system, measurements are given
in feet and inches throughout.
To avoid confusion over terms relating to floor levels the
standard terms used are "ground floor" and "first floor".
Finally, the dating of houses relies mainly on the information contained in the original building plans. It is therefore assumed, in the absence of other information, that the houses
were constructed reasonably close to the dates on the plans.

The Singapore House, 1819-1942
© Times Editions, 1988
Times Centre
1 New Industrial Road
Singapore 1953

© text Lee Kip Lin

Photography and copy work by Lee Kip Lin, Ho Yue Weng,
Whang Tar Kway, Eugel Yeo, Mr Joseph Soh
and Mr Lee Chee Kheong

Typeset in Goudy by Superskill Graphics, Singapore
Colour separation by Far East Offset, Kuala Lumpur
Printed in Singapore by Tien Wah Press

ISBN 981-204-023-4

Cover and Frontispiece: Hand-tinted photograph of a
Singapore house circa 1920, location unknown.
Endpapers: Measured drawing of the house of
Madam Teo Hong Beng at Kerbau Road,
built in 1905 and still standing.
Title page: Detail of a map of Singapore in 1881 showing
residences in Tanglin and Claymore.
Pages 8-9: Interior elegance. The living room of Panglima
Prang photographed in June of 1971,
before the house was demolished.
Pages 10-11: Seaside charm. Choa Kim Keat's bungalow in
Katong painted by Low Kway Soo in 1928.
Pages 12-13: Life at Rosedale. A page from the album of the
Chia family shows the house as a backdrop to
everyday life in the 1930s.
Pages 14-15 and 142-143: Two interior views of Grasslands
from an album inscribed: "Photographs taken by Dr Chia
Boon Leong during the wedding of Mr Tay Wee Soon to
Miss Chia Gay Lian Neo on 24th January, 1927 at
"Grasslands" No. 8 St Thomas Walk, Singapore." The first
picture is inscribed "Side view of drawing room (portico)"
and the second ""Bridal Chamber".
Pages 226-227 Verandah in Penang circa 1910.

CONTENTS

PART I   THE HISTORY

PART II THE ALBUM

PART III APPENDICES

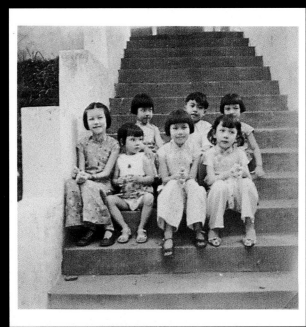

THE

HISTORY

~

1.1 View of the town by Lt Philip Jackson dated June 5, 1823.
The height of Bukit Larangan, in the centre of the drawing,
has been exaggerated. Raffles' house is on the hill while the
shore is lined with what appear to be timber and attap houses.
1.2 This detail from Jackson's drawing (opposite) shows the
house of Francis Bernard, the police superintendent. It is
obviously in timber and the high pitched roof appears to be
covered in thatch.

The First Years

1819-1829

Singapore's modern history began when Stamford Raffles landed on January 29, 1819 to establish a British trading factory. A survey, conducted by Captain Daniel Ross the same month, identified only two villages along the entire coastline from Tanjong Pagar to the "red cliffs" at Tanah Merah — the Temenggong's village near the mouth of the Singapore River and a village at Kampong Glam. Other settlements, both Malay and *orang laut*, were later discovered along the periphery of the island in Kallang, Geylang, Serangoon, Punggol, Seletar and Kranji, and a large settlement of *orang laut* at Keppel harbour.

Inland, apart from the 20 Chinese gambier plantations on the hills close by the future town, the island was uninhabited virgin jungle. "The whole of the country as you well know on our first arrival presented nothing but one vast forest of the largest and most impenetrable kind" wrote the first Resident, Lieutenant-Colonel William Farquhar, in 1821. An agreement was reached between Raffles and Sultan Hussein and the trading factory formally established on February 6, 1819. The next day, Raffles left and the British began to organise their cantonment on the only open ground, between the Singapore River and the present Stamford Canal.

Raffles did not spend much time in Singapore yet he played a vital role in the planning of the settlement. On his second visit, from May 31 to June 28, 1819, he formulated his plan to divide the town into communal neighbourhoods or "Campongs". The Europeans were to reside in the Beach Road area, between Stamford Canal and Arab Street; the Chinese were to be located south of the Singapore River; and the followers of the Temenggong, the local chieftain, and other Malays were to be moved to the upper reaches of the river. Land on the north

bank of the Singapore River was also set aside for use by the government. In June of 1819, shortly before his departure, Raffles declared with great satisfaction to his superiors in the East India Company that Singapore's population exceeded 5,000 souls and "an extensive China Town has been marked out on the opposite side of the River and the Bugginese have established themselves in considerable numbers on the margin of the Eastern Bay near which His Highness the Sultan has also fixed his residence."

By March of 1822, Farquhar marvelled that merchants "of all descriptions" were "collecting so fast that nothing is heard in the shape of complaint but the want of more ground to build upon. The swampy ground on the opposite side of the River is now almost covered with Chinese houses and the Bugis Village is becoming an extensive town." Already over 15 miles of roads had been laid, including High Street, Hill Street, North Bridge Road, Beach Road as well as the roads around Fort Canning and Mount Sophia and about two miles of road in Chinatown and Telok Ayer.

The European merchants, however, found the Beach Road area allocated to them by Raffles unsuitable for landing goods from ships because of the continual surf. The north bank of the Singapore River suited their purpose best, compared to the opposite bank where the land was low, swampy and subject to constant flooding. When Raffles returned on October 10, 1822 for his nine-month final visit, he found to his annoyance that Farquhar had allowed merchants to occupy the more suitable north bank and Reserved Plain. He acted quickly, planning a major reorganisation of the town and forming a committee to oversee its implementation. Lieutenant Philip Jackson was appointed executive engineer and placed in charge of public works, a position he held

1.3 Singapore from Government Hill circa 1823-1824. The
two parallel roads to the sea are Bras Basah Road and High
Street. The road connecting the two and running behind the
tall tree in the centre is possibly St Andrew's Road. The
Esplanade has several houses on it. The buildings, as in
Jackson's sketch, appear to be temporary timber structures.

1.4 Two early Penang houses drawn by James Wathen. The house on the left is Ah Mee's and on the right is Dr McKinnon's.

until his early retirement due to ill-health in 1827. George Drumgoole Coleman, an architect living in Batavia who would soon move to Singapore and play an important role in the fledgling settlement, was also consulted.

Raffles then issued his well-known Instructions of November 4, 1822. He now proposed forming a commercial centre south of the river by levelling a hillock and clearing, filling and draining the marshlands. A Chuliah or Indian Campong was to be formed on the northern fringes of the Chinese Town. Beyond Fresh Water Stream (Stamford Canal), the Bugis Town was realigned and an Arab one added. Squatters along the beach at Kampong Glam were evicted and seven lots of land on Beach Road issued previously to absentee landlords were resold. Large numbers of people were required to move. Some 200 acres at Telok Blangah were cleared and prepared for the removal of the Temenggong's village from the north bank of the Singapore River. The Chinese, on the southwest bank, were moved inland to make way for the "principal mercantile establishment". Those who had occupied land on the Reserved Plain were told to move as well. The Instructions included directions that streets were to be laid out in regular right-angled grids wherever possible. Houses were to have a uniform front and "a verandah open at all times as a continued and covered passage on each side of the street," stipulations which were to result in the singularly unique character of the towns of Singapore and, later, Malaya.

By the time of Raffles' final departure on June 9, 1823, many changes had been set in motion. In addition to those already mentioned, the Chinese Town had been reorganised and Commercial Square (Raffles Place) was taking shape; the marshes had

been filled and warehouses were already being built along the south bank. The construction of the first bridge across the river, designed by Jackson and an important milestone in the expansion of the town south, would be completed in August. To John Crawfurd, who would soon arrive to succeed Farquhar as resident, Raffles stressed that "... to the beauty, regularity and cleanliness of the Settlement, the width of the different roads and streets should be fixed by authority and as much attention paid to the general style of building as circumstances admit."

Much, in fact, remained to be done and Crawfurd faced a difficult task in managing the infant settlement. He received minimal financial support from the East India Company because it was by no means certain that the British would retain Singapore until an understanding was reached with the Dutch on conflicting territorial claims to the islands of the region. Finally, in March of 1824, by the Treaty of London, the Dutch relinquished all claims to the Malay Peninsula and Singapore in exchange for Java and Sumatra. Singapore's future was further assured in August when the Sultan ceded the entire island to the British.

Development now proceeded with confidence. Crawfurd, practical and far more resolute and independent-minded than his predecessor, was convinced that Singapore's success depended on material progress. Aware that funds were short, and that much of the government reserved land on the north bank of the river and in the Esplanade area would remain undeveloped, he issued grants and temporary leases to those who applied and to others who had remained in occupation of the reserved land. Among those who benefitted was the Java-based merchant John Argyle Maxwell who received

a grant in November of 1825, amalgamated it with an adjoining lot and built a house in 1827 which still stands as Parliament House.

When John Prince succeeded Crawfurd as resident in 1827, the town and suburbs extended from Kampong Glam to Telok Ayer and inland from the sea to a line roughly along the present North Bridge Road, Hill Street and South Bridge Road as far as South Canal Road. Prince was to reverse Crawfurd's policy of granting land on the Reserved Plain and it is to him that the survival of the Esplanade as an open space is due.

The hills surrounding the town were considered more valuable, and as early as 1821 there began a scramble for their possession by the European settlers. Farquhar liberally issued land grants to those who applied and by mid-1822 Scott's Hill (Ann Siang Hill), Mount Erskine, Pearl's Hill, Flint's Hill (Mount Sophia) and Bukit Cawa (Mount Emily) had been de-forested. The hills commanded excellent views of the town and harbour and in due course houses were built on their summits. Mount Palmer was one of the first to boast of a small bungalow, by 1822, and Pearl's Hill probably shared this distinction. Raffles completed his bungalow on Bukit Larangan in January of 1823 and Flint moved into his house on Mount Sophia about five months later. Colonel Nahujis, a Dutchman who visited Singapore in 1824, remarked

of the settlement: "The land is mostly hilly and is thickly covered with trees. Many of the hills in the neighbourhood of the beach are already adorned with houses of the various Europeans and amongst these the most noteworthy are the houses of the harbour-master, Captain Flint, and of the merchant Scott."

The first houses erected by the new arrivals were timber with attap roofs and walls lined with *kajang*, waterproof matting of *pandanus* or *mengkuang*. These were similar to the houses of the original inhabitants and undoubtedly similar to those erected in Penang after its establishment in 1786. James Wathan, an artist who visited Penang in 1811-12, depicted two such structures (1.4). The house of Dr McKinnon had a jack-roof and encircling verandah and was very similar to houses of the period in India. Mr Amee's house was a single-storey bungalow raised higher than usual on timber posts. It was entered by a flight of steps that led to the open verandah which projected from the main body of the house. The window shutters were timber, framed in attap, and top-hung, after the fashion of the indigenous houses.

It should be noted that the Europeans already had about 250 years of experience building in the East by the time the British arrived — in Malacca, Macao, the Dutch East Indies and India. In Singapore the

1.5 View of Singapore Town and Harbour taken from the Government Hill, circa 1830. The buildings appear more permanent and substantial. The first Institution building and Maxwell's house can be seen, and the Esplanade has been cleared of buildings.

original houses were in timber, the main building material of the region, and were only gradually replaced by brick ones. At first, bricks had to be imported from Penang, where brick houses were fairly common, and probably from Malacca where they had been manufactured since Portuguese times. Captain Pearl, who arrived in Singapore at the same time as Raffles, was said to have sold bricks that were used on his ship as ballast from which he had "deducted an excellent percentage by taking advantage of the market." Kilns were established by the government after the arrival of the first Indian convicts from Penang.

The earliest visual records of Singapore houses are a sketch dated June 5, 1823 (1.1) and an undated lithograph circa 1824-25 (1.3). In both, the buildings are shown as squat, compact and simple with steep attap roofs. In the 1823 sketch are two houses which can be identified with certainty: Raffles' bungalow on Government Hill and the house of Francis Bernard, the first police superintendent (1.2). The undated lithograph shows some of the early roads

and the Esplanade before it was cleared of buildings. It lacks details, however, and probably gives only a general impression of the early buildings.

There were few houses in the first years, and the East India Company records show that by December of 1823 the settlement could boast of 631 dwellings — 29 in brick, 52 in timber with tiled roofs, 200 in timber with attap roofs and 350 huts. By 1824, there were 822 dwellings — 74 in brick, 59 in timber with tiled roofs, 314 in timber with attap roofs and 375 huts. By the end of 1825 there were 1058 — 147 in brick, 399 in timber with attap roofs and 105 huts, the decrease in the number of huts due to a fire in Chinatown which destroyed 130 buildings.

Residences and godowns are, not surprisingly, hard to differentiate in early illustrations since merchants lived and worked in godowns concentrated mainly along the river front, in Commercial Square, in High Street and along the southern edge of the Esplanade. A few prominent merchants and government officials had, however, built houses in North Bridge Road and Beach Road as the decade came to a close.

Born in Singapore. Children and their parents in portraits
from the early 20th century.

The people who first came to live and work in Singapore were merchants, traders and adventurers from all over the region. With the exception of the original inhabitants and immigrants from the Indonesian Archipelago, the population was mostly male and transient — a phenomenon that continued well into the present century.

In 1824, there were 2,956 Chinese men and only 361 women. Ten years later, the Chinese population had risen to 10,767 of which less than 10 per cent were women. The ratio of women increased slowly: 20 per cent in 1901, 26 per cent in 1911, 32 per cent in 1921 and 38 per cent in 1931. Among Europeans, there were 23 women and 51 men in 1824. From the 1830s up to the mid-1930s women accounted for a stable one-third of the European population. In

Family gatherings. These Singapore photographs also date
from the early 20th century.

contrast, among Indians there was only one woman for every four men right up to World War Two. The proportion of Eurasian females was higher; in the 1830s women accounted for 40 per cent, by the 1860s 50 per cent, and until World War Two slightly more than half. Malay men and women remained in about equal numbers throughout the whole period.

Equally significant, the number of houses built relative to the population was small and continued to be small up to World War Two. The majority of Asian immigrants lived in shared quarters above shophouses and godowns in the Chinese and Chuliah kampongs while many Europeans were bachelors who lived in offices or godowns, shared a house or boarded with families initially in the Beach Road area and later in Tanglin.

2.1 This 1846 map of the town by J.T. Thomson shows the European, Arab, Malay and Bugis residential areas, coloured in orange, north of the Singapore River. South of the river, and coloured in grey, are the more congested Chinese and Chulia areas. The residential areas did not extend beyond the confines shown on this map until the 1860s. *2.2* Houses in the Coleman and Hill Street area in 1863. From a photograph by Sachtler & Company.

The Early Houses

1830-1869

Several events during the 1820s paved the way for the growth of the town from the 1830s onwards. The treaties of 1824, already mentioned in chapter one, had dispelled doubts over Singapore's future and the mood of self-assurance was reflected in the dramatic rise in the colony's population from 4,727 in 1821 to 16,634 in 1830. In December of 1826, the government was reorganised, and the three settlements of Penang, Malacca and Singapore were united under the administration of a governor seated initially in Penang until 1832 but in Singapore thereafter. In 1826 G. D. Coleman arrived. His contribution to the development of the town and its architecture were to mould its general appearance.

The town area began to take on a neater appearance. By 1830, the swamps south of the Singapore River were filled and drained; Chinatown, the Chuliah Kampong and Commercial Square were established, and the Esplanade was a permanent feature. By 1842, there were some 3,609 houses and the town extended east-west from Rochor Canal to Pagoda Street and inland from the sea to Selegie Road, Hill Street, across the new Coleman's bridge, completed in 1840, and along New Bridge Road.

The extent of the town remained virtually unchanged for the next 20 years although the population more than doubled, from 35,389 in 1840 to 81,734 in 1860. The increased density was especially felt in Chinatown and Kampong Glam in the vicinity of the Sultan's domain which, by 1840, was relatively urbanised. Even the main European residential area around Beach Road and the Esplanade had, by the standards of the day, become overcrowded. Gordon Forbes Davidson, a businessman, wrote of the area in his book *Trade and Travel in the Far East* (London: 1846): "Pleasant, however, as is this part of the suburbs, it is gradually being deserted for country situations, where the hot winds of July, August, and September are not so much felt, and where the nights are cooler than on the sea-shore." By the 1860s many houses in the Beach Road and Esplanade area had been converted into hotels or boarding houses. John Cameron in his book *Our Tropical Possessions in Malayan India* (London: 1865) wrote:

To the line of buildings fronting the beach on this side of the river, extending from the church for a quarter of a mile eastward, more perhaps than to any other feature, Singapore owes its pretty appearance, viewed from the harbour. These, as I have said before, though the finest of them are hotels now, were once the residences of the early merchants, and are large and of elegant construction; they each cover a considerable space of ground and have compounds or gardens around. It is a very fine sight from the beach to see these houses lit up at night, the brilliant argand lamps in use shedding a flood of light round the lofty white pillars and colonnades of the upper storeys, while the lower parts of the buildings are hid by the shrubbery of the gardens in front. Every door and window is thrown open to admit the cool night breeze, and gathered round their tables or lolling about in their easy chairs, may be seen the wearied travellers or residents.... Indeed, on a fine starry night, standing there, on the sea-wall of the bay, with the stillness around only broken by the gentle ripple of the wavelets at one's feet, it is not difficult while gazing on the houses, the lights, the figures, and the heavy leafed shrubbery in front, to imagine oneself amid the garden palaces of the Arabian Nights.

It was the opening up of the island by the Europeans for agricultural estates from the 1830s to the 1860s which accelerated the expansion of the town westward. To the northeast, the swampy, low-lying lands between Serangoon Road and the

2.3 South Bridge Road circa 1870.

Kallang River deterred development for another 30 years or so. Initially the Europeans were reluctant to invest in land too distant from town, in spite of government encouragement. Lack of proper roads made access difficult and until 1851 only four led beyond the town into the country — Bukit Timah, Serangoon, Thomson and Changi. Lawlessness was also prevalent and a deterrent to living in relative isolation. A more important reason was the shortness of the land leases issued. In 1828, however, 20 year leases were given with an option for a further 30 years renewal. Further encouragement came in 1843 when land was granted in perpetuity.

By 1835, Europeans were planting nutmeg and other spices on a commercial scale north and west of the town. Much of the forest, particularly in Tanglin, had already been cleared by Chinese squatter gambier and pepper planters who felled the trees surrounding their plots for firewood to boil the gambier leaves in order to extract its commercial product. When the soil was exhausted, they moved to virgin land and this process of continual shifting led to the clearing of large areas of forest. J. T. Thomson, government surveyor, 1841–1853, observed that "The district of Tanglin in the beginning of 1843 consisted of barren looking hills covered with short brushwood and lallang".

One of the first Europeans to move into the country was Dr. Thomas Oxley, the colony surgeon. In about 1837 he acquired 173 acres and formed Killiney estate, described in the 1840s as "the finest nutmeg garden". About the same time, William Cuppage, an officer in the postal service, occupied Emerald Hill, and Charles Carnie, a businessman, built the first house in Cairnhill in 1840. Soon other Europeans were moving to "country situations" in the nearby districts of Claymore and Tanglin.

By about 1860, the nutmeg trees succumbed to a blight caused by a species of beetle. The estates, which by now stretched from Pasir Panjang to Adam Road through Tanglin, Claymore and Bukit Timah Road, gradually failed. Some owners retained their holdings and erected houses for rental. Cuppage, for example, built Fern Cottage circa 1850 as his residence and rented out the first house he had built, Erin Lodge, on Emerald Hill. His son-in-law, Edwin Koek, added Claregrove on purchasing the entire estate after his father-in-law's death in 1872. When George Garden Nicoll offered his 150 acre Sri Menanti estate for sale in 1859 there was already a house on the estate. Other owners sold their estates which were then parcelled out into building lots and resold by the new proprietors. The process was continual, and the land was subsequently further subdivided into ever smaller lots. By the 1870s, nearly all of the nutmeg plantations had been transformed into large, pleasant and exclusive residential suburbs.

The houses that stood on the wooded and undulating hills of Tanglin and Claymore between 1850 and 1880 were named after the estates of their European owners and many of the names survive to this day as road and place names — Tyersall, Chatsworth, Ardmore, Dalvey, Irwell Bank, Orange Grove and Cairnhill. A network of roads was formed along the original plantation carriageways or along their boundaries. Grange Road, Dalvey Road, Emerald Hill Road, Scotts Road, Duxton Hill, Oxley Road, Prinsep Street and Spottiswoode Park Road, to name a few, were roads which originated in this way.

Thomas Oxley's nutmeg estate provides a good example of what transpired after the failure. The land lay within an area bounded by Orchard Road, Grange Road, Leonie Hill Road, River Valley Road and Tank Road. In 1850, Oxley began to dispose of his land in lots. By 1862, there were 38 houses within the estate, mostly along St Thomas Walk and the area between Killiney and Oxley Roads. By 1880, a network of roads was completed — the present Somerset Road, Devonshire Road, Exeter Road, St. Thomas Walk, Eber Road, Dublin Road, Lloyd Road and Oxley Road. Oxley Drive was a private driveway that led up Oxley's Hill where there were five houses: Pavilion, Bargany House, Bargany Lodge, Killiney Bungalow and Killiney House, Oxley's own residence.

A number of Chinese merchants and traders also owned plantations. In the mid-1830s, Seah Eu Chin was reputed to own the largest gambier and pepper plantation on the island — an estate that extended from Tanglin Road to Bukit Timah. Choa Chong Long, who died in China in 1837, was probably one of the first Chinese to manage a plantation in the country while he continued to live in Commercial Square. He owned a hill in Telok Blangah which was named after him. Hoo Ah Kay, or Whampoa, went as far as Katong to plant coconuts even before Thomas Crane started planting cotton there in February of 1836. Eventually some of the Chinese merchants settled outside the town while others built holiday bungalows on their country estates which, if not too distant from town, became homes for the secondary wives. Alfred Russel Wallace, who was in Singapore in the 1850s, remarked in his *The Malay Archipelago* (London: 1869) that the Chinese merchant

...has a handsome warehouse or shop in town and a good house in the country. He keeps a fine horse and gig, and every evening may be seen taking a drive bareheaded to enjoy the cool breeze. He is rich, he owns several retail shops and trading schooners, he lends money at high interest and on good security, he makes hard bargains and gets fatter and richer each year.

2.4 The Singapore River circa 1870.

Agricultural activity was not limited to the Tanglin and Claymore areas, however. Further east, Joseph Balestier, the American consul, speculated in sugar planting in Serangoon. Balestier's estate of over 1000 acres lay between Balestier Road and Kallang River. Beyond was Montgomerie's Kallangdale estate, also about 1000 acres, acquired in 1825. Both were planted around 1830 but failed by the late 1840s due to poor sugar prices in the world market.

The eastern part of the island, which would one day become the densely populated residential suburbs of Katong, Geylang and Siglap, was opened up mainly by European planters. Francis Bernard, Farquhar's brother-in-law, was probably the first European to own land in the district — a coconut estate in Tanjong Katong in 1823. From 1830 onwards, plots of land in the area stretching from Siglap Road to the Geylang River and from Geylang Road to the sea were granted to individuals in large parcels ranging from 20 to 500 acres. By about 1840 most of the land had been planted with coconut trees as the sandy soil of the area was well suited to their cultivation. Access to the area was mainly by sea as the overland route entailed crossing the Kallang River, bridged only in 1842. Gordon Forbes Davidson wrote of this developments:

To the eastward of the town of Singapore, extends a considerable plain, on which the sugar and coconut plantations stand. To the westward and inland of the town, the country consists almost entirely of hill and dale; and its aspect is very striking and picturesque. On many of these miniature (for they are but miniature) hills, stand pretty bungalows, surrounded with nutmeg and fruit trees: they are delightful residences.

Other pioneer estate owners on the eastern part of the island were Thomas Dunman, Thomas Owen Crane, Sir Jose d'Almeida, the Little family, John Armstrong, W.R. George and Hoo Ah Kay. Crane and d'Almeida at Perseverance estate, at the eastern corner of Paya Lebar Road and Changi Road junction, tried cotton planting without success. Thomas Dunman eventually extended his holdings through purchasing Crane's and George's estates; by the 1870s his plantation, The Grove, was 688 acres. D'Almeida also owned Confederate estate, between Haig Road and Still Road. When the cotton failed, he planted coconuts, and produced rum and molasses. Next to Confederate estate were two other well-known plantations: John Armstrong's 325-acre estate, which extended from the sea inland to Changi Road and from Still Road to Siglap Canal; and beyond, the 450-acre Siglap estate owned by Dr Robert Little.

2.5 A sampling of early houses photographed circa 1870 includes the three along the Esplanade (opposite middle); the house of Thomas Owen Crane in Katong (above); a house near the newly-built Government House (opposite top); and a house on Mount Elizabeth (opposite bottom).

As the colony settled to a secure future, timber houses and godowns built in the early 1820s were replaced by more permanent and substantial structures. A view of the town circa 1827 (1.5) shows several rather large and permanent looking houses amidst the simple squat buildings, including some by Singapore's first resident trained architect, G. D. Coleman. Hardly any houses from the period 1830 to 1870 have survived. Records are also scant and include mainly prints of the settlement, some photographs and traveller's descriptions. Yet an accurate picture of Coleman's houses is possible as three were reconstructed on plan in the 1950s from site evidence: Maxwell's house (2.6), Coleman's own house in Coleman Street (2.9), and the Caldwell house (2.8), which still stands near the corner of Bras Basah Road and Victoria Street. The elevational treatment of the three was in the Palladian manner still current in England during the Regency period (1800–1830). All three were symmetrical in plan. Maxwell's had a verandah above a projecting carriage porch; in Coleman's, the verandah was over a driveway which ran along the entire front of the house, instead of projecting, and the main lounge and dining room were on the first floor. The verandah on the first floor of Maxwell's house suggests that the main lounge or drawing room were on that level as well, an assumption strongly supported by Maxwell's own description:

The following is the description and accommodation of the upper part of the house: Central Room — 49 feet long. Front side Room 28-1/2 × 21-1/2. Four Bed Rooms — about 20 feet square. Two of the Bed Rooms having a Dressing Room and private verandahs to each. The verandah facing the sea measures 60 feet long × 15 feet broad and the one over the Portico is 41-1/2 feet × 28 feet. The central projection on the side next the River is to contain two small apartments on a 3rd and 4th storey, communicating with the Terrace on the top. There is an eliptical staircase at the front and there is a backstairs. The Baths can be supplied with water from a cistern lined with lead situated over the Roof and capable of containing more than 700 cubic feet of water conveyed to it by gutters from the roof. The Basement Storey (ground floor) is nearly similar in its arrangement and number of apartments with the principal storey with the exception of such a difference as a reference to the Plan will readily suggest to be unavoidable.

Three other houses attributed to Coleman, built between 1830 and 1840 along the Esplanade (2.5 and 2.7), are particularly interesting because they ex-

hibit several architectural features which became common to houses built in Singapore for the next century — verandahs over projecting carriage porches, gable-end roofs supported by what appear to be Doric columns resting on podiums with arched openings, and outhouses which accommodated the kitchen, stables, and servants' quarters. The three houses were described in some detail by John Cameron in *Our Tropical Possessions in Malayan India* as

… handsome lofty mansions, which years ago, while the present suburbs of the town were yet jungle, constituted the residences of the merchants and government

2.6 This sketch of Maxwell's house, or the court house as it was called, by J.T. Thomson is dated 1846.

officials. They are all large buildings, generally kept snowy white with pillared porticoes and balconies, and green-painted latticed doors and windows; to each also is attached a compound or garden of fair dimensions, tastefully laid out with trees and shrubs. Few of these houses are now in use as private residences, some of the best are taken up for hotels, and one is used as the masonic lodge.

Coleman also built a house opposite his own residence for Miss Takoyee Manuk (2.11) around 1840. It was symmetrical in form with semi-circular wings on each side and had, as in Coleman's house, a carriage porch along the entire front of the building.

The best of the European houses were probably designed by Coleman who was the only trained architect in Singapore for many years. The buildings executed by him (the architect often offered a package deal, both designing and contracting to build for clients) were not the usual utilitarian builder's designs. His few surviving buildings, as well as those demolished but seen in photographs, are distinguished by fine detailing and elegant proportions which testify to his architectural abilities.

2.7 The view of the Esplanade circa 1840 shows the court house on the left, the three
houses along the Esplanade, and St Andrew's Church.

A native of Drogheda County Louth, Ireland, Coleman was born in 1794. His father was a merchant and so was his mother's family, the Drumgooles, from whom he took his second name. Little is known of his early life, although it is certain that he received some form of architectural training before leaving Britain at the age of 22. His career began in 1816 in Calcutta where, to quote his own words:

I exercised my professions of Architect and Surveyor, until 1820, when being applied to by Mr Palmer on the part of Mr Vanbram of the Dutch Java Government I went to Batavia to build a Cathedral, for which I had about a year before given the designs, but during my passage Mr. Vanbram died and on my arrival, there was no existing intention to building a Church. I then engaged in some extensive surveys and remained in Java until 1822, when I came to Singapore with an introduction to Sir Stamford Raffles, who immediately directed me to draw designs for a Church. These he did me the honour to approve of but declined building he said, in consequence of my returning to Batavia where I was engaged in an agricultural speculation until February 1826, when

I returned here and have since remained engaged in my professional pursuits.

During the 15 years that Coleman was in Singapore, he was engaged by the government to carry out revenue and topographical surveys and to lay out and construct roads and bridges. In 1830, he was officially appointed government surveyor and in August 1833 he was made superintendent of public works, overseer of convict labour and land surveyor, a post he held until his retirement in June of 1841. At the same time, he maintained a flourishing private practice as an architect-contractor, designing and building a considerable number of projects. His buildings include the Armenian Church, the first St Andrew's Church, the Telok Ayer Market of 1837, Boustead's godown at Boat Quay, and Raffles Institution. According to Robert Ibbetson, the resident 1830–1832, Coleman was paid 15 per cent professional fees as an architect. To this was added the profits he earned as a contractor, which prompted Colonel W. J. Butterworth, governor 1843–1845, to remark: "Mr Coleman, whose services were highly

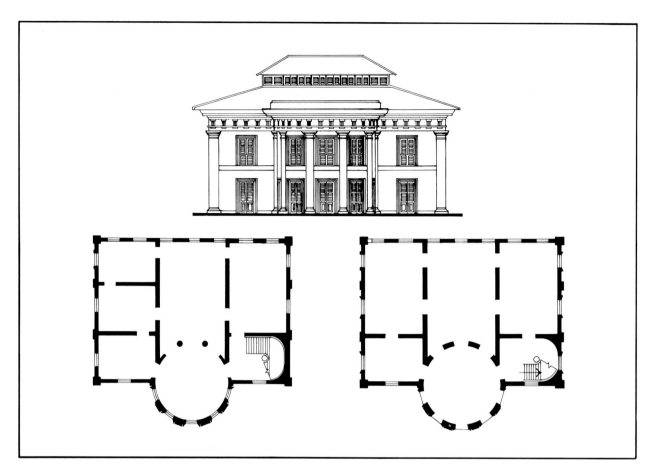

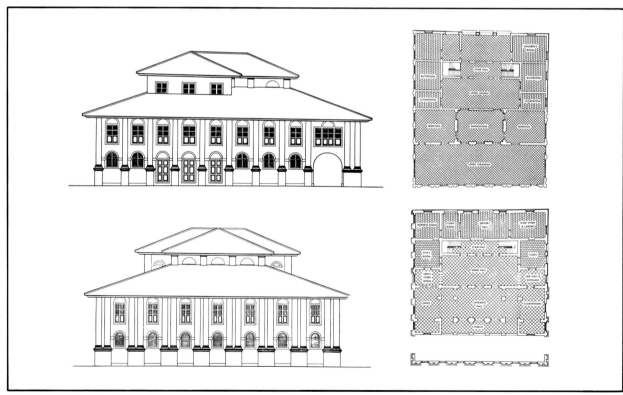

2.8 Elevation and plans (top) of Caldwell's house *2.9* Elevations and plans (above) of Coleman's house *2.10* The notices (opposite) date from the 1840s. *2.11* Following pages: Coleman's house is on the left and Takoyee Manuk's on the right.

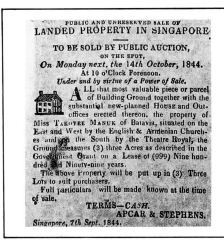

recognised on his vacating office, told me that he made the greater part of his property (he possesses lands and houses) by this means."

Little is known of Coleman's personal life. By all accounts he was witty, popular and respected. J. T. Thomson, his successor as surveyor, paid tribute to him when he said: "It was Coleman who laid out the city of Singapore in that expansive and well-arranged plan admired by all strangers." After retiring, he left Singapore on July 4, 1841 and married in England in 1842. There is, however, a record in the St Andrew's Church register of a baptism on the July 20, 1837 of Eda Elizabeth, born March 10, 1828. The father's name was given as G. D. Coleman but the mother's name was omitted, which was unusual. She may have been Miss Takoyee Manuk, Coleman's neighbour.

That Coleman was in a position to build his own large house only three years after settling here was proof of his rapid success. On March 17, 1828, he obtained a lease for land on the street which today bears his name. The spacious building of 14,500 square feet with three large bedrooms was completed the following May. Here he lived in style, for Governor Bonham (governor 1837–1843) commented that "Mr Coleman maintains an Equipage second only to my own." He planned a second residence when he returned to Singapore after his two-year absence. To be built at Bukit Pasoh, the plans were described as "magnificent" and "in the Italian style of architecture with ornamental gardens, stables, etc." Unfortunately it was never built. Coleman died four months after his return, on March 27, 1844, aged 49 years. He was buried in Fort Canning Cemetery.

It was not known if Coleman built any houses outside the town but certainly the early European houses in the countryside were not vastly different in appearance from those in town. Records consist mainly of drawings, sketches and a handful of early photographs. Three of the earliest (2.13) that can be identified with certainty are the houses of Charles Carnie in Cairnhill; William Wemys Ker overlooking the entrance of Keppel Harbour; and Broadfields, built about 1835 by one of the founders of Paterson Simons & Company. All three were two-storey rectangular buildings with enclosed verandahs above projecting carriage porches. The main roofs were hipped. The roof above the projecting verandah in Carnie's house was gable-ended, but hipped in Ker's house and Broadfields, which in particular had the appearance of a neat white stuccoed building so typical of the period. All three had louvred French windows. Broadfields was wider at the wings, and, like Carnie's house, had side verandahs which were probably added later.

The evidence available suggests that all of the early two-storey houses were remarkably consistent in form and style. Conspicuously absent were the encircling verandahs which later became so common. Most were built on low budgets except those for which an architect, such as Coleman, had been engaged. Presumably most of the houses were dressed sparingly in Classical features; only Coleman seems to have fully understood the Classical Orders, which he applied elegantly and in full measure.

The symmetry and compact form of the houses of this period were derived mainly from Britain's Georgian country houses. It was inevitable that the British brought not only their social customs to the East but their house plans as well. The merchants emulated the landed gentry at home who had built the great Palladian-inspired country houses of the late 18th and early 19th century during the period of the country's greatest prosperity. The style of the Italian Renaissance architect Andrea Palladio (1518–1580), whose restrained classicism was extremely appealing to the English taste, had become widely adopted in England from the 18th century. The Georgian house was compact,

symmetrical in form with a central portico. According to John Betjeman in *Pictorial History of English Architecture* (London: 1972), in plan it was "an oblong divided in two on the long or horizontal axis and in three on the short or vertical axis, resulting in six rooms with a communicating hall and a saloon in the centre." Following Italian custom, the *piano nobile*, or main floor, was placed above the ground floor. All important rooms — the drawing, reception and dining rooms — were on the *piano nobile* which was reached by an external staircase.

The drawing room was considered the most important of the rooms and was usually located near the bedrooms. This arrangement originated in the 17th century with the custom of ladies withdrawing after dinner while the men remained in the dining room or adjourned to the study or library, the male preserves. They were permitted to join the ladies in the drawing room later on, after having sobered up a little. In the grand houses, the drawing room occupied the entire first floor.

The ground floor was referred to as a basement and was enclosed within a podium that appeared as a base to the building. The basement included the cellar and kitchen services. In some houses, the dining room on the *piano nobile* was reserved for formal occasions while the family dining room, breakfast room, parlour and other private rooms were on the ground floor, the main entrance hall was also sometimes located. If the important rooms were on the *piano nobile*, the main entrance was on that level and, as mentioned, approached by a broad flight of external steps.

The similarity in form between Coleman's houses and their antecedents in Britain is not surprising. Born in 1795, he was inevitably influenced by trends in England as well as in India where he practised in Calcutta from 1816 to 1820. A description of a typical Georgian House by Alan Powers in *The National Trust Book of the English House* (London: 1985) also applies to the residence Coleman designed for Maxwell: "No English house had ever looked like this before, but in the course of the next 50 years, the central portico, the rusticated basement storey and the square-shouldered silhouette were to become distinguishing marks of even the most provincial country house."

The plan of Maxwell's house and the placement of the large central room on the first floor conformed with late Georgian fashion. The plans of Coleman's own house and Caldwell's were distinctly Georgian; in Coleman's own house, all of the main rooms, including the dining room, were on the *piano nobile*. The purer classicism imposed on the symmetrical facades was also distinctly Georgian. Many of the houses credited to him had a box-like appearance created by the concealment of the gutters behind projecting cornices or parapets that partially screened the roof from view. In two of the houses, Maxwell's and the house of Dr Montgomerie, the middle of the three houses along the Esplanade, the square-shouldered solidity was further enhanced by side wings and verandahs above projecting carriage porches. The two houses were even more Palladian in character and bear comparison with Villa Piovene in Lenodo, Italy by Palladio (1508–1580) and Queen's House, Greenwich (1618–1635) (2.14) The balusters on the parapets at Maxwell's house were a Palladian detail.

Not all Georgian houses had podiums and neither did all of Coleman's. French theorists objected to the raising of the portico on a basement storey and maintained that the portico provided shelter while columns were best viewed when they rose directly from the ground. Sir William Chambers (architect, 1723–1796) adopted the theory in a house built in England in 1762 and others followed. Coleman followed in Chambers' footsteps in the elevations for his own house, Caldwell's and Miss Takoyee Manuk. In all three the podium was replaced by giant classical columns rising from the ground.

The *piano nobile* was gradually abandoned in English country houses. In large town houses, however, it lingered until the mid-18th century, when the dining room moved to the ground floor while the drawing room remained upstairs. In Singapore the custom lingered on well into the present century, as shall be seen in the chapters that follow. Even when the Asiatic Petroleum Company (Shell) built a house in 1924, the enclosed verandah above the projecting carriage porch served as a drawing or sitting room.

2.12 Killiney House, built by Dr Thomas Oxley, was renamed Belle Vue by Manasseh Meyer who purchased it about 1890.

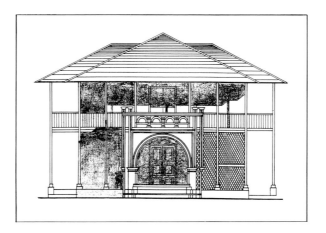

2.13 More country houses, clockwise from top: Belle Vue Cottage, 1870; Broadfields, circa 1835; Bukit Chermin from a sketch dated 1846; Cairnhill house from a painting by J.T. Thomson; and White House on Dalvey estate.

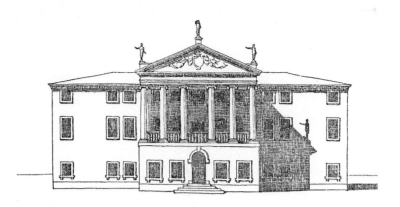

Thus far the discussion has centred on two-storey houses. Bungalows, however, were commonly built in Singapore as well. These were usually raised on sleeper walls, brick piers or timber posts about two to five feet off the ground. The term "bungalow" originated in 17th century Bengal from the word for indigenous huts, *bangla* or *bangala*. The *bangala* hut was a simple mud-walled structure raised a foot or two above the ground, encircled by a verandah and with a roof curved at the ridge. The Europeans probably adapted the *bangala* hut to suit their needs by enclosing the sides for bedrooms and bathrooms but retaining the front and rear verandahs to ventilate the central portion.

The bungalow was introduced into Singapore and Malaya by the British. The suspension of the floor on brick piers or timber posts was a local adaptation. In India, bungalows that were raised two to three feet off the ground were laid on a hard core of broken bricks and rubble; when raised three to four feet, they were sometimes suspended on brick walls that appeared as a solid base to the building. In Singapore, brick walls supporting the floors had arched openings to ventilate the underside of the timber floors, a necessary feature in the damp and humid climate. Alternatively, air bricks or ventilating grills were built into the walls. For a description of this house type we again turn to Cameron:

Bungalows, a term often applied to any style of dwelling-house in the East, are, properly speaking, only of one story, elevated some five or six feet from the ground upon arched masonry. A moderate-sized building of this description might be 90 feet long, 60 or 70 deep, usually a

2.14 The early houses followed European traditions, as illustrated here. The Villa Piovene by Palladio (top) and Queen's House, Greenwich by Inigo Jones (above). House plans opposite are from top: by James Gibb, 1728; Ramsbury Manor circa 1680; and Chevening Place, 1630; The Roman Doric and Tuscan Orders (opposite bottom). *2.15* Following pages: Three of the unidentified Singapore houses have carriage porches with Tuscan or Doric columns.

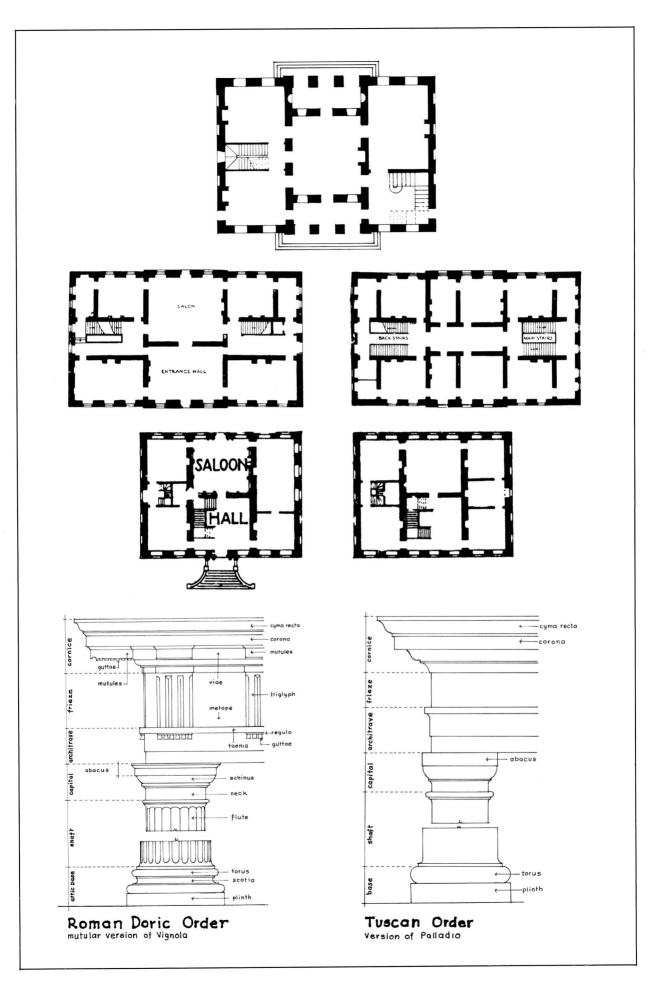

Roman Doric Order
mutular version of Vignola

Tuscan Order
Version of Palladio

parallelogram in form, but sometimes varied in shape to suit the arrangement of the rooms inside. The walls from the flooring to the roof are seldom less than fifteen feet high, which gives a lofty ceiling to the apartments and the roof is covered with tiles. The most striking feature of these buildings, however, is the broad verandah which runs right round the house about eight or ten feet in width, resting on the plinths of the pillars that, extending upwards in round columns with neatly moulded capitals, support the continuation of the roof which projects some four feet beyond the pillars, forming deep overhanging eaves. On the verandah, which is surrounded by a neat railing, all the doors of the bungalow open, and as these

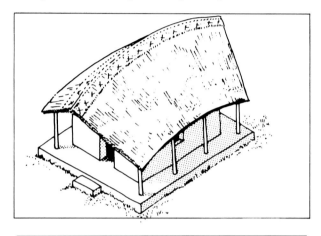

2.16 A *bangala* hut.

also serve the purpose of windows, they are pretty numerous; they are in two halves, opening down the centre like cottage doors at home, with the lower panels plain and the two upper ones fitted with venetians to open or close at pleasure. From the centre of the building in front a portico projects some 25 or 30 feet, and generally about 25 feet broad, covering the carriage way and a broad flight of stone steps leading from the ground to the verandah. The pillars and walls are chunammed to a snowy whiteness, the doors are painted a light green, the tiled roof in time becomes a dark brown and the whole forms a very pleasing picture, especially in its contrast with the foliage around.

Only a handful of pre-1880 bungalows can be identified with certainty, including the Court House in George Town, Penang, built probably as a dwelling house in the 1830s. Another is St James, built in 1846 by James Guthrie at Telok Blangah and illustrated in *L'Extreme Orient* by Paul Bonnetain (Paris: 1887). Stylistically, St James was derived from the Anglo-Indian bungalow. A third, Panglima Prang, built circa 1860 for the wealthy Chinese merchant Tan Kim Seng, was in appearance a European house.

It had stout Doric columns resting on tall plinths, similar to St James which was built 20 years earlier. The main building in its original form was almost a perfect square measuring 94×92 feet. The high, hipped roof and deep overhang of the eaves, extending 17 feet beyond the outer walls, lent a sheltered and comfortable air of quiet self-assurance to the house which was complemented by the unpretentious symmetry of its elevation.

The similarities between these three early bungalows is striking (2.17): the raised floors, the broad flights of brick steps under carriage porches with roofs supported by Doric columns on tall plinths, high stepped roofs and broad open verandahs under extended eaves — all were common features of other early Singapore bungalows as well. In contrast, a bungalow probably built in the 1840s by the Alsagoff family (page 161) sat directly on the ground. It was undoubtedly after a style common in India and Sri Lanka, and it could represent a type that was more common in 19th century Singapore than we suspect.

By the 1860s, there had evolved a simple, elegant style of domestic architecture which conformed to English traditions but made concessions to the tropical climate. The style persisted well into the 20th century, although changes began to occurr in the 1870s with the influence of Victorian Eclecticism. The most compelling evidence is the photograph of the town taken from the tower of St Andrew's Cathedral in 1863 (2.18). All of the houses are square and compact in form, with plain, unadorned plastered wall surfaces and high, hipped roofs with short ridges. The "main houses", two-storey or bungalow, have projecting porches for horse-drawn carriages. Outhouses accommodate the kitchen, servants' quarters, stables and coach houses and are linked to the main houses by covered walkways. The two-storey houses invariably have verandahs over the projecting carriage porches. In plan, the houses were compact, symmetrical and divided into three bays, or sometimes five, along the front with the entrance along a central axis.

The "three-bay plan" was copied from English middle class houses of the same period. A typical example by Peter Nicholson (1765–1844) for middle class housing is shown in 2.19. The plan was accepted with little variation in Britain during the first 50 years of the Victorian era (1837–1887). A classic Singapore example which illustrates the similarities between England and Singapore is W. E. Hooper's house at Paterson Road (2.20). Although built fairly late, in 1889, the plan and style of the house belong to the period under discussion. Only the drawing

2.17 Early bungalows. The Court House in Penang (top left) was designed as a residence in the 1830s. Panglima Prang (top right) was built by Tan Kim Seng around 1860. St James (above) was built in 1846 by Alexander Guthrie. The rare interior view is also of St James. *2.18* Following pages: Panoramic view of the town of Singapore 1863 by Sachtler & Company. All of the houses are square and compact in form with high, hipped roofs with short ridges.

room above the projecting carriage porch and the verandahs at both levels distinguish it from an English house. The internal divisions were virtually identical, and the dining rooms were in the same position. Hooper's billiard room was in the same location as the English parlour. The rear of Hooper's house was given to stores and a pantry while Nicholson's house had a kitchen and library. Staircases were placed in the centre bay of both and bedrooms were confined to the first floor and similarly arranged.

Following English custom, the drawing room and bedrooms were on the first floor in all two-storey houses. Most houses, according to Cameron, had billiard rooms on the ground floor where a study or additional bedrooms were also located. Bathrooms, before the introduction of piped water and modern sanitation, were on the ground floor and directly accessible from the bedrooms or dressing rooms by separate stairs. An external door in each bathroom facilitated the removal of the chamber pot by the *tukang ayer*, the domestic help whose duties included drawing water from the well, chopping fire-wood and preparing the baths for the *tuan* and *mem*. Most European residences had only three or four bedrooms as large families were the exception rather than the rule. When the travelling time between Europe and the East was considerably reduced by the opening of the Suez Canal in 1869, many chose to leave their children behind to be educated and families were reunited every few years during home leave.

Few interior views from this early period have survived. One is the interior of St James (2.17). The centre of the room has a carpet, the ceiling is alcoved and the walls plastered and decorated with pictures and mirrors. The straight-backed chairs are plain and appear to have woven rattan seats. Behind the table in the centre of the room is the inevitable reclining seat with pivoted leg rests concealed from view. The room is not opulent; only the screen and the fans on the wall give an oriental touch. Cameron, in *Our Tropical Possessions in Malayan India*, also gave a description of the interiors of the time:

The interiors of all the houses are lofty, for in addition to the side walls being seldom less than fifteen feet high, the ceilings of the principal rooms are alcoved. There are numerous columns and arches inside as well as outside, and the Chinese builders make very neat cornices to the doorways and ceilings. The rooms are never papered, but the entire plasterwork — ceilings, walls; and pillars — is kept beautifully white with chunam. The floors are matted, not carpeted, and the apartments not overcrowded with furniture. The wooden doors leading from room to room are usually thrown open, there being silk screens on hinges attached to each doorway which, while they maintain a sufficient privacy, admit of a free ventilation throughout the house. From the ceilings are suspended a very liberal supply of hanging argand lamps, which, when lit up, give a brilliant effect to the rooms. Punkahs are used in the dining-rooms, but not in the sleeping apartments, as is the case in India.

The kitchen, stables, and servants' rooms are always built at a good distance from the house, and connected with it by a covered passage. There is little remarkable about these, except perhaps in the internal arrangements of the kitchens, which, though for the use of Europeans, are thoroughly oriental in their character. There is no fireplace, but in the centre of the room a table of solid brickwork is built with slabs of stone or brick tiles laid on the top; at one end of this a small circular chamber is built to serve as an oven; a strong fire is placed inside, and when the brickwork is thoroughly heated, the fire is raked out, and whatever dish is required to be baked placed inside and the aperture closed up, the heat given out from the bricks being sufficient to cook it in a short time. The rest of the table is divided into a series of little fireplaces, over which proceed the ordinary processes of cooking. Wood or charcoal only is used as fuel.

The elevational treatment of Hooper's house was simple, elegant, typical of the period, and can be further illustrated by three houses built between 1880 and 1901 — Magenta Cottage at Killiney Road (page 176), the Bishop's residence at Stamford Road and Syed Mohamed Alsagoff's house at Thomson Road (2.21). Magenta Cottage, which is still standing, has verandahs confined to the rear and the projecting front. The front verandah is supported by two pairs of brick piers. The hipped roof over it is, in turn, carried by two pairs of Doric columns, as in Panglima Prang. The thick walls are bare of ornamentation except for the cornices around the building and the pilasters at the corners. The louvred French windows have semicircular fanlights, a common feature since timber louvres darkened the house. The Bishop's residence, built in 1886, and Syed Mohammed Alsagoff's house, built in 1901 to the designs of Lermit and Westerhout, had open verandahs above projecting carriage porches flanked by pairs of Doric columns, and hipped roofs with decorative eaves boards.

The Classical Orders played an important role in the architecture of Singapore. With few exceptions, all buildings were in the classical style until the arrival of the Modern Movement in the 1930s. The classicism of the early years, however, differed fundamentally from the later period in its comparative plainness. Coleman and those after him designed with Palladian restraint. The preference was for the simpler Roman Doric or Tuscan Orders (2.14) applied in a manner reminiscent of the refined elegance of the Regency period such as one sees in the work of John Nash (1752–1835). The buildings shown in early prints and photographs all appear dressed in the Roman Doric or Tuscan Orders; the only exceptions being Takoyee Manuk's house and the first floor of Maxwell's house, where Coleman used the Ionic Order.

The Roman Doric and the Tuscan Orders are the simplest and the easiest to construct of the Classical Orders, the Ionic, Corinthian and Composite being more complex. The Tuscan is, in turn, simpler and coarser than the Doric; it is basically a simplified Roman Doric and its classification as a separate Order was due to the Italian Renaissance architect-writers of the 15th and 16th centuries. The Tuscan column, by their rules, was seven diameters in length compared to the eight diameters of the Doric column. Other differences: the Tuscan base is usually a plain torus moulding on a plinth whereas the Roman Doric column stands normally on an Attic base; the Tuscan capital has a larger abacus than the Doric and it rests on an unfluted shaft under a plain entablature without triglyphs. The austere subtlety of the Greek Doric was rarely employed in India, never in Malaya and only once in Singapore, in the Seaman's Hospital by J.T. Thomson, the reason being that Greek Revival architecture in England had run its course by the beginning of the 19th century. It was also difficult to construct: the triglyphs and fluting of the columns, both essential, could not be omitted, and the fluting required skill to render in chunam.

The Tuscan Order seems to have been more commonly used than the Roman Doric, although the latter, being the more refined, was probably preferred. As with most classical details, they were usually applied in ignorance or neglect of the rules. The consequent distortions resulted in a Doric column that resembled a Tuscan and vice versa. The original intentions of the builders, in most instances, will never be known. Yet the results were naive and charming, and befitted the rustic settings of the early plantation houses and rural bungalows. On the whole, however, the Classical Orders were applied sparingly throughout this period as their proportions were exacting. Ordinary brick piers were cheaper and easier to construct.

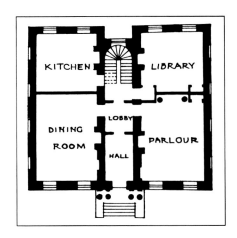

2.19 Typical early 19th century English house plan reproduced from *Practical Builder* by Peter Nicholson circa 1823. 2.20 Elevation and plans of house of W.E. Hooper (portrait at right) at Paterson Road, 1889. Only the drawing room above the projecting carriage porch and the verandahs on both the ground and first floors distinguish it from Nicholson's plan.

2.21 Following pages: The symmetrical three or five-bay across the front plan was dressed in a variety of facades as these examples from the 1880s to 1916 show.
Top left to right: Bishop's residence at Stamford Road, 1886; Song Soon Guan at Bencoolen Street, 1884; Mandalay Villa at Amber Road, 1902; Sultan of Siak at Chancery Lane, 1907.
Second row: New Harbour Dock Company, 1897; Syed Mohd Alsagoff at Thomson Road, 1901; Frederick d'Almeida at Lloyd Road, 1901; J. Motion at St Thomas Walk, 1900.
Third Row: Pang Teck Joon at Killiney Road, circa 1905; Pang Teck Joon at Scotts Road, 1901; Bungalow at 13 Amber Road, 1901; J.A. Pickering at Tyersall Road, 1903.
Bottom: A.W. Stiven at Cluny Road, 1901; Veerloop at Mt Elizabeth, circa 1901; T. Sarkies in Tanglin, 1908; Puey Yuen Chan at Grange Road, 1916.

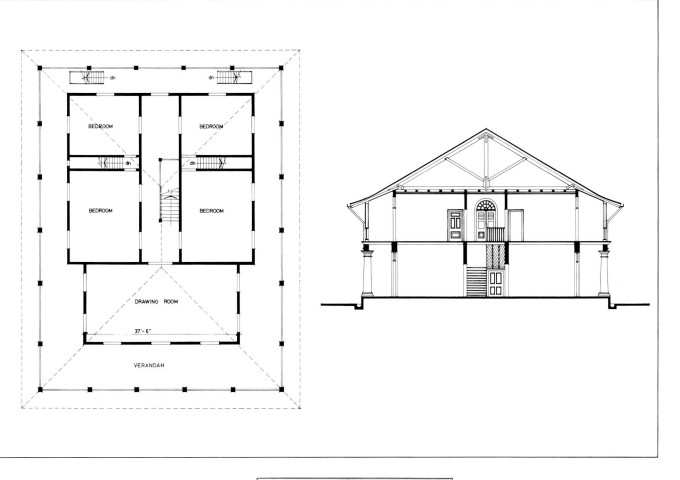

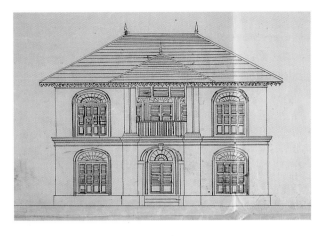

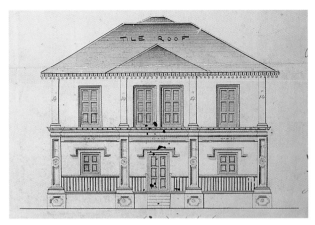

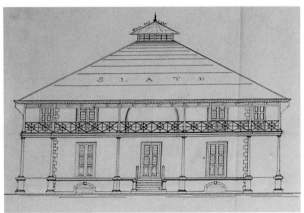

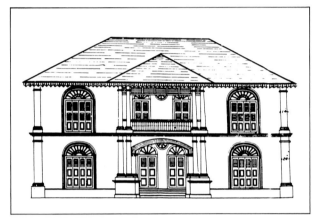

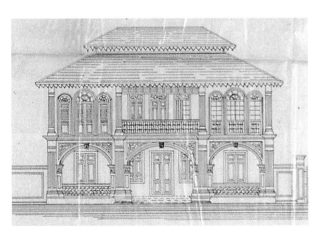

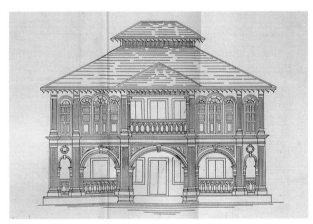

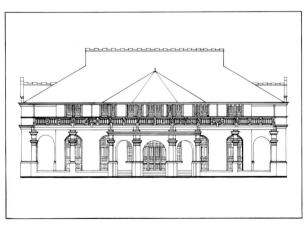

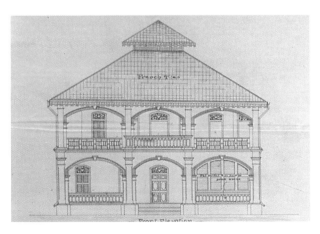

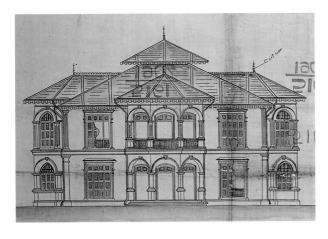

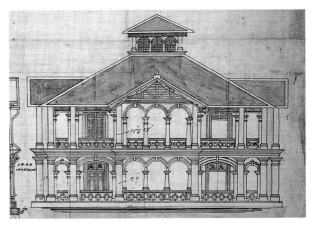

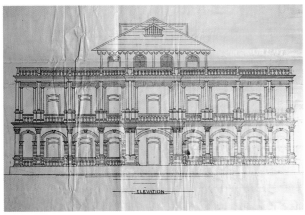

ELEVATION

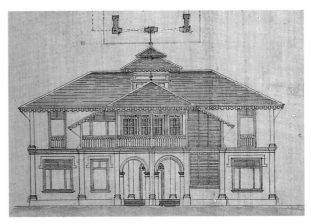

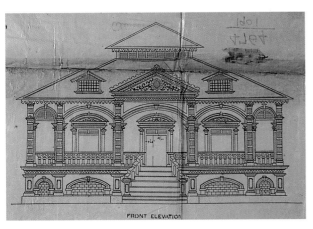

FRONT ELEVATION

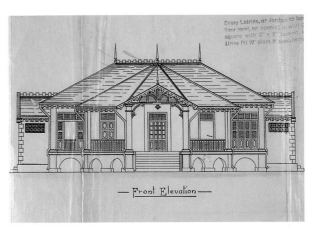

—Front Elevation—

PROPOSED NEW HOUSE
TANGLIN SINGAPORE
FOR T. SARKIES ESQ.
SCALE 8 FEET TO AN INCH

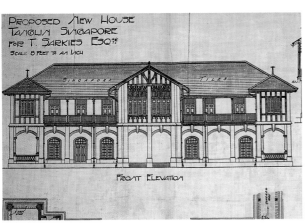

FRONT ELEVATION

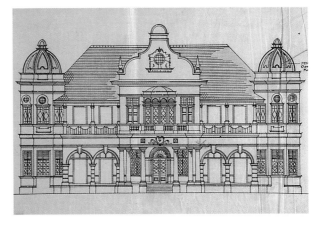

49

Singevore,.................................... Verandah of European Dwelling-house.

Life on the verandah circa 1910.

The verandah was an important feature of the 19th century colonial house and served as a cool and comfortable sitting area or, occasionally, as a more formal drawing room. G. F. Davidson, a visitor, commented of Singapore that "the houses generally ... are large and roomy, with verandahs in front and rear, enclosed with Venetian blinds. These are kept shut from ten a.m. till four p.m. which darkens the house .... " Writing about the verandah in India in *Stones of Empire* (Oxford: 1983) Jan Morris observed: "It was the one place the Imperialists had for just messing around on. Everything was easy going about the verandah. Its furniture was meant for lounging ..." The same could be said for Singapore.

Some houses were completely encircled while

others had verandahs along one side. The verandahs were either open to the outdoors, with timber balustrades and rattan chicks to give protection against the weather, or enclosed by walls and ventilated by French windows with timber louvres. Certainly it was the extended eaves, the verandahs with timber balustrades, and the steep roofs hipped on all sides for the efficient discharge of rain water that gave the colonial houses of this period their unmistakable tropical look.

Enclosed verandahs were usually confined to side wings or located above projecting carriage porches. Open verandahs were located on any or all sides but often completely encircled the house on both levels. Open verandahs probably originated with the *bangala* in India, where the verandah was

Family photographs on the verandah circa 1900.

created by the extension of the eaves on all sides of the house for better protection from the weather. In Singapore, the eaves usually extended slightly beyond verandahs of about eight to ten feet, providing sufficient cover and protection from the sun and rain for doors to remain open at all times in order to ventilate the rooms.

In some houses, the eaves were simply extended around the house and supported by brackets as an additional form of weather protection or as an alternative to the verandah. In other cases, the eaves were supported by timber posts raised from the ground. This can be seen in a number of early houses including Belle Vue, Cairnhill and Spring Grove. At Grasslands (page 206), the extension of the eaves along the front instead of the sides

was unusual. The structures suggest they were all later extensions and not part of the original design.

From the 1880s onwards, such spacious verandahs became less common. The introduction of glazed windows, the increases in building costs, and changes in building materials all contributed to their decline. (By 1870 there was hardly any jungle left in Singapore.) After reinforced concrete was introduced, most verandah floors were in that material in preference to timber which required regular maintenance when continually exposed to the weather. The deep overhanging eaves were also reduced in depth around this time. For stylistic rather than practical reasons they reappeared in the 1920s and 1930s in the houses designed by architects who were influenced by the Arts and Crafts Movement.

3.1 Tyersall, the Singapore residence of the Sultan of Johore, was one of the grandest homes built in the Victorian Eclectic style. The photograph by G. R. Lambert & Company shows the projecting carriage porch. The twin Corinthian pilasters attached to the massive piers add weight to the building. 3.2 The relatively slow forms of transportation, such as this horse and buggy, discouraged residents from living much beyond two-and-a-half miles from the centre of town.

Eclecticism

1870 - 1899

The establishment of the Straits Settlements government in 1867, which ended the authority of the East India Company, and the opening of the Suez Canal in 1869 accelerated the development of the colony. During the next half century, the town area began to expand beyond its confines. New residential suburbs were opened while new modes of transport were introduced that influenced the spread of residential areas; and a new, more elaborate style of architecture was introduced that sharply contrasted with the simplicity of earlier houses.

By far the most important development within the business centre was the construction by Colonel George Chancellor Collyer of the quay (3.3) named after him. It was completed in 1864, and by 1866 a line of new commercial buildings facing the quay were in place. The first Town Hall at Empress Place, completed in 1862, marked a new phase in the general development of the colony as it progressed. As a result of the need for direct communication between the town and New Harbour (Keppel Harbour), land reclamation was carried out at Telok Ayer basin between 1879 and 1890. A plan to reclaim the bay by private speculators in 1865 had been abandoned because it was considered to be too expensive. When the government decided to reconstitute the defence works at Mount Palmer (prompted by fear of war between England and Russia), the scheme was revived as the works necessitated the levelling of Mount Palmer and the earth removed could be used as fill material for the reclamation. On the reclaimed land Anson Road was formed in 1880, Cecil Street by 1885 and by 1900 all the new roads were completed. Clyde Terrace was formed following a second and smaller land reclamation near Rochor River in the 1870s.

The expansion of the town was basically radial, beginning initially as ribbon developments along the main trunk roads — Tanjong Pagar Road, River Valley Road, Orchard Road, Bukit Timah Road, Thomson Road, Serangoon Road and Kallang Road. The completion of the Telok Ayer reclamation paved the way for the expansion of the town towards Tanjong Pagar. Until about 1870, the residential suburbs were confined generally within a radius of about two to two-and-a-half miles from the centre of town. People were not inclined to live beyond that if they worked in town, as did most of the traders and merchants, as the horse and carriage was slow and the rickshaw, first introduced in February of 1880, had similar limitations.

Between River Valley Road and Thomson Road many middle class residential areas were being established. The outward movement of the Straits Chinese families from the overcrowded central areas of Telok Ayer, Tanjong Pagar, Neil Road and Duxton Hill began from the late 1890s when the first and some of the finest terraced houses were built in the area of River Valley Road, Kim Yam Road, Mohamad Sultan Road and Tong Watt Road as well as at Emerald Hill Road, Cuppage Road and Koek Road. Along Orchard Road the first shophouses were built in the 1880s, shortly before the first market in the area was established by Edwin Koek, a lawyer and son-in-law of William Cuppage.

Predominantly European enclaves were already well-established in the Tanglin and lower Bukit Timah districts by 1870. In the 1890s, property investment companies such as Fraser & Cumming by John Fraser and James Bannerman Cumming were established. The company leased a saw-mill in Johore, manufactured bricks at Balestier Road, and purchased White House estate on which three

3.3 Collyer Quay circa 1890. The buildings on the left were constructed shortly after the quay was completed around 1860. Before then, the backs of the godowns at Commercial Square fronted the sea where the quay was built on reclaimed land. The photograph also shows the various means of transport including the rickshaw which was introduced in 1880. 3.4 Following pages: Views of the town and countryside around the turn of the century. Half of Jalan Besar and the entire length of Lavender Street passed through what was still countryside as can be verified in the map of 1905 (page 56). Large coconut estates (page 57) stretched from Changi to Geylang as shown in the map of 1885. The postcard titled "Neil Road" shows the Jinricksha headquarters, completed in 1902.

houses were built, namely Glencaird, Sentosa, and Cree Hall. The estate was sold to Mansfield & Company in 1908 which built additional houses.

To the east of the town, between Serangoon Road and the sea, much of the land was low-lying and swampy, originating in Serangoon and Kallang, and continuing between Bukit Timah and Thomson Road to the water catchment area where Macritchie Reservoir was built in 1863. Jalan Besar, on the opposite side of Rochor River, was formed in 1878 but did not reach what is now Lavender Street until about 1890. The earliest shops and terraced houses in the area, between Sungei Road and Race Course Road, date from just before 1900. Six large kampongs (3.4) formed a ring around the southern edge of the swamp where it extended through the Kallang district as far as the Geylang River and inland to Serangoon Road — Kampong Kapur, occupied mainly by Malays; Kampong Boyan; Kampong Bugis; and Kampongs Kallang, Rokok and Laut which were originally occupied by various groups of *orang laut*. To live beyond this area increased the distance from town by three-and-a-half miles or more.

Much of the large low-lying area between Serangoon and Geylang roads remained rural until after World War Two. The development along both these roads and into Katong and Siglap was, however, inevitable due mainly to the increase in the Asian population and the lack of available land in the established middle-class residential areas in Bukit Timah, Tanglin and Claymore. The four main roads important to the eventual development of the Katong and Geylang areas were Tanjong Katong Road, Grove Road (now Mountbatten Road), East Coast Road and Joo Chiat Road. Tanjong Katong Road had been formed in the mid-1830s. Grove Road was constructed through Thomas Dunman's coconut plantation in 1905 and completed in 1909. In 1906–1907 East Coast Road was extended westwards from Haig Road to join Tanjong Katong Road.

The increase in population and subsequent demand for housing resulted in the gradual fragmentation of the plantations in the eastern part of the island and the establishment of residential suburbs beginning about 1910. In Geylang, d'Almeida sold his Perseverance estate about 1860 to John Fisher, a mechanical engineer who planted lemon grass, or *serai*. He was evidently successful as the estate won awards for citronella oils in the 1863 and 1865 Nagapore Exhibitions. In 1887, Fisher sold his business to C.M. Allen, his manager since 1881. The Allen family remained proprietors of the estate until after Allen's death in 1900. It is uncertain if the Alsagoff family purchased the land from the Allen

family or from Fisher, but sometime before 1907 the land was leased from Alsagoff & Company and managed by D.R. Cowan. Around the Geylang Police Station, which stood near the junction of Paya Lebar and Geylang Roads, the Chinese village established in 1852 spread into the abandoned estate and became a predominantly Malay village. It was named Geylang Serai — after Fisher's lemon grass.

About 1900 Chew Joo Chiat, who had purchased Confederate estate from the families of Dr Robert Little and others, paved the main estate road that was to be named after him. A.W. Cashin cut a new road, later called Haig Road, through property that was originally part of T.O. Crane's coconut plantation. Further east, John Armstrong's 325-acre coconut plantation (purchased by Mathew Little in 1868) was subdivided, and in 1885 Little sold that part of it known as Annandale Coconut Plantation to three individuals, including Armogum Anamalai, surveyor and architect, and Alfred Lermit's partner in the firm of Anamalai & Lermit. The greater part of Anamalai's lot of about 20 acres, located between East Coast Road and the sea, was bought in 1917 by Moona Kadir Sultan, a well-known cattle merchant, who built Karikal Mahal (8.1).

On the western side of the island, the entire hilly area stretching from Tanglin to the sea was interspersed with swamps. Alexandra Road, one of the main roads in the area, remained sparsely inhabited for many years. In 1862, Tan Kim Seng had acquired about half of the area between Telok Blangah and Clementi Road — a total of 2,859 acres! It was probably the largest single parcel of land ever owned by a private individual in Singapore. Much of the area was occupied by tenant farmers or squatters, while on the slopes of the hills at Telok Blangah large pineapple plantations were established. By about 1900, the west coast area had opened up as far as West Coast Road and a residential suburb with houses along the road and on the hills fronting the sea had begun to develop.

Thus, by the early years of this century, the town had expanded considerably from what it had been a mere 50 years earlier. The suburbs extended generally in an easterly direction, but their furthermost limits were still not more than three to four miles from town. The urbanisation of Geylang, Katong, parts of lower Tanglin and the Serangoon-Jalan Besar area would intensify after World War One.

The completion of the Town Hall in 1862, mentioned above, was a milestone in Singapore's architectural history. It was the first of a number of buildings constructed

Singapore.

Jalan Besar, Singapore

Lavender Street, Singapore

Campong Kallang

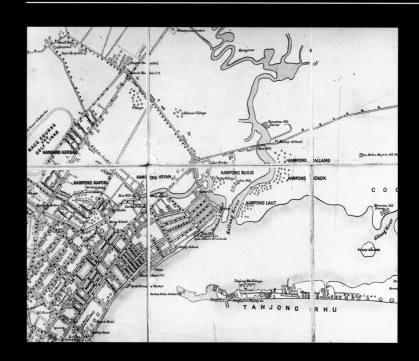

Singapore. Bukit Timah Bungalow.

H. No. 333 Thompson Road Singapore

Singapore. Gaylong Road.

Singapore. Nell Road.

3.5 These examples of Victorian buildings vary considerably. The Town Hall, 1852-1862, (top) possibly introduced Eclecticism to the colony while the Post Office, circa 1874, (above left) and the Exchange building, circa 1870, (above right) were other early examples. All three are fairly restrained. Later buildings include the Central Police Station (opposite, top left) and the Police Court (opposite top right), both circa 1870. The Hong Kong and Shanghai Bank (opposite, bottom left) of 1877 is perhaps the most eclectic of all. Boustead Institute, circa 1890, (opposite, bottom right) is a late example and reflects the renewed interest in classicism towards the end of the century.

Police Court, Singapore

The Police Court, Singapore

on a scale and grandeur hitherto unseen in the colony, and was influenced by changing architectural trends in Europe. The tendency towards an extravagant application of classical motifs and decorations to all types of buildings began in Britain in the early 19th century when the pendulum of taste began to swing from Palladian simplicity to highly decorative Victorian Revival architecture. The main contestants were the Gothic and the Classical styles. The "Battle of the Styles," as it became known, raged from 1830 to the end of the century and widened to include every known period. As time went on, there was less concern for historical accuracy, and the desire for innovation and novelty led to an extravagant and excessive eclecticism. It was said that the eclectic architects and builders raked history for embellishments and added to their houses distorted fragments of Norman castles, French chateaux and Swiss chalets. Roger Dixon and Stefan Muthesius in *Victorian Architecture* (London: 1978), remarked that "after 1860 until the turn of the century most architects felt free to choose, and to vary their choice and combination of styles..."

The origin of Victorian Eclectism can be traced to the Picturesque Movement, which flourished in England circa 1750 to the 1830s, and exerted a

significant influence on domestic architecture. Dixon and Muthesius remarked that under the influence of John Nash (1752–1835) and Humphrey Repton (garden designer 1752–1818), "the house itself was seen as a picturesque element in the landscape. Irregularity of outline was one of the main characteristics of the Picturesque, and hardly a single house was without some asymmetrical element." The most extreme examples were the remodelling of the Royal Pavilion at Brighton in 1815-1821 by Nash, and Castle Goring in West Sussex built in 1795–1815 for Sir Bysshe Shelley, the poet's grandfather, and designed by John Biagio Rebecca (?–1847). The Royal Pavilion had an Indian exterior and interiors of a Chinese character mixed with the Gothic. The castle, on the other hand, was described by David Watkin in *The Buildings of Britain* (London: 1982) as "an astonishing split personality house with a Classical south front and a Gothic north front."

Eclectism in domestic architecture was continued by the architects of the Arts and Crafts Movement including John Ruskin (1819–1900), William Morris (1834–96), Philip Webb (1834–96) and George Edmund Street (1824–81), the latter being best known for his design of the Law Courts in London, built in 1866. In a growing reaction to the

HONGKONG & SHANGHAI BANK, SINGAPORE.

Singapore. Boustead Institute.

3.6 Government House, now the Istana, in an early postcard.

age of the machine, these men preached the revival of crafts, the vernacular, individuality and an architecture free of imposed formality and styles. In his design of the Red House at Bexley Heath, built in 1859 for William Morris, Philip Webb used Gothic arches as well as 18th century sash windows. The "picturesque possibilities" of a mixture of motifs derived from widely different styles were readily taken up by other architects.

In Singapore, it was from the 1860s to the early 1900s — between the simple styles of the early years and the onset of a classical resurgence — that Victorian Revival and Eclectic architecture flourished. The mixture of styles ranged from the various classical modes to the Gothic, the former being more commonly adopted.

Probably the first building to reflect the new trend was the Town Hall (3.5). Work began in 1856, but because of financial problems took six years to complete. It was designed by John Bennett, an engineer, who was among the first to introduce this richer style of architecture into the colony. He was more lavish with details, unlike the chaste and orderly architecture of the earlier decades. He was disciplined in his exploitation of the Ionic Order, used instead of the usual Doric or Tuscan, but also applied a profusion of stylistic elements and details, particularly in the corner blocks topped by a minaret-like ornament.

The Town Hall was followed by three important buildings in Fullerton Square in the 1870s (3.5) — the Exchange Building (1865–70), the General Post Office (1874) and a new building for the Hongkong Shanghai Bank (1877). Within the same decade, the Central Police Station and the Police and District Courts at South Bridge Road were built (3.5). All of these buildings were less in-

hibited in the use of the Orders, which were not confined to the Doric and Tuscan alone. In most of the buildings at least two Orders were used; following classical rules, the Doric Order is always on the ground level and the Ionic and Corinthian on the upper levels. The General Post Office might have been one of the first to adopt the Corinthian Order.

Nearly all of the eclectic houses built in Singapore during the period under discussion were essentially classical in style, in the broadest sense, ranging from the ornate Victorian Renaissance to the simpler Roman Classical, with touches of Gothic, Chinese, Malay and other influences. Two of the earliest, and grandest, were Government House, or the Istana, designed by Major J.F.A. McNair, RA, the colonial engineer, and completed around August of 1870 (3.6), and Tyersall, the Singapore residence of His Highness Sultan Abu Bakar of Johore (3.1).

The Istana is a symmetrical building with a dignified front of open verandahs in the Ionic upon Doric Orders. The central portion of the building is carried to a third level tower in the Corinthian Order and crowned with a mansard roof. But for the mansard roof in particular, and the ornate details of the cornices and balustrade of the roof parapet, the house was designed in the best Anglo-Indian tradition, although quite in contrast to Coleman's Palladian classicism. Tyersall, on the other hand, had a touch of the Gothic in its decorative eaves boards and its pierced balustrade. These, together with the ornamental vases resting on the balustrade, gave the palace an oriental look. The twin pilasters and the enclosed verandahs created a heavier appearance.

Of the smaller houses of the 1860 to 1900 period, a number of examples have been documented, mostly built after 1884. These include Belle Vue Cottage circa 1870 (page 37) as well as Magenta Cottage (circa 1882), W.E. Hooper's house (1889) and Syed Mohammed Alsagoff's house at Dunearn Road (1890), which have been mentioned in chapter two. Stylistically they belong to the earlier decades. To these may be added Carrington House (page 186) which belongs to the type with surrounding verandahs, like Hooper's. All of these were in the simpler style of the earlier years and there were probably few, if any, houses other than Government House and Tyersall that were built in the formal classical manner during this period.

The introduction of Victorian Eclecticism in Singapore, however, resulted in the gradual emergence of a "Coarsened Classical" style, so-called because of the ignorant application of the Classical Orders and other classical elements. One of the earliest houses in the more flamboyant style was Bonnygrass, built by Ong Ewe Hai (3.7). The plans of the house were submitted in 1889 by the Eurasion architect Henry D. Richards. It had a standard three-bay across the front symmetrical plan but was unusual for its great depth and the internal air well. The elevations, without doubt, were strongly influenced by Victorian Eclecticism. The facade treatment was elaborate: the simulated stonework on the balusters and walls, the plaster relief decorations on the spandrels to the ground floor arches, and the fluted pilasters on the first floor.

The application of the classical motifs and decorations was also somewhat more restrained, as compared to houses built 20 years later, in the houses of Cheang Hong Lim (1884) at Kim Yam Road (3.7) and Botan House (circa 1880) (page 172) at Neil Road. Henry Richard's design of the Norris bungalow (1888) at Bukit Timah Road (page 183) also showed some restraint in the treatment of the rather Grecian pediments, the Doric or Tuscan columns being somewhat dated. The Cheang Hong Lim house and Bonnygrass in particular may perhaps be regarded as the precursors of the more elaborate and decorative style of coarsened classicism that was to last well into the present century and be given new impetus during the Edwardian period as will be discussed in chapter eight.

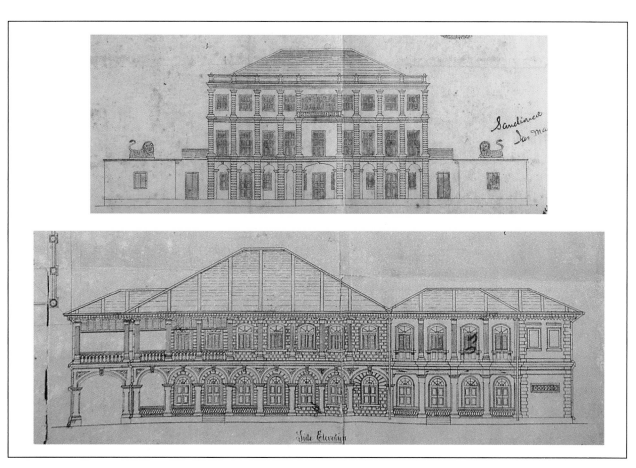

3.7 Elevation of a house for Cheang Hong Lim, (top) and side elevation of Bonnygrass (above), both precursors of the Coarsened Classical style.

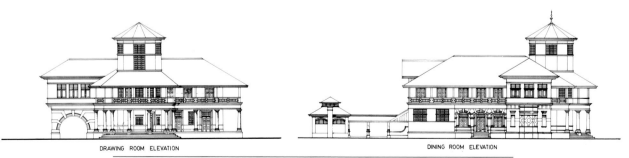

3.8 Glencaird, 1897, was one of the earliest houses with an asymmetrical plan. John Fraser (top) was the original owner of the house. The elevations are measured drawings based on the original building plans.

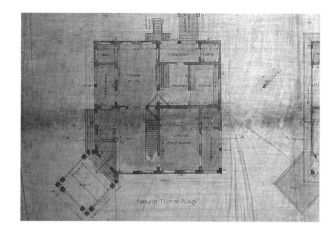
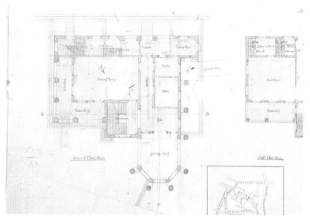

3.9 Two examples of asymmetrical plans: house for Dr Galloway at Cairnhill, 1913 (left) and house at Mount Sophia for Singapore Land, 1892 (right).

There were, in addition, changes introduced in regard to the floor plans of houses. The standard symmetrical three-bay across the front colonial house, derived from the compact plans of the Georgian and Regency periods, survived in Singapore until the outbreak of the Pacific War. Towards the end of the century, however, a number of houses were built that departed completely from the standard plan, a change influenced by trends in Britain that popularised, among the prosperous middle class, country houses and the picturesque cottage-like house, or cottage *orne*, as holiday houses or country retreats. The cottage *orne* was a rustic building, usually of asymmetrical plan. This phenomenon, as well as the challenge to classicism as the basis of good taste and the Picturesque cult, brought about the asymmetrical and eclectic facade. Behind the irregular exteriors, house plans began to vary. Asymmetrical planning, in turn, created clearer distinctions in the functions and sizes of rooms. By the 1840s, the transformation was complete.

The change was introduced into Singapore probably around 1890. The earliest extant architectural drawings of an asymmetrically planned residence are of a house at Mount Sophia Road built in 1892 for Singapore Land Company (3.9). It was designed by Crane Brothers, a firm of auctioneers, land valuers and architects. The first floor plan strongly suggests that the building was of three bays and traditional in plan while the asymmetry was effected by the position of the carriage porch on one side. In other respects the location of the rooms was traditional; the dining room on the ground floor and the drawing room above the carriage porch and next to the bedrooms.

One of the architects responsible for the

introduction of the new plan concept was Regent Alfred John Bidwell (1869–?). Bidwell, who came to Singapore in 1895, received his professional training in articleship with Lockyer, Son & Cox, London. Subsequently he worked in other private offices and the London County Council before coming East to join the Public Works Department in Kuala Lumpur, where he was for some years. He moved to Singapore to work for Swan & Maclaren and became a partner in 1899. By the time of his departure from the firm in 1911 to begin his own practice, Bidwell had executed some of their best work, including the Teutonia Club (now part of the Goodwood Hotel), Chased-El Synagogue, Singapore Cricket Club and Telegraph House. Bidwell seems to have stopped practising during World War One and disappeared thereafter from the records.

In his use of the asymmetrical plan in three houses, Bidwell retained the outhouses: Glencaird, a two-storey house built in 1897 for John Fraser (3.8); Atbara, a bungalow built in Gallop Road in 1898 for John Burkinshaw (page 180); and a two-storey house at Cairnhill Circle built in 1913 for Dr D. J. Galloway (page 220). In all three, the plans departed from the compact, symmetrical three or five-bay across the front with a projecting porch and verandah placed centrally to the main axis. Although Glencaird, which is still standing, is divided structurally into three bays, it deviates from the standard plan in the division of rooms and the placement of the entrance porch leading into the stairhall that projects at the side. The planning obviously took into consideration the best prospects offered by the site by placing the drawing room at the rear corner to face the most desirable views of White House Park in two directions: eastwards towards

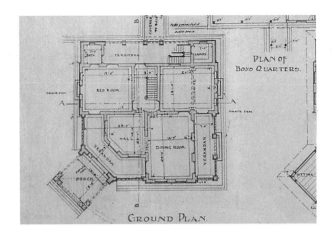

PLAN OF
BOYS QUARTERS.

GROUND PLAN.

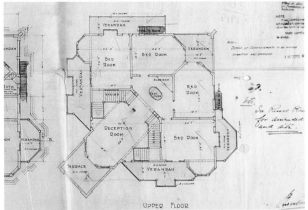

UPPER FLOOR

3.10 An asymmetrical plan was used by David McLeod Craik in a house at Nathan
Road in 1913 (left) and by J.B. Westerhout in a house at Oxley Rise in 1919 (right).

Cree Hall and southwards towards an undulating expanse that sloped across Dalvey Road. The entrance porch faced west and above it, quite sensibly, was the morning room. The asymmetry of the elevations was accentuated by the three-storey stairhall which rose above the roof as a prospect tower.

Charles McArthur's house at Gallop Road, called Inverturret (page 184), was also compactly planned with minimum passages and circulation areas. Designed by Swan & Maclaren in 1905, it could also have been planned by Bidwell who was then already a partner of the firm. As in Glencaird, the architect wanted to take advantage of the fine views and the rooms were asymmetrically arranged with the important ones facing east towards Atbara, and the valley below it, and north towards a grove of tall Tembusu trees on a stretch of green sward that dipped to the winding road below.

Bidwell's example was followed by others, including David McLeod Craik in Mohammed Ali Namazie's house at Nathan Road in 1913 and J. B. Westerhout in Meyer's house at Oxley Rise in 1919 (3.10). Succesful in his profession, Westerhout (1871–1937) designed many fine houses. He was born in Malacca and was of Dutch descent. His grandfather, Johannes Bartholomew Westerhout (1779–1856), was a native of Utrecht and governor of the District of Naning, Malacca. Westerhout, who adopted his grandfather's name, worked as a draughtsmen in the Public Works Department, Malacca from 1889 to 1893. He came to Singapore in 1896 and worked for Crane Brothers as an architect. From 1898 until his death in 1937 he had his own practice; in partnership with Alfred Lermit from 1889 to 1893 and with William Campbell Oman from 1924 to 1929.

David McLeod Craik, one of the most talented architects to work in Singapore, spent his early childhood in Scotland but later moved with his parents to Swansea where he received his education. After leaving school, he was articled in Bucknall & Jennings, architects, from 1889 to 1894. He worked thereafter in Glasgow, Edinburgh, Belfast and was in London in 1898. He was elected Student, RIBA in 1896, Associate in 1900 and Fellow in 1913.

Craik arrived in Singapore in 1902 to work for the Singapore municipality but resigned in 1907 to set up his own practice. While employed by the municipality, he designed the Jinrikisha Station at Tanjong Pagar and the lodge, gate and chapel at Bidadari Cemetery. He joined Swan & Maclaren in 1913 but went on home leave the following year when World War One broke out. He enlisted in the Royal Engineers, was wounded in action in France in 1917 and returned to Singapore after the Armistice. He retired with the rank of Captain RE, and was demobilised in August of 1919 in Singapore. On rejoining Swan & Maclaren, he was put in charge of their Penang office. He withdrew from the partnership and was on his own again in 1928. He retired and lived on Penang Hill in the late 1930s until circa 1940, after which nothing is known of him. He was successful in private practice and among his projects were the Arcade, St. Joseph's Cathedral and parochial buildings, the Wesley Church at Fort Canning, the Masonic Lodge, and the Banque de L'Indochine, built in 1912.

In his plan for J. P. Hallaway's bungalow (3.11), Craik was unconventional; the plan is similar to Bidwell's Atbara. The main house was long and narrow, which improved through ventilation, and access to the bedrooms was along the open verandah. A wing accommodating the servants' rooms and kitchen replaced the conventional outhouse. Built

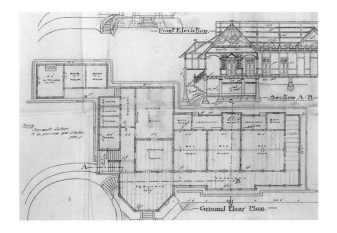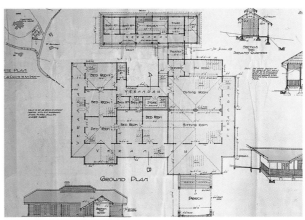

3.11 Asymmetrical plans were also used in J. P. Halloway's bungalow at Mount Victoria (left) and Mrs E. Johannes bungalow in Cairnhill Road (right).

in 1905, it could possibly be the first house planned and built without an outhouse.

The long, narrow plan of one-room depth and a verandah, or corridor, exemplified in the plans of Atbara and the Hallaway bungalow, was a concept often used by the early Arts and Crafts architects in Britain. Bidwell, again, could possibly be credited for its introduction into Singapore. Other examples of houses similarly planned were T. Sarkies' house in Tanglin (3.14) and Mrs. E. Johannes' bungalow at Cairnhill Road (3.11). In both, the main buildings were long and narrow, of one-room depth, and with open corridors or verandahs along the fronts, rears or sides. The narrow plan was well-suited to the tropics since it improved ventilation.

In many government bungalows built in the 1920s, the long-and-narrow plan was employed, including the houses along Malcolm Road designed in their fimiliar "black-and-white" mode derived essentially from the "Mock Tudor" style popular with government architects (page 224). The Malcom Road houses were Class III government quarters designed by H. A. Stallwood, ARIBA, of the Public Works Department in 1925, and they are still standing Two storeys in height, the houses are technically bungalows. Except for the stair-hall and garage, the ground floor is open. Built on sloping ground, the houses are linked to outhouses on the upper level of the slope. The main portion of each house is long and narrow and of one room depth with a continuous verandah along the front and sides; private verandahs to bedrooms and the dining room are at the rear. The plan and front elevations, however, are symmetrical. The houses built at the former British naval base at Seletar were similarly designed and planned.

The "butterfly" or "sun-trap" plan was another

Arts and Crafts innovation. A variant of the long-and-narrow plan, the house was curved or angled to let in as much fresh air and sunlight as possible. The plan was regarded especially suitable for seaside houses, and was adopted by Bidwell in 23 Amber Road, designed in 1912 for A.W. Cashin (page 211). The crescent-shape was unusual. The open verandah facing the sea served as access to the various rooms placed along the length of the building. The house was designed in the neo-Renaissance style, and symmetrical in plan and elevation but for the outhouse placed at the side.

It does seem incredible, on evidence so far available from extant houses of the period and the earliest drawings dating back to 1880 in the National Archives, that the asymmetrical and informal plan arrangement initiated over half a century earlier in England was not introduced into Singapore until the 1890s by Bidwell, and later Craik, in their irregular, compact and linear corridor plans. In some houses, such as the Crane Brothers' plan of Captain J. Blair's house at Spottiswoode Park built in 1895, asymmetry in a basically traditional three-bay symmetrical plan came about more by the requirement of a large dining room on the ground floor and the separation of the drawing room from the open verandah on the first floor rather than by consideration of site and orientation as in Glencaird. Similarly, in Veerappa Chitty's bungalow (page 218) the asymmetry was the result of projecting the sitting room, a form that continued into the 1930s as at nos. 2 and 4 Poole Road (page 219).

The delay can perhaps be accounted for by the relative isolation of the colony from Europe caused by sheer distance and the slow and often irregular communications. The opening of the Suez Canal in 1869 overcame, to some extent, these disadvant-

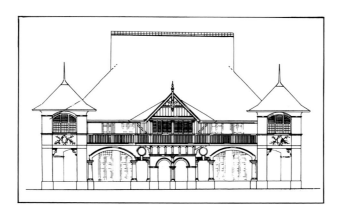

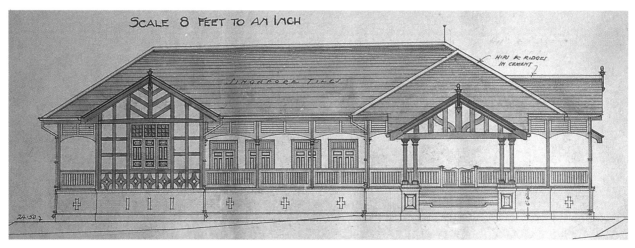

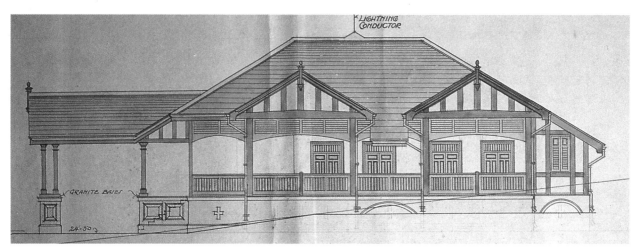

3.12 Patchitt's house (top) and Mrs Johannes' bungalow (above) are early examples of the popular Mock Tudor style. The Patchitt house, however, is less pure as it is Tudor on the first floor and classical on the ground floor and thus more in the spirit of Victorian Eclecticism. 3.14 The Mock Tudor is also evident in the house of T. Sarkies (following pages). The original building plans are a fine example of the beautiful rendering that was characteristic of the period. Note the corridor access to the rooms and the shallow depth of the building.

ages and facilitated the flow of new ideas and in-fluences. The new crop of important buildings of the 1860s and 1870s was a direct consequence of the growing prosperity that followed, and they popularised the eclectic facades. Yet the asymmetrical plan was introduced late here as in British India, where a remarkable parallel in the development of the bungalow appears to have taken place. Wrote Janet Potts in *Old Bungalows in Bangalore*:

Although the general plan of porch, verandah, central living room flanked by bedrooms, dressing rooms and bathrooms usually remained the same, by the beginning of the 20th century, the symmetry was less important and in some bungalows there was an alternative plan with an entrance at the corner or side of the building.

In contrast, the eclectic facade appeared much earlier, possibly in the 1860s or 1870s, about 20 to 30 years after its appearance in England. The houses of the 1830s through the 1850s were designed with disarming simplicity and subtle elegance. As we have seen, between the 1860s and the 1870s Victorian eclecticism was introduced first in public buildings, probably by Bennett. McNair on the other hand, was essentially a revivalist: St. Andrew's Cathedral, completed in 1862, was Gothic while Government House was classical.

The asymmetrical forms were dressed in a variety of eclectic facades. Stylistic tendencies depended on the current vogue or the architect's whim. Craik and Bidwell, for example, who may be regarded as contemporaries, were not always consistent in their choice of styles. Both adopted Gothic as well as classical modes in the eclectic manner. In their designs for Hallaway's bungalow and Atbara the Gothic character is apparant. Bidwell's prospect tower at Glencaird was a picturesque element with popular appeal.

The Gothic style was never widely adopted in Singapore, except for a few ecclesiastical and educational buildings. The gateways to the Fort Canning Cemetry, reputedly by Coleman and built in 1833, were probably the earliest Gothic Revival structures. Other examples include St Andrew's Cathedral; the old St. Andrew's School building at Stamford Road built between 1875–1885; St Joseph's Church designed by Craik in 1911; the old Convent of the Holy Infant Jesus Chapel and the Church of our Lady of Lourdes at Ophir Road built in 1888. Other examples are Wesley Church at Fort Canning, also designed by Craik in 1908, and another building known as the Parochial House at Victoria Street designed by Craik in 1912.

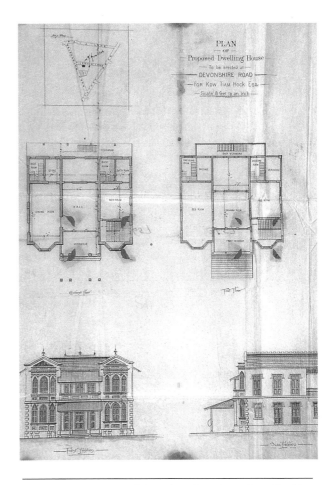

3.13 The conventional three-bay plan of Kow Tian Hock's house was dressed in a purer Gothic facade, complete with lancet windows, decorative ridge pieces and finials.

Gothic details, however, became extremely popular in domestic work. The finials fixed to some house roof tops were Gothic in origin as were the ornamental ridge pieces and the decorative eaves boards. Although executed by local craftsmen, the forms were imported. A good example of more apparent Gothic influence can be seen in the bungalow at Tyersall designed in 1903 by Lermit & Westerhout for James Arthur Newton Pickering (see 2.21) who was listed as a stockbroker in 1904 (and who is not to be confused with W.A. Pickering of the Chinese Protectorate from 1871 to 1889). Thoroughly eclectic, it had a rather strong Gothic accent. The half-round arches of the supporting walls, the Tuscan columns and piers and the windows were classical. The ridge pieces, eaves boards, the finials and the bargeboards of the "monkey tops" over the carriage porch were distinctly Gothic. The rounded gable ends of the bathroom wings were baroque if not Dutch.

The Gothic influence can also be seen in Adis Lodge on Mount Sophia, built in 1904 (page 187). The verandahs along the front and sides were

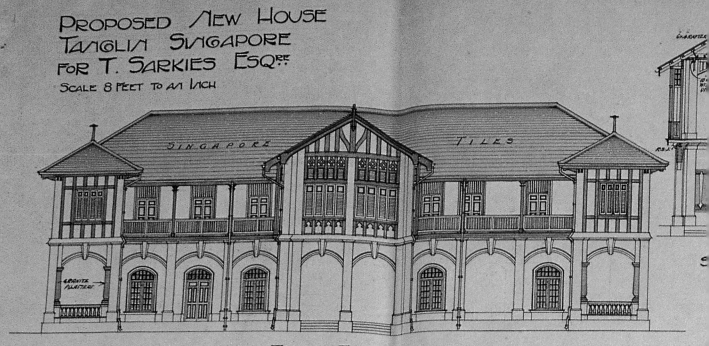

PROPOSED NEW HOUSE
TANGLIN SINGAPORE
FOR T. SARKIES ESQRE
Scale 8 Feet to an Inch

FRONT ELEVATION

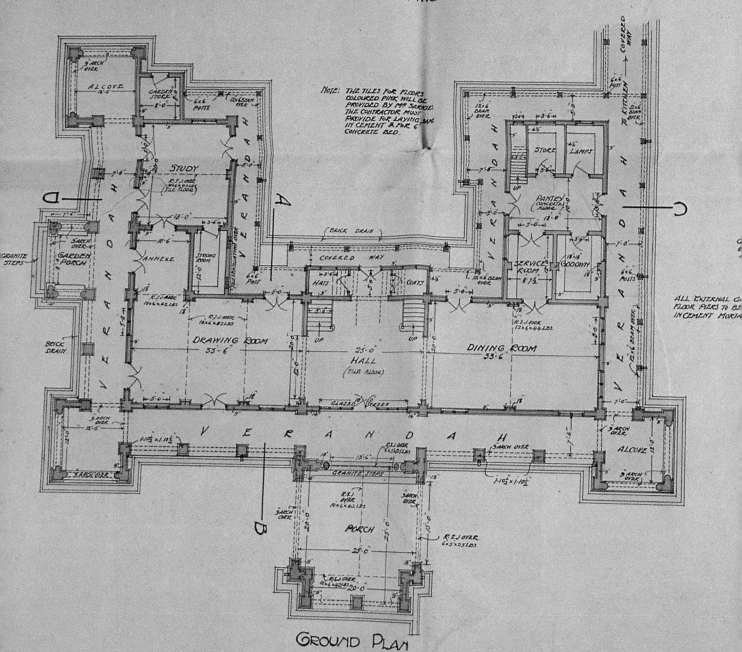

NOTE: THE TILES FOR FLOORS COLOURED PINK WILL BE PROVIDED BY MR SARKIES THE CONTRACTOR MUST PROVIDE FOR LAYING SAME IN CEMENT & FOR 6" CONCRETE BED.

ALCOVE

STUDY

DRAWING ROOM
33-6

HALL
(TILE FLOOR)

DINING ROOM
33-6

VERANDAH

PORCH

GROUND PLAN

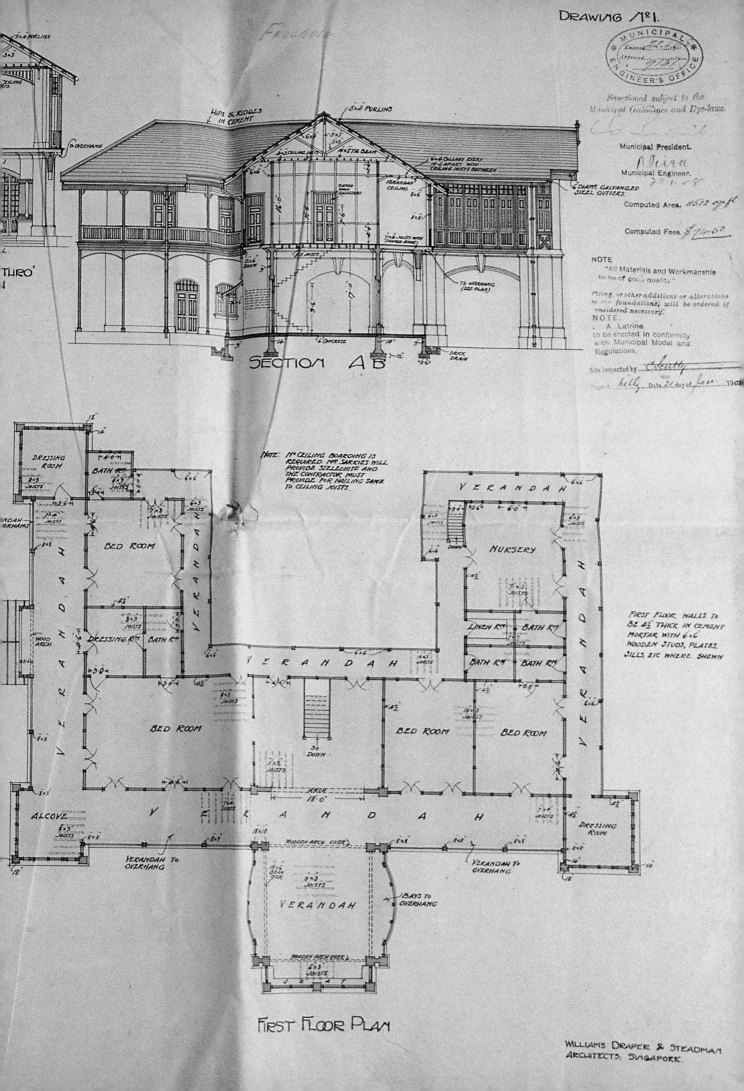

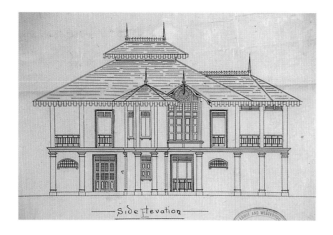

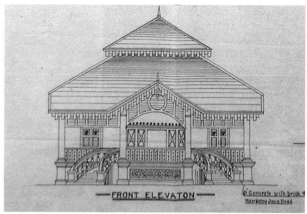

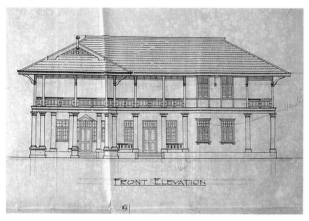

3.15 The houses of G.F. de Souza and at Bushy Park (above left and right) show half-timber construction.

supported by Corinthian piers with timber screens above balustrades of Victorian Renaissance design; but the bay windows of the rear bedrooms were Gothic and so was the treatment of the gables above the windows. A rare example of more complete Gothic treatment is Kow Tiam Hock's house at Devonshire Road, designed by Lermit &

3.16 The Gothic influence is apparent in the houses shown here built in the early years of this century.

Westerhout in 1900 (3.13). Lancet bay windows were used on either side of the front entrance veran- dah while other windows, including those at the sides, were Tudor. Other Gothic features were the bonnetts over the bay windows, the decorative eaves boards, the treatment of the bargeboards, the finials and the decorative iron ridge pieces. The simulated stone quoins of the ground floor walls were early Renaissance, however.

Gothic influences were also apparent in the Tudor and the half-timbered Old English style of architecture, first revived in Britain by Norman Shaw and others in the 1860s and described locally as Mock Tudor. The earliest known example is a house at Cluny Road designed in 1903 by Swan & Maclaren for W. Patchitt (3.12). Two other early examples are Sarkies' house at Tanglin (3.14), and a bungalow at Cairnhill Road, both built in 1908 and designed by Williams, Draper & Stead- man. The Sarkies house is, in fact, another example of Victorian eclectism in which the upper half of the building was Mock Tudor and the lower classical, as is evident in the arches and Renaissance

Scal[e]

Front Elevation

3.17 More Gothic details. The house of William Dunman at Mount Alma.

balustrade on the ground floor. Half-timbered construction also occurs in numbers 1, 2 and 3 Bushy Park (3.15), built in 1918 for the Straits Trading Company and designed by Swan & Maclaren, and G.F. de Souza's house at St. Michael's Road designed by J.B. Westerhout in 1920 (3.15). It was confined to the roof gables in D.M. Craik's design of the bunga-low at Mount Victoria built in 1905 for J.P. Hall-away (3.11) an engineer who was later in charge of the municipal gas department.

The style was fondly adapted, as mentioned earlier, by government architects in houses that have survived to this day at Goodwood Hill, Seaton Close, Adam Park and elsewhere. In some, the half-timbered construction was confined to the upper levels while the lower part of the two-storey houses as well as the bungalows were of load-bearing brick walls, piers and columns. Here, too, eclecticism persisted in the blend of the half-timbered Old English of the first floors with the classicism of the supporting structures of the ground floors, as in the arches and classical mouldings of the cornices and the bases of the piers and walls. In some instances, Doric or Tuscan columns were inevitably used to support the projecting verandahs.

The Mock Tudor and various classical styles continued to be popular in Singapore well into the present century; but as the 19th century came to a close, changes were imminent that would eventually alter the course of domestic architecture.

3.18 The house of George d'Almeida at Cuppage Road.

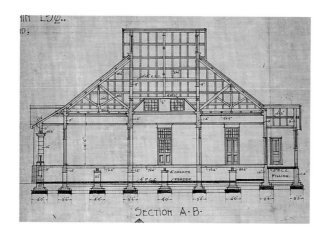

Sectional drawing of house of A.W. Cashin at Rochalie Drive
reveals construction details.

Colonial houses were basically of load-bearing brick-wall construction. Walls were normally ten inches thick except on the ground floor of some two-storey houses where they were 14 inches thick. Chinese bricks, either manufactured locally or imported, were used. They measured ten inches in length, four inches in width and one-and-a-half inches in thickness and were smaller than the imported English or Indian bricks. Local bricks were produced to British standards by Indian convict labour and first manufactured on a large scale probably when the Public Works Department opened their brick fields in Serangoon in 1858. Curved bricks were specially made for round columns.

The floors of bungalows raised above ground level were constructed of timber joists and one-and-a-half inches Chengai (*Balanocarpus heimei*) or Jati (*Tectona grandis*) floor-boards. The ground below the floor was slabbed over in brick or concrete and screeded over in cement. The first floors of two-storey houses, similarly constructed of timber joists and floor-boards, were supported on load-bearing brick walls or timber bressumers — the front edge or main beam that supports secondary beams — often Balau (*Shorea materialis*) or Berlian (*Eusideroxylon zwaggeri*) and occasionally on cast-iron or steel beams. Intermediate supports were sometimes provided by means of cast iron columns, usually imported from Calcutta or Glasgow.

FOUNDATIONS AND FLOORS
Strip foundations to walls and piers were sometimes in lime concrete but usually in bricks, bedded in lime mortar and, where required, laid on Bakau piles. The lime was produced from local shells and coral and the Bakau piles logged locally. Ground floor slabs were either of brick, six inches of concrete composed of granite chips, brick dust and lime mortar, or Portland cement. The slabs were laid on a six-inch thick hardcore of broken bricks or granite and finished in neat cement or tiled.

Red Malacca clay floor tiles were used in most houses. These measured approximately 15 inches square and one-and-a-half inches thick. Some were hexagonal, measuring 14 inches across the sides and 16 inches across the angles. Tiles were laid with a one-inch joint pointed in blue. Marble slabs, usually white and imported from China, were laid in wealthier homes. Imported European patterned ceramic floor and wall tiles and mosaic tiles were introduced probably in the 1880s. Patterned cement tiles were produced locally at the turn of the century. Unpolished granite slabs, usually four inches thick, were used sparingly either as the trimming to floor edges, airwells and verandahs or as paving in airwells, courtyards and patios. In traditional Chinese houses, some of the columns and lintels above door openings were in solid granite.

CEILINGS AND ROOFS
The ceilings of ground floor rooms were usually the exposed floor-boards of the rooms above, varnished or painted. In Chinese homes, red lacquer was sometimes applied instead of ordinary wood varnish. Suspended or false ceilings were not common. Ceilings under roofs were boarded and alcoved in the earlier houses or, later, covered in asbestos sheets which were secured by timber battens.

Roofs were timber framed and covered in attap, wood shingles, half-round Malacca tiles or imported slate. French tiles and concrete tiles were introduced towards the 1930s. Roofs were often trussed to meet wider spans. In traditional Chinese houses, the elaborate and decorative roof trusses were fabri-

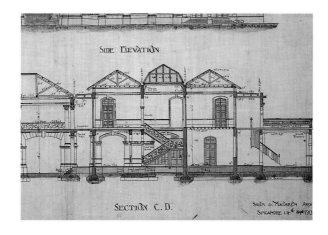

Sectional drawing of house of E.S. Manasseh at Ladyhill.
Note the concrete floor of the first floor.

cated and imported from China; roller joists were sometimes fixed to support roofs of smaller spans.

In homes of Chinese families, traditional or otherwise, crescent-shaped eaves tiles were sometimes fixed to the ends of green glazed earthenware over-tiles on overhangs above door openings and verandah ways. Decorative eaves boards were fixed to main roofs of some houses regardless of the nationality of the occupant or architect, the most common being of the pattern seen on the house at Kerbau Road built for Teo Hong Beng (see endpapers). The eaves soffits, if covered, were either boarded and with vent holes or covered with asbestos sheets. Gutters were of galvanised iron sheets, and rainwater hoppers and down-pipes of cast iron.

The hipped and gable roofs were the two most common roof forms. Jack-roofs were often added to the main house and outhouses to improve ventilation. A half-hipped or gambrel roof was occasionally adopted as was the jerkin-head or "Sussex" hipped gable. Attics were rarely constructed and mansards were found mainly on the larger houses. Decorative ridge tiles of terracotta or galvanised iron often adorned the ridges. The apex and gable ends of roofs were crowned with a *buah buton*, or timber finial. Houses designed in the traditional Chinese style had more elaborate roof ornamentation.

WINDOWS

Until the introduction of glazing, sometime between 1870 and 1880, window openings were frequently door length, with wooden louvres on the top half and panelled below. When glass became less expensive at the turn of the century, fixed lights were incorporated above the windows.

Two pairs of windows were sometimes fixed, the inner pair being glazed the outer timber louvred. Most often found in Chinese homes, the glass panels of the inner windows were divided by glazing beads into a regular pattern of hexagons and rectangles. In traditional Chinese-style houses windows were boarded. Patent steel windows were first introduced in the early 1930s, and these were replaced by sliding aluminium windows in the 1960s.

STAIRCASES AND BALUSTRADES

Before the introduction of reinforced concrete, staircases were of timber with cast-iron or timber balustrades and timber handrails. Some were of elaborate design, such as the Jacobean stairs at Cree Hall. Cast-iron spirals were used as secondary stairs in large houses and were common in terraced homes where space was limited.

Balustrades on first floor verandahs were usually of timber or cast-iron with timber hand rails. The heavier bottle or vase-shaped balusters of green glazed earthenware, or concrete and brick coping with plastered mouldings, more often lined ground floor verandahs.

WALLS

External and internal wall surfaces were rendered in lime plaster. In the early years, however, chunam plaster — composed of shell lime, coarse sugar and egg white mixed with coconut husks to form a paste — was also used. The surface applied when dried was then dusted with fine soap stone powder and rubbed down to a fine white gloss with rock crystal. No painting was then required.

External plaster reliefs, or pargetting, were in cement or lime plaster. According to Mr Chew Tat (tiler, born in 1927 in Guangdong province), the plaster relief work he saw in China in the 1930s was in lime plaster reinforced with husk and wire

Photograph of the staircase at Cree Hall circa 1880. The stairs
led from the carriage porch to the front hall of the house.

mesh. Mouldings and capitals to pilasters, columns and piers were pre-cast in timber moulds and fixed to walls. Mouldings on wall surfaces were fixed in the same way. Cement plaster was often used in the later years.

Wall surfaces of lime plaster were painted in lime wash, the colours of which varied. White, pale yellow and light green were common, the last being a popular choice among Chinese owners as can be observed in a number of houses built in the 1920s. This was possibly due to the fact that symbolically green represented youth and longevity to the Chinese. Red was used in temples and occasionally pink for houses, both symbolising prosperity.

The peeled surfaces of some old Chinese buildings in Singapore sometimes reveal indigo blue which was an odd choice, since blue and white were regarded as mourning colours. But blue could well have been the common choice before the turn of the century. An American visitor to Singapore in 1882, William T. Hornaday, remarked in his book *Two Years in the Jungle* (1885), "Architecturally considered, Singapore has little to boast of except solidity and uniformity. With but few exceptions the buildings are all Chinese and perfectly innocent of style. It is a two-storey town throughout, solidly built of brick, plastered over and painted a very pale blue or light yellow." Hornaday was obviously referring to the terrace houses and shops in the central area of the town, but if his impressions about uniformity are correct, a similar taste for colours in detached Chinese homes in both the town and the country could well have prevailed.

Doors and windows were usually painted. If two sets of windows were installed, the inner glazed windows were often varnished in red lacquer. In Chinese homes, the external windows were often full panelled with decorative patterns and Chinese characters inscribed on the panels and painted in gold against a red lacquer background. Such windows were fixed under verandahs at the front of houses on either side of the main entrance door.

Colours for doors and windows varied. According to Cameron, light green was the usual colour for the windows of European houses and it was probable that in the harsh tropical sunlight here, green was considered restful to the eye not only for houses but also in public buildings, an example of which can be seen in a watercolour sketch of Raffles Institution in 1841 by J.A. Marsh.

WATER SUPPLY

The population of the entire island depended on wells for their water supply. In the early years, water was probably also drawn from the present Stamford Canal, the water of which originated from a natural stream and was certified by Dr Montgomerie as safe for consumption.

In 1852, J.T. Thomson proposed a project for the supply of water from the headwaters of the Singapore River, but nothing came of the scheme. Tan Kim Seng's offer of $13,000 in 1857 to bring water into the town from Bukit Timah was spent instead on a fountain to commemorate his generosity. The first public water supply came from an impounding reservoir constructed between 1863 and 1868 at Thomson Road. It was enlarged in 1894 and again in 1904 to its present size when it was named after James MacRitchie, the municipal engineer.

Pierce Reservoir was completed in 1910. Service reservoirs were built on Mount Emily circa 1878, on Pearl's Hill in 1901–1904 and on Fort Canning circa 1925. There was no water filtration until 1889 when the first filter bed was constructed at Bukit

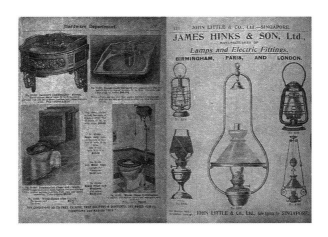

Among the items advertised in the John Little catalogue circa 1912 were essentials such as bathroom fixtures.

Timah Road. It was extended several times but when the first filter bed was constructed at Bukit Timah Road. It was extended several times but was inadequate to deal with the increasing demand, so that additional sets of filter beds were constructed at Woodleigh around 1910.

SEWERS

In the beginning, sewage was disposed of in sandpits or discharged directly into canals and open drains in the town. In 1899 the bucket system was introduced and it continued to be used in parts of Singapore until recently.

Around the turn of the century, Singapore's sewers were pronounced "unsuitable for a town in the tropics with an ignorant population." Recommendations in a report by W.J. Simpson of the University of London were considered costly but finally a sewage scheme proposed by Robert Pierce, the municipal engineer, in 1911 was accepted.

In house compounds, latrine huts were located usually at the corner of the compound or sometimes within the outhouses. These were often used only by domestic servants while chamber pot stands of timber or wrought iron were placed in bathrooms in the main house. Before the introduction of piped water, bathrooms were usually on the ground floor below bedrooms and accessible directly by stairs.

ELECTRICITY

Streets were lit by oil lamps from 1824 and by gas lamps from 1864. Electric lighting was first introduced in 1906, the supply for which was purchased from the Singapore Electric Tramway Company by the municipality for distribution to only a small section of the town.

Extension of the electric cables to Tanglin district was completed only in 1922. Although the extension scheme was first planned in 1914, it was not implemented until 1921 because of the outbreak of World War One. In 1924, the municipality decided to supply its own electricity and terminated its contract with the Shanghai Tramway Company which had taken over the Singapore Electric Tramway Company in 1913.

While the St James generating station was being constructed, supplies were obtained from the Singapore Harbour Board on a short term agreement that ended in 1927 when the station was completed. Generators were, however, installed in some private homes before the public supply reached them. A large generator plant was built in 1911 by Manasseh Meyer to supply electricity to the Sea View Hotel as well as to his house at the junction of Meyer Road and Amber Road on land now occupied by the Eastern Mansion flats.

TELEPHONES

The telephone made its appearance in Singapore in 1879 when an exchange of about 50 lines was operated privately by a Mr Bennett Pell. The Oriental Telephone Company Limited, a multinational company registered in London on February 4, 1881, five years after Alexander Bell registered his first patent, bought Pell's exchange. Pell was appointed the first manager of their Singapore branch which opened in 1882 with 43 exchange lines and 16 private lines. The first sub-exchange lines were opened in Tanglin in 1899. In 1898, the central exchange moved from Collyer Quay to 91 Robinson Road. In 1906 it moved to Hill Street and merged with the Tanglin exchange. Sub-exchanges were opened in Pasir Panjang and Katong in 1930. There are no records of the first houses to have telephones.

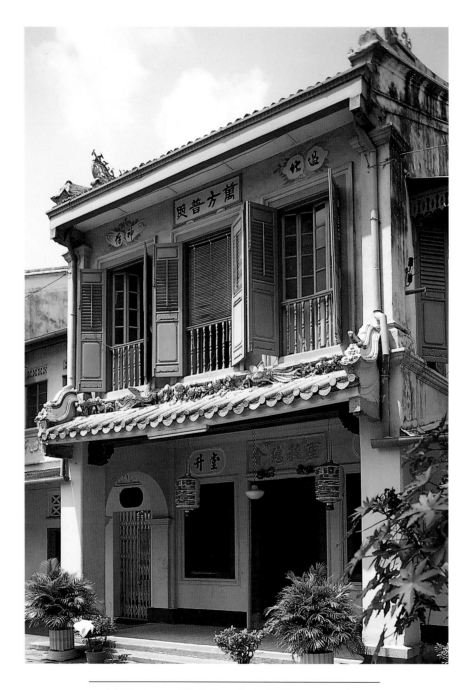

4.1 The house of Seah Song Seah, 1896, appears to be a
shophouse but is partially detached. The facade is an eclectic
mixture of European and Chinese elements found in Chinese
residences of the period. 4.2 A lithograph circa 1837 shows a
Chinese-style house along High Street which is thought to
have been either Yeo Kim Swee's or Tan Che Sang's.

Chinese Cognate

In the uncertain years before 1825, the Chinese were not inclined to build elaborately and they, like their European counterparts, lived in simple timber and attap houses. After 1825, brick structures, terraced in form and following Chinese architectural traditions, predominated in the town. Even the wealthy members of the community built relatively simple houses which conformed to Chinese traditions but did not require imported elements and highly skilled craftsmen.

In China, seclusion of the family was important. Houses were inevitably "inward looking," surrounded by solidly built boundary walls, symmetrical and planned as a progression of spaces. Rooms were arranged around airwells, or courtyards if large enough, which gave the necessary ventilation. A large house was composed of a series of courtyards along a common central axis with courtyards or airwells along the sides as well if the house was sufficiently wide. Deviation from this principle was rare. Individual buildings or rooms within a large compound were sometimes connected by colonnades. The main part of the house was the front ancestral hall. Here guests were received. Family rooms were located behind the reception hall while the kitchen area, servants' rooms and stores were at the rear. The form, layout and orientation of traditional Chinese houses were based on cosmic theories, particularly geomancy, which determined orientation. Roofs were supported by an elaborate system of transverse beams, stepped to allow for the curvature of the roof and to admit more light into the interiors. The eaves were supported by complex sets of brackets and projected to provide additional weather protection.

It is not known how many detached houses in the pure Chinese style were built in Singapore during the 19th century. Only a few can be identified with certainty. The first is seen in a lithograph circa 1837–38 (3.2). It is set back from the street and has gable ends rounded at the ridges. A large open courtyard appears to have linked the front building with a two-storey block at the rear. The house, at High Street between Maxwell's house and North Bridge Road, possibly belonged to Yeo Kim Swee. If so, it was built in 1832–1834 on land purchased from Stephen Hallpike and later owned by Seah Eu Chin. However, it more likely belonged to Tan Che Sang who is known to have purchased land on the river side of High Street in 1823 from D.S. Napier.

Tan Che Sang was one of the most prominent and wealthy of the early Chinese pioneers. Born in Canton in 1763, he emigrated to the Rhio Islands and lived in Penang and Malacca before settling in Singapore in 1816, where he accumulated great wealth and wielded considerable influence. He was probably the first Chinese to erect a permanent building on Boat Quay, which in February of 1823, according to Raffles, was "... in active improvement. Messrs Mackenzie, Napier and Scott, Che Sang, and others, building substantial warehouses, according to an approved plan ..." Regarded by most Europeans as dissolute and a notorious gambler, it was said that he made a vow never to gamble again by cutting off a finger after losing heavily at a gambling table. He was also reputed to be a miser; the room in which he died in his High Street house in 1836 was said to be full of coffers of silver and other valuable goods.

Another four traditonal Chinese houses are mentioned in Song Ong Siang's *One Hundred Years' of the Chinese in Singapore:* Tan Seng Poh's house at Hill Street built in 1869; Seah Cheo Seah's at Boat Quay built in 1872 (which probably replaced Yeo Kim Swee's house, purchased by Seah Eu Chin, and mentioned above); Wee Ah Hood's at Hill Street

4.3 Tan Yeok Nee (top) built his house in traditional Chinese style at Tank Road in 1882. It is the only one of its kind which stands today. The photograph of Telok Ayer (above) is from Mount Wallich. The overcrowding of the Chinese town, apparent in this view, led to the outward movement of the expanding Chinese population in the 1880s and 1890s.

built in 1878 on the site of the present Chinese Chamber of Commerce building; and Tan Yeok Nee's house at Tank Road built in 1882, the only one standing today. A final example was the house of Goh Sin Koh on Sin Koh Street which was built in 1896 and demolished in 1984. The houses of Tan Yeok Nee and Goh Sin Koh are the only two for which there are plans (4.6). Both are symmetrical and are composed of groups of buildings around courtyards. Both have, in addition to a central courtyard, smaller side courtyards which link the main part of the house with single storey wings.

Tan Yeok Nee (1827–1902) was born in China and came to Singapore at an early age. He earned a living as a cloth peddler and by 1866 had established himself as a pepper and gambier planter in Johore. After his death, the house was occupied by the Tank Road railway station master. It then became the St Mary's Home and School for Eurasian Girls until it was bought in 1938 by the Salvation Army which occupies the building today. The house is remarkably well preserved, although much of the main courtyard and the front reception and entrance hall have lost their original character. Louvred windows have been added. Some of the doors are original and these pivote between granite lintels and the threshold instead of hung on hinges.

Little is known of Goh Sin Koh. From 1884 to about 1905 he was in the shipping business under the name of Goh Guan Loo & Company and he owned several saw-mills in Kallang. When he was convicted of inciting a riot in 1902, a group of influential Chinese merchants submitted a memorial on his behalf to the government. He was acquitted on the grounds that the police evidence was contradictory. The plan of the house is similar to that of Tan Yeok Nee's and was probably the last of the traditional Chinese houses built in Singapore. Although the architects were d'Almeida & Kassim, it is obvious that the building was planned and designed by Chinese builders; the architects merely submitted the plans (4.9) for approval to the authorities.

For the majority of the Chinese, however, life was lived in terraced houses often with businesses on the ground floor. The terraced form was due to the original subdivision of the land into narrow lots for reasons of economy as well as to Raffles' directive of November, 22 1822 requiring that houses have uniform fronts with covered footways. Raffles stipulated that "for the sake of uniformity and gaining as much room as possible, a particular description of front for all brick or tiled houses should be attended to." He added that "a still

4.4 Roof detail from Tan Yeok Nee's house.

further accommodation will be afforded to the public by requiring that each house should have a verandah of a certain depth, open at all times as a continued and covered passage on each side of the street."

If the building form was predetermined by practical considerations, the basic principles on which the immigrants planned their terraced homes were dictated by tradition — private, inward-looking, and a progression of spaces with courtyards or airwells. The houses ranged from a single airwell or two within a long and narrow site to a more complex but symmetrical arrangement of living and working areas around airwells, or courtyards on wider lots. The roofs invariably spanned the depth of the building in sections rather than the narrower width.

The extent to which elaborate details were adopted in the terraced houses depended on the budget and the craftsmen available. The elaborate beam-and-bracket roof support system was rarely used. Normally five-inch diameter purlins of Bintangore (*Calophyllum*) were fixed at three feet intervals to support roofs which were covered with the cheaper Malacca clay tiles instead of imported Chinese tiles. The maximum purlin size of about 20 feet consequently limited the width of the building and in turn influenced the plan arrangement Chinese architectural features included the rounded gable ends — that were stepped, bow-shaped, or rounded like the "ears of the Chinese cooking pan" — which dominated the townscape for decades. Windows and doors were relatively plain. Before the introduction of European ironmongery, doors and windows were pivoted on granite sills and lintels. Some facades had decorative friezes of floral and fauna motifs in ceramic pieces below first floor windows. The early Asian immigrants would have had little contact with Europeans before their arrival

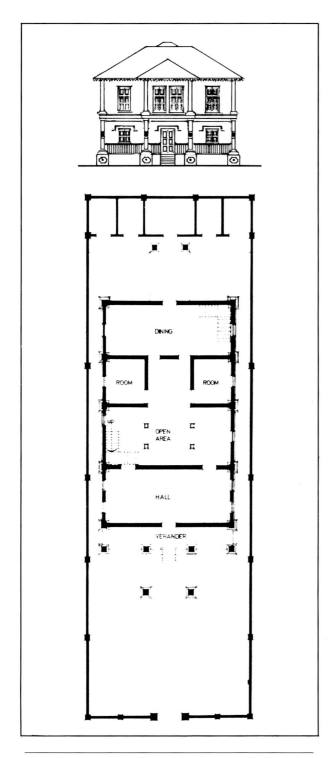

4.5 House of Song Soon Guan at Bencoolen Street, 1884.
Note the outhouse built to the boundary walls.

in Singapore and were not, at least in the beginning, influenced by European architecture. European architectural elements and motifs were introduced gradually and there evolved "a sort of compromise" and between European and Chinese features (see chapter eight).

The wealthier Chinese merchants continued to live mainly in the crowded areas of the town until the later part of the 19th century. Due to the absence of detailed planning regulations, and the liberal attitude of Crawfurd and his successors towards Raffles' insistence on regular street frontages, it is likely that merchants were allowed to amalgamate two or three lots in order to build larger houses. Consequently, some partially contiguous houses were built, the result of a detached house between shophouses.

The house of Seah Song Seah, one of the four sons of Seah Eu Chin, built in 1896 at River Valley Road (4.1 and 4.7) and still standing, is one example. Externally the house appears to join its neighbours, but it was not totally "terraced" since only the front and rear portions were built right up to the boundary and party walls. The roof spans the depth of the building in two sections with an airwell in between. The brick pilasters and cornices are European, as are the louvred windows, while the rounded gable end wall, the overhang above the ground floor front verandah, and the wall decorations are Chinese. The main portion of the house is 111 feet long and 21 feet wide. A forecourt about 30 feet in depth separates the house from the public footway. As with most traditional Chinese houses, there is an ornamental entrance gate.

Other Chinese families lived in houses that were an interesting accommodation of architectural trends, cultural needs and the limitations of the site. The house of Teo Hong Beng at Kerbau Road (page 194) and still standing is one example. Originally built as a detached house, the front portion of the first floor is a later addition that projects over the footway in the manner of shophouses. The main entrance opens to the public five-foot way. The house is surrounded by a boundary wall which encloses a garden and outhouses at the back. Built in what was even then a relatively urban area, the house demonstrates a possible solution to housing on a narrow site in a crowded city. Song Soon Guan's house built in 1884 at Bencoolen Street (4.5) had the appearance of a typical colonial house with a projecting carriage porch, first floor verandah and outhouse, but in plan it was similar to a terraced shophouse. The form was most likely dictated by the narrow site.

One footnote to history. There is no basic difference on plan between a Chinese residence and temple. It was not uncommon practice in China for a senior official or a rich merchant to donate his residence to the service of religion and have it consecrated as a temple. The practice prevailed in Singapore, and the houses of Seah Song Seah and Goh Sin Koh were eventually donated by their descendants for use as temples.

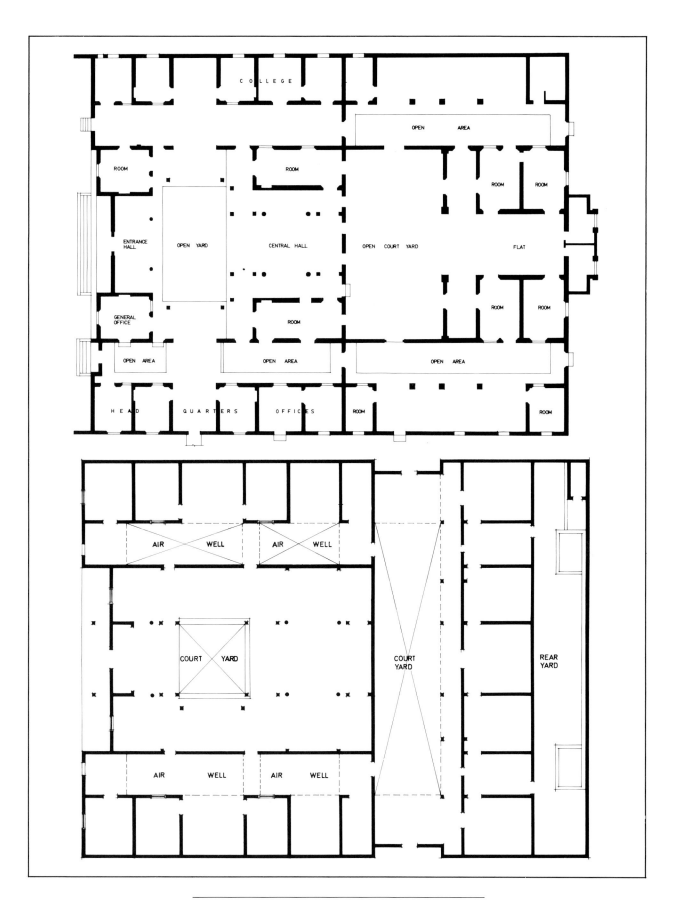

4.6 The plans of Tan Yeok Nee's house (top) and Goh Sin
Koh's (above).

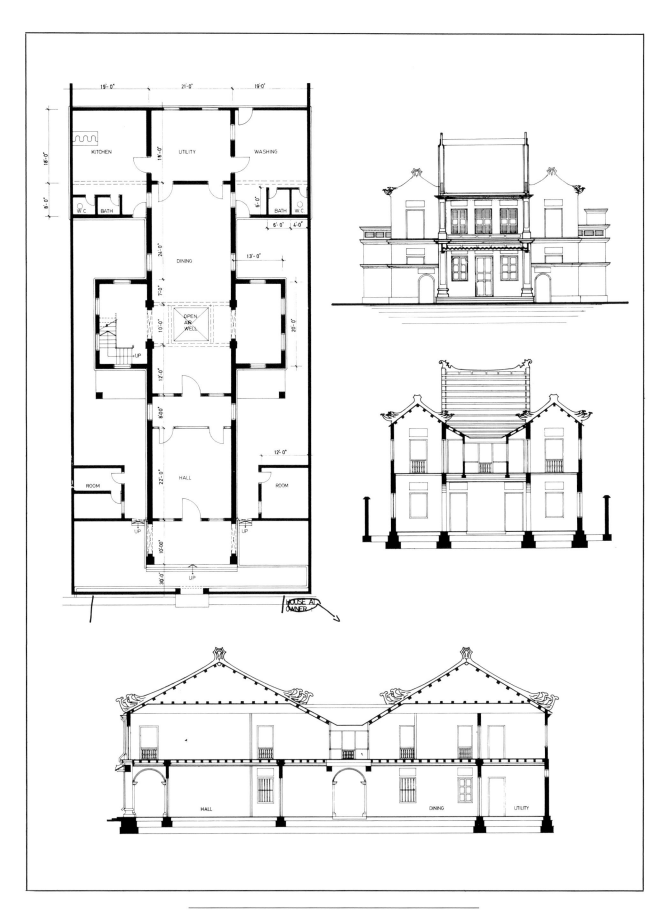

4.7 Plans, elevation and section of Seah Song Seah's house at
River Valley Road, 1896.

82

RIVER VALLEY ROAD RESIDENCE.

SEAH SONG SEAH.
COUNTRY HOUSE, THOMPSON ROAD.

4.8 Seah Song Seah, following the custom of many Chinese merchants, had two residences. His country house has been demolished but the River Valley Road house still stands and is now a Chinese temple. 4.9 Following pages: A page from the original building plans for Goh Sin Koh's house, 1896, probably the last traditional Chinese-style house built in Singapore. Although the architects were d'Almeida & Kassim, the building was probably designed by Chinese builders; the architects merely submitted the plans for approval to the authorities.

CROSS SECTION

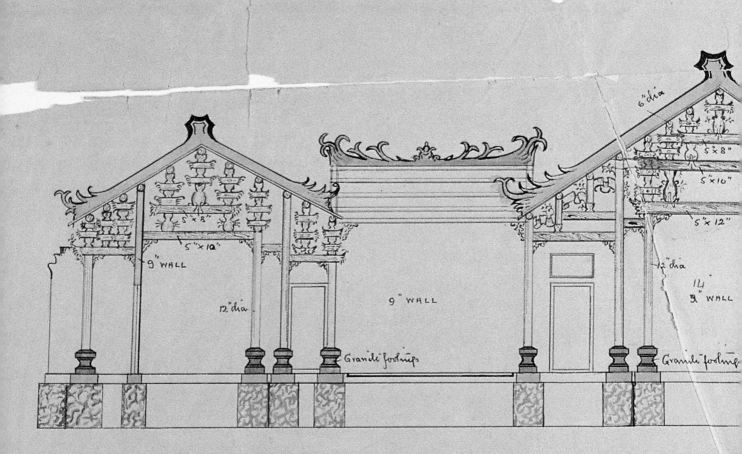

LONGITUDINAL

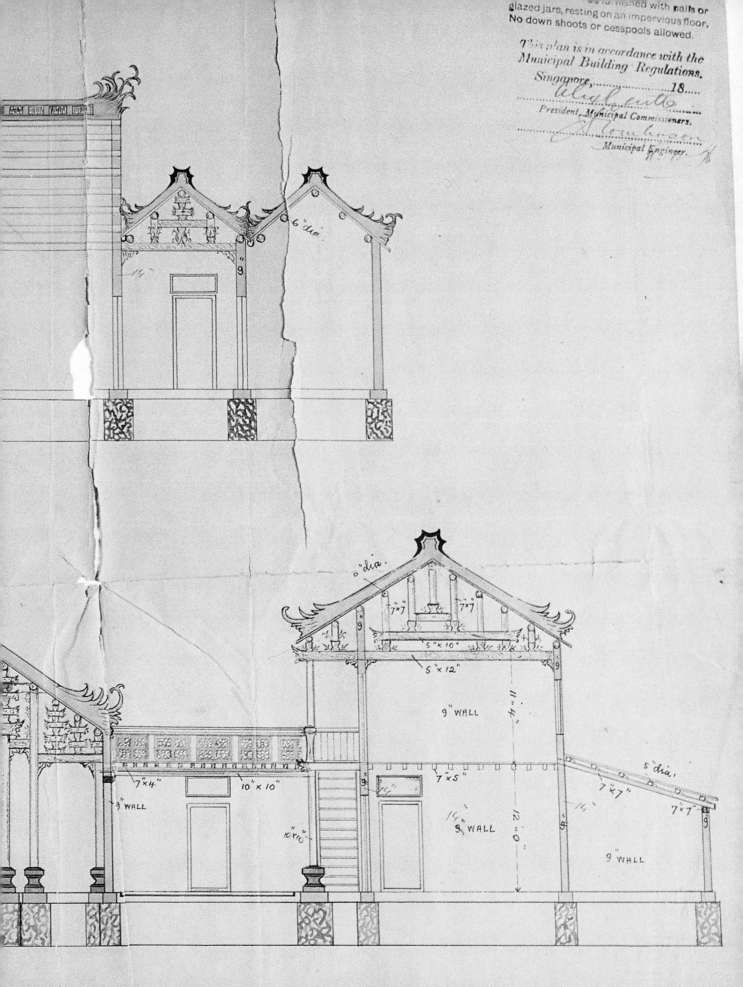

TION.

5.1 Kampong Rochor in 1846 from a sketch by J.T. Thomson.
The view was drawn from the site of the present Victoria
Bridge. Note the Bugis houses on the right and the Chinese
on the left. 5.2 Malay houses in Telok Blangah circa 1860.

Malay Traditions

The *orang laut* and the Malays were Singapore's earliest inhabitants. The former lived in boats and the latter in houses which were generally similar to those in Peninsular Malaysia where there were regional differences. The arrival of the British did not initially affect their domestic lives or their social and religious customs. For many years, the *orang laut* continued to live in boats and the Malays in their traditional houses.

It is commonly believed that the colonial house was partly Malay influenced. However, features in the later Malay houses suggest probable European influence, casting some doubt as to which building type influenced the other. Malay houses were traditionally of timber throughout and raised on stilts or posts from five to eight feet above the ground. The *rumah bumbong panjang*, which had a gable-end roof, was the earliest type and existed before the arrival of the Europeans. Some examples can be seen in J.T. Thomson's sketch "Campong Rochor 1846" (5.1). The *rumah bumbong panjang* was a flexible living space that could be added to or even moved to another site. The house had three basic components: the front hall or reception verandah, the main body and the kitchen. In the *serambi*, or reception verandah, guests were received. The main house, or *ibu rumah*, accommodated the private family area (*balai*) and the sleeping area, usually a raised platform (*pentas*) with a corridor (*lorong*) between them. If more sleeping accommodation was needed, an attic was added. Permanent partitions were rare, but light screens were sometimes used for privacy.

The kitchen was in a separate building which varied in position and was sometimes linked to the main house by a *saloran* (verandah). Other components included an *anjong*, a short projection that served as an entrance lobby, and a *jemoran*, or open deck, which was used for conversation in the early evening or for outdoor tasks if located near the kitchen. Some of the variations or additions to the basic house form may have been the result of immigrant influence. In the Campong Rochor sketch, for example, all of the houses, except the one in the distant background, have projecting additions. Since the kampong had a large Bugis population, the additions were probably Bugis in origin.

The *rumah bumbong panjang* continued to be built until as recently as the 1930s and 1940s. The gradual flow of European and other influences, however, resulted in two later types of Malay houses: the *rumah bumbong lima*, and the *rumah bumbong Perak* or *rumah bumbong potongon Belanda* (5.6). The hipped and gambrel roofs which respectively identify these two types were commonly used from about 1880 onwards. As is noted in chapter six, some Malays lived in European colonial houses. Sultan Hussein built a European house for himself in 1830 and the custom continued in Sultan Ali's house at Serangoon Road (page 188) and in Syed Mohammed Alsagoff's house on Dunearn Road (page 182). The acceptance of particularly the colonial bungalow and the continuing European influences led inevitably to the development of hybrid forms.

Both the *rumah bumbong lima* and the *rumah bumbong Perak* had projecting verandahs, were raised three to four feet off the ground and were basically similar on plan. A typical *rumah bumbong lima* (5.7) showed some European influence in the interiors. The house was still composed of three main elements — the front hall, the main body and the kitchen. The main body retained the subdivision into an internal hall and a *lorong* between two bedrooms, but the partitions were permanent, a consequence of European influence. The *serambi*, which tradi-

5.3 Four views of Malay kampongs in the early years of this century.

tionally ran across the front, was divided by the addition of a front hall, *surong*, taking the form of a projection similar to the colonial bungalow. The twin steps on either side of the *bilek tetamu* were also European influenced.

There were, therefore, many similarities between the two later types of Malay houses and the smaller and simpler colonial bungalows. The *surong* and the *bilek tetamu* were identical with the projecting verandahs of the colonial bungalows. It is difficult to distinguish whether the European bungalow gave rise to the Malay house or vice versa. The European roof forms on the *rumah bumbong lima* and *rumah bumbong Perak* suggest that these house types evolved from the colonial bungalow. On the other hand, it is possible that the modest colonial bungalow, so common in Geylang and Katong, was the result of the influence of these two later Malay house types.

An unusual house essentially in the colonial style but adapted to fit the needs of a Malay household is that of Salaman (5.5), built in 1885 at Dickson Road. It was almost certainly inspired by a Malay house despite its colonial appearance, the

tiled hipped roof supported by king-post trusses and the continuous open verandah on three sides. The fourth side could be assumed to represent an enclosed *serambi*, or reception hall, with an *anjong* projected beyond the main body of the house as was the preferred style in Malacca and Negri Sembilan. The intimate family area within the core, where guests were not admitted, was raised a few steps above the level of the *serambi* and included the kitchen, since the site was too small for an outhouse. (In colonial dwellings, the kitchen was always in the outhouse.) The four flights of stairs were probably European-inspired and their position was untraditional but logical since entrance stairs sometimes led to a *rumah tangga*, an open platform or deck, which in this case was substituted by the continuous verandah. Salaman's bungalow cannot be classified as a *rumah bumbong lima* despite its roof of five ridges because of the absence of a typical and characteristic element — the projecting front verandah or *surong*.

A bungalow at Newton Road (5.5) built for Seah Chye Joo in 1896 actually resembles the *rumah bumbong lima* more closely because of its projecting front

5.4 A view of Kampong Kallang in the 1890s. Note the houses along the river.

verandah, similar to a *surong*, and from the fact that it stood low over the ground on short piers. The only unusual feature was the gambrel roof. The house is typical of a type that was built throughout the suburban areas, particularly Katong and Joo Chiat.

European details common in Malay houses generally were louvred windows, glazed fanlights, balusters around the *serambi* and *anjong*, the use of laterite steps and, later, brick steps decorated with European-made ceramic tiles. The only significant Chinese influence was the use of the Malacca roofing tiles in some houses. A number of features of colonial houses were thought to have been influenced by Malay architecture but this is doubtful. The timber louvres to windows were used in Europe from the 16th century. The decorative eaves boards of sawed timber or galvanised iron were Victorian Revival, although some of the patterns and designs, such as the *awan larat*, could have been Malay. Also European in origin were the decorative ridge pieces of terracotta or galvanised iron and the carved timber or cast iron grills to fanlights. The *buah buton*, or finial, was Gothic-inspired and, like the decorative eaves boards, common in British Indian bungalows.

There was some similarity in the timber frame construction of the Malay house and some colonial bungalows. Early Malay houses had walls·of *kajang*, later replaced by timber boarding. In the colonial bungalow, brick or lath and plaster in-fill was used. In the alterations to H.C. Veerloop's house at Lloyd Road in 1892, the specificaton for the work stipulated that "the whole of the present plant partitions and walling to be removed and lath and plaster walling to be substituted in lieu of." In Mrs Dallan's house, built in 1904, the whole of the habitable upper portion of the bungalow was timber framed with brick in-fill. The substitution was a practical step since brick or lath and plaster was more durable and offered better projection from the weather than timber boarding while timber framing was more economical than load-bearing walls. The similarity in construction and appearance of early Malay houses of *kajang* matting in-fill and some timber-frame colonial houses is striking and could have influenced the British architects who introduced the Mock Tudor style.

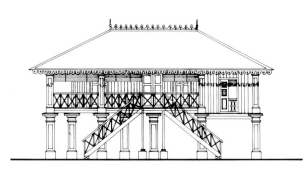

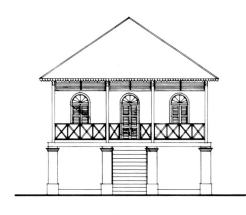

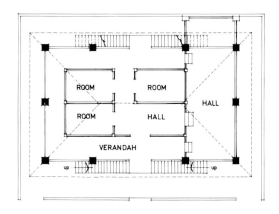

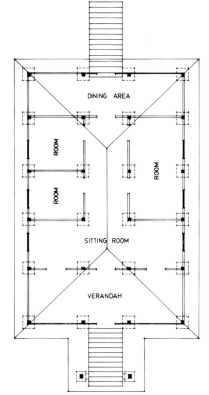

DINING AREA

ROOM

ROOM

ROOM

SITTING ROOM

VERANDAH

ROOM   ROOM

ROOM   HALL

HALL

VERANDAH

up   up

5.5 Salaman's house at Dickson Road (top right) is European in appearance but Malay in plan. Although it has a roof with five ridges it is not strictly a *rumah bumbong lima* because of the absence of the projecting verandah. The house of Seah Chye Joo at Newton Road (top left) resembles a *rumah bumbong lima* more closely because of the projecting verandah.

5.6 The three basic Malay house types, defined according to the roof form, are from left: the *bumbong Perak*, the *bumbong lima* and the *bumbong panjang*.

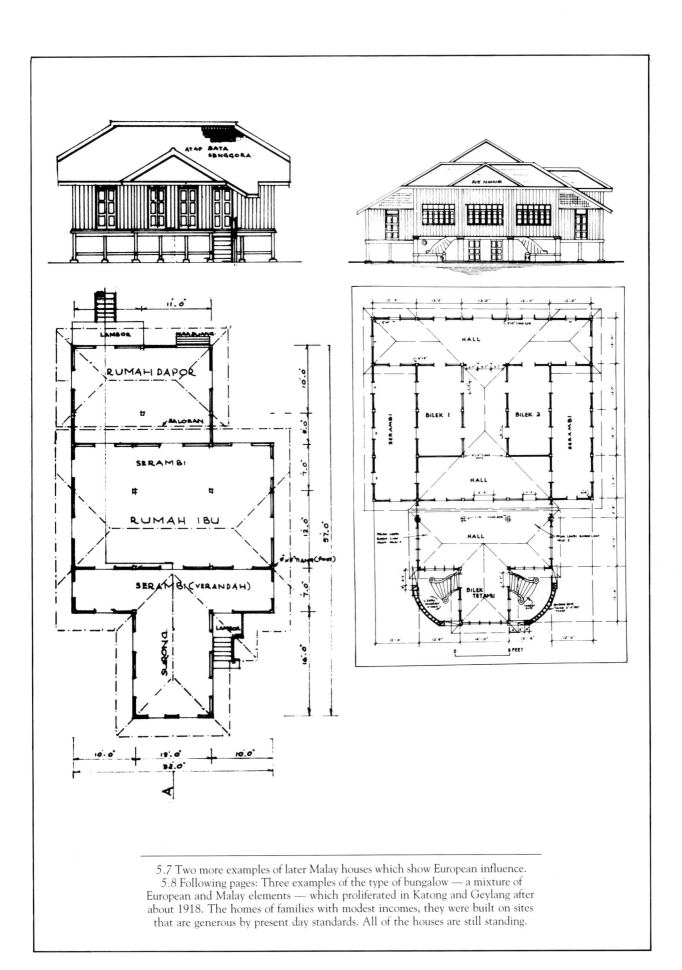

5.7 Two more examples of later Malay houses which show European influence.
5.8 Following pages: Three examples of the type of bungalow — a mixture of
European and Malay elements — which proliferated in Katong and Geylang after
about 1918. The homes of families with modest incomes, they were built on sites
that are generous by present day standards. All of the houses are still standing.

6.1 Portrait of a young nonya woman circa 1910. Note her hairstyle, the beaded slippers, and the details of the dress including the set of brooches — all typical of the time. 6.2 The rattan chair above is similar to furniture advertised in a John Little catalogue from the same period.

The Adoption

Fig. F 526. Lady's Long Chair, $3.85

Fig. F 581. Fancy Rattan Table, $3.95

Fig. F522. Rattan Table, $5.40

By the late 19th century, many Asians, especially the more affluent, were living in European-style homes. The adoption was the inevitable result of the spread of European influences, especially education in English. The first English school had been established in 1823 and towards the turn of the century English education became more widespread. It nurtured in Asians a taste for things European. Western dress, for example, was gradually adopted by Straits Chinese men from about 1875, although the women retained their *sarong* and *kebaya* and the traditional Chinese dress for many years. Continual contacts between Asian merchants and the British community was also an important contributory factor.

The first Asian known to have adopted the colonial house was a Malay, Sultan Ali. George Bennett, a naturalist and surgeon, observed during his second visit to Singapore in 1833, that "since my last visit (in 1830) His Highness had caused a house to be constructed after the style of the European residents at Singapore ... We were ushered into the new house, the rooms of which were furnished after the English style, with wall lamps, bookcases, tables, chairs, etc; ascending to the upper room, chairs were placed ... and the pungka was caused to be moved to cool our frames ..." From this brief comment, it can be assumed that the Sultan had adopted a European-style house without adapting it to suit an Asian lifestyle. When, 50 years later, in 1892, another member of the Malay royalty, Sultan Abu Bakar of Johore, built a European-style palace at Tyersall, the accommodations included a ballroom and a billiard room.

It is not known precisely when the Chinese adopted the European-style house or bungalow. Certainly the cost of building a traditional Chinese house was prohibitive and, as has been noted, after 1900 no such houses were built. Whampoa may have been the first. In about 1840 he purchased land at Serangoon on which to build a timber bungalow.

The colonial houses occupied or owned by Chinese families were distinguishable externally from European residences by some architectural details. These included the *ji-ho*, the sign hung above the entrance door, and the *pintu pagar* or fence door. Security bars to windows, absent in European houses, were inevitable. The *pintu pagar* with panelled tracery of Chinese design was also fixed between rooms, especially bedrooms. In European homes short, swing doors were commonly fixed between rooms.

Chinese homes were also, in the case of the middle and wealthy merchant classes, distinguished by their size and the greater number of rooms. More rooms were a practical necessity that arose from the extended family household tradition. Mandalay Villa, for instance, had six bedrooms which accommodated an extended family of 14 persons in the 1930s compared to an average of three to four bedrooms in a typical European house; althought in the early years, there were some large European families who built houses with many bedrooms. In an eight-bedroom house across the road from Mandalay Villa, there lived from 1924 to 1941 a matriarch with her eldest son and his wife, a daughter, a widowed daughter-in-law, four grandchildren, two of whom were married, and eight great-grandchildren — a total of 19 persons. The domestic help included one male cook, one houseboy, four maids and one female Batak slave from Sumatra who died in 1938 at the ripe old age of 80. The house accommodated altogether 26 adults and children.

Inside Chinese homes, the arrangement of the rooms was generally the same as in European homes

6.3 Carved and gilded built-in cupboards of Chinese design
were often used to store exportware or Peranakan porcelain.
The cupboards were found in both terrace houses and
bungalows built in the late 19th and early 20th century.

but the manner in which the main rooms were used reflected the different social customs. In the Chinese home, guests were never conducted to the sitting areas or verandahs on the first floor. These were regarded as strictly private and used only by the family or close relatives. Guests or visitors were confined to the ground floor front hall or verandah and to the adjoining sitting or lounge area. Only relatives or close family friends were admitted beyond. When guests were invited to dinner, dining tables were placed in the sitting room area.

The colonial house was, on the whole, remarkably well-suited to the needs of Chinese families. The axial symmetry and internal room divisions conformed generally to the traditional Chinese house. The front hall or sitting room area functioned as the reception hall of the traditional Chinese house, and the dining room, rear verandah and side rooms formed the private family area. The altar piece was placed in the front hall and the family altar and tablet at the rear, as was the practice in traditional houses. The location of the two altars, however, depended on the family's religious convictions, and quite often the family altar was in the front hall where tall mirrors in their Victorian frames were sometimes hung on the side wall to confuse or discourage evil spirits from entering the house.

Often the dining room was only used on social or formal occasions. A space at the rear of the house was set aside for daily meals. For large dinner parties,

6.4 The dining room at Panglima Prang photographed in 1971. The long dining table served 16 and was used on formal occasions. Behind it is the family ancestral tablet and altar placed on a traditional Chinese altar table. With the exception of the altar table and some Chinese porcelain, all of the furniture in the room is European. The ceiling is boarded and alcoved. Above is a page from a John Little catalogue circa 1912 advertising English china.

tables were laid on the lawn under canvas canopies in case of rain. The evening's fare included music and dancing, especially at dinners to celebrate birthdays, weddings and anniversaries. A Chinese *seronee*, a small musical ensemble, alternated with the Malay *ronggeng* on the verandah overlooking the lawn where the tables were laid or on the garden patio. The *ronggeng* girls sang in accompaniment or danced to the music and the male guests joined in the singing as well as the dancing well into the late hours of the evening. This form of entertainment was a long-standing custom which lasted until a few years after the Pacific War.

European furniture became widely used in the houses occupied by Asians. In most of the European-style houses occupied by Chinese, the interiors were furnished with a mixture of Chinese and European furniture. In the front hall, where the altar stood, blackwood chairs and side tables inlaid with mother-of-pearl lined the walls above which were hung large mirrors with carved frames of Victorian design. These were sometimes flanked by scrolls of Chinese calligraphy. In the centre was sometimes placed a table with a set of high-backed Victorian chairs.

On either side of the altar were a pair of red lacquered chairs with tall backs, important items used on ceremonial occasions such as weddings when the betrothed couple paid their respects to their elders who were seated on the chairs. In large houses where there was a living room, cushioned settees were placed and other furnishings included display cabinets, where the family silver and ceramics were kept, dressers and chairs of either Chinese

Dining furniture was usually European and mostly imported. Round tables were often topped with marble and long dining tables had tops of polished teak. Sideboards and dressers were European as well. In large families, a second table was required which was often placed at the rear verandah for lesser family members. In Straits Chinese homes, meals were served on Chinese exportware porcelain but silver forks and spoons were used instead of chopsticks.

Wealthier homes had European ceiling and wall lamps and chandeliers in important rooms. In the ground floor front verandah a pair of Chinese paper and bamboo framed lanterns were hung. On festive days a *chai kee*, a long piece of red cloth, was draped round the main entrance door as a customary festive gesture. Bedroom furniture included wardrobes, cupboards and dressing tables. Beds were often iron and brass four-posters, and a traditional Chinese wedding bed, for ceremonial purposes only, was always at hand.

The number of colonial homes that were structurally modified to suit Asian customs was probably

quite small. The houses of Alsagoff (page 182) and Sultan Ali (page 189), both dating from the early years of this century, are interesting examples of European-style houses that appear to have been deliberately and thoughtfully planned and adapted to the needs of their Muslim owners. Both followed the standard colonial bungalow plan in their internal divisions of space and elevational treatement. In the Sultan Ali house, the covered link to the outhouse was divided in two, an arrangement that separated the male domestics from the female, as practised in some Muslim families.

Adaptations of the European-style house by Chinese are not unknown. The adaptation was sometimes in the creation of courtyards that separated the front from the rear of the house as in the traditional Chinese house. The house of Pang Teck Joon at Killiney Road, built in 1901 (page 48, third row left) is an example. The two-storey rear block was linked to the main house by a passage, one full bay in width, with courtyards on either side which were enclosed by screen walls and two outhouses. The rear enclosure to the house of Liem Ie Ging (page 191), built in 1900, served probably as a work yard.

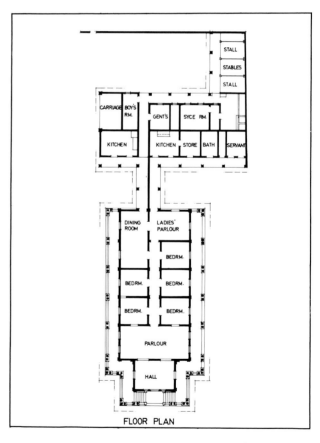

6.5 Plan of the house of Sultan Ali at Serangoon Road, 1899. Note the separation of the women's quarters.

6.6 East meets West. Portrait of child and amah (top) shows typical blackwood
furniture inlaid with mother-of-pearl. The family altar (middle) is from Rosedale.
And a young Chinese woman (above) poses in front of the family car.

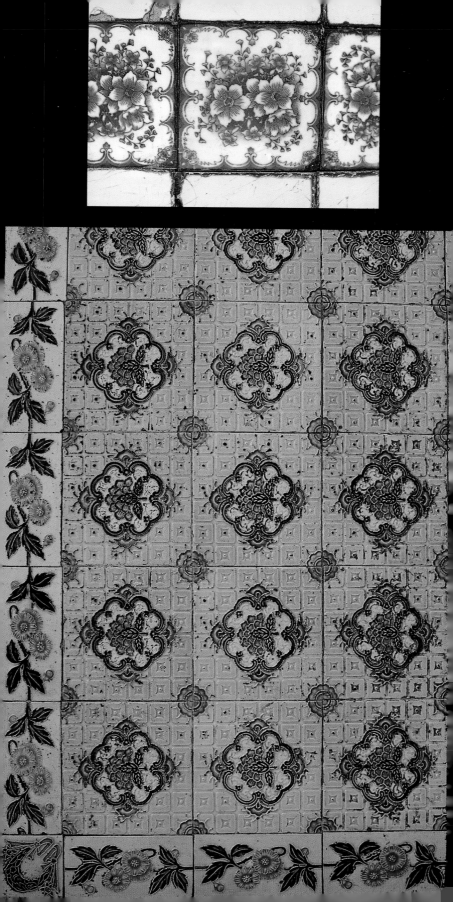

Flower Stands.—continued.

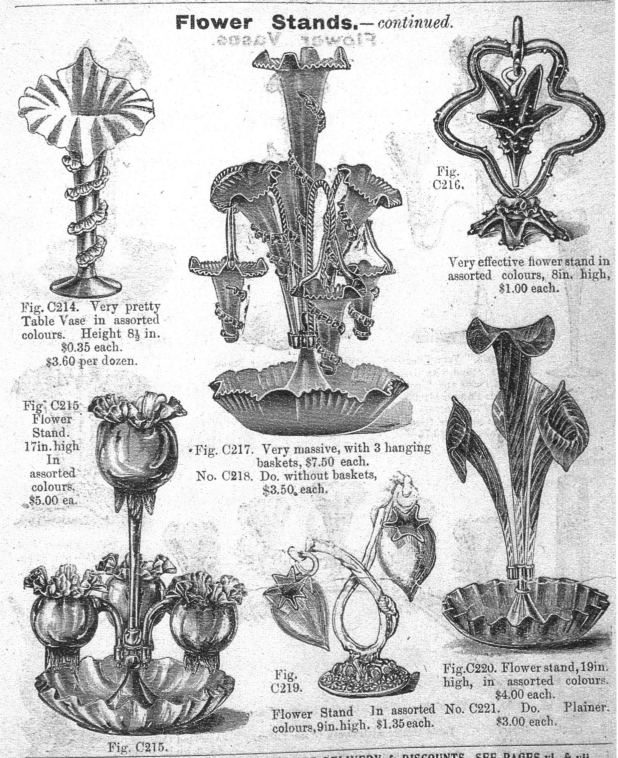

Fig. C214. Very pretty Table Vase in assorted colours. Height 8½ in. $0.35 each. $3.60 per dozen.

Fig. C215 Flower Stand. 17in. high In assorted colours, $5.00 ea.

Fig. C216.

Very effective flower stand in assorted colours, 8in. high, $1.00 each.

•Fig. C217. Very massive, with 3 hanging baskets, $7.50 each.
No. C218. Do. without baskets, $3.50 each.

Fig. C219.

Flower Stand In assorted colours, 9in. high. $1.35 each.

Fig. C215.

Fig. C220. Flower stand, 19in. high, in assorted colours. $4.00 each.
No. C221. Do. Plainer. $3.00 each.

FOR CONDITIONS AS TO FREE PACKING, FREE DELIVERY & DISCOUNTS, SEE PAGES vi. & vii.
EXCEPTIONS ARE MARKED THUS *

103

6.7 Chinese families, in particular the Peranakans, comfortably adopted European-style houses. A typical wedding photograph, at the house of Pang Teck Joon (pages 100-101) also shows floor and wall tiles. The wall tiles opposite are European in origin. Another wedding photograph (pages 102-103) shows the popularity of European ornamental objects which were available through sources such as the John Little catalogue. Floor tiles (right) were advertised in a 1912 catalogue and captured in the photograph of the young woman above.

RILEY HARGREAVES & Co., Ltd. SINGAPORE.
ORIGINAL DESIGNS FOR FLOOR TILING.

No. 350.

No. 351.

No. 354.

No. 355.

CERAMIC MOSAIC PAVEMENTS.

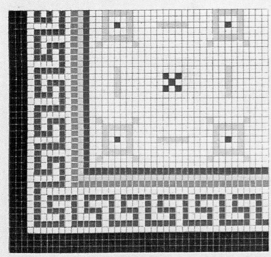

No. 365.

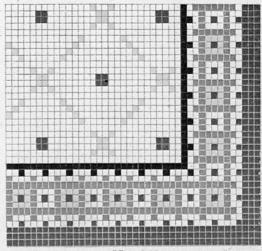

No. 363.

SCALE 1 INCH TO A FOOT.

We are SOLE AGENTS for Messrs T. A. SIMPSON & Co., Ltd. BURSLEM, ENGLAND.

FURTHER DESIGNS FREE ON APPLICATION.

7.1 A 1909 photograph of the house of Pang Teck Joon shows
the formal layout of the driveway so typical of houses lived in
by Chinese families. 7.2 Garden furniture advertised in a Riley
Hargreaves & Company — engineers, contractors and suppliers
of building materials — catalogue in 1912.

Landscape and Garden

No. 2284.
Garden Chair.

No. 2285.
Garden Seat.

The earliest country houses were situated on large plantations which varied in size. Bukit Chermin was 51 acres, Mount Echo and Mount Victoria, both owned by Jose d'Almeida Junior, were 30 acres and 100 acres respectively. Seri Menanti estate, where G.G. Nicol built Chatsworth, was 150 acres. Charles Carnie's estate in Cairnhill was, according to J. T. Thomson who surveyed it, about 68 acres, of which 16 were low-lying swamp. Emerald Hill, owned by William Cuppage, was 36 acres. One of the largest plantations belonged to Joseph Balestier, the American consul, who held 1,000 acres of land of which 200 acres were planted with sugar cane. William Dunman's coconut estate in Katong was 688 acres. Dr. Little's coconut estate at Siglap was about 150 acres.

The houses were usually built on the highest ground of the estate, often in the middle of the vast domain, in quiet seclusion at the end of a long winding carriageway. In the Tanglin district, where the land undulated, the houses were inevitably on top of a hillock. The estates were planted right up to the immediate grounds of the building. Viewed from a distance, the white stuccoed houses stood in splendid isolation against a somber backdrop of forest uncleared or only partially cleared. Cairnhill House, as seen in the watercolour by Charles Dyce in 1842 (page 153), stood on a hill planted with nutmeg trees and was set against partially cleared forests. A pre-1860 photograph of White House at Dalvey Road (page 37), is similar, although the open ground surrounding the house appears some-what barren since the nutmeg trees were not fully grown. The uncleared jungle is just visible in the distance. In both illustrations the plantation dominates the landscape. Only within the immediate vicinity of the houses were there clipped lawn and trimmed hedges.

When the spice plantations were abandoned from the 1850s, the large estates were subdivided into plots varying from half an acre to 30 acres. John Cameron, writing in the 1860s, has given a description of the European gardens typical of this period:

Those [houses] nearer town. where ground is more valuable, are built tolerably close together, with perhaps one or two acres to each; those at a greater distance are more apart, generally crowning the summits of the innumerable little hills, which are such a geological peculiarity of Singapore, and surrounded by ten or fifteen acres of ground, either covered with patches of jungle, or planted with nutmeg and fruit trees...

The ground around the European residences are for the most part tastefully kept. A couple of gardeners cost eight or nine dollars a month, and to such good effect can nature be cultivated that the expenditure is seldom begrudged. The beauty of the hedges, which are either of bamboo or of wild heliotrope, and the greenness of the grass, are features not often seen in a tropical climate, but which are particularly noteworthy about Singapore. The grass is a very coarse, short, thick sort, and so vigorous is it of growth that a considerable body of men are maintained throughout the year at the public expense to keep the roads clear of it.

Few of the private gardens as yet yield much fruit, owing to the fact of the greater part of the grounds around Singapore not many years ago having been laid out with nutmegs, a crop which made magnificent returns for many years, and then suddenly gave way from some unknown disease or blight. Fruit trees, however, are now growing up in their place.

(Cameron's comment about fruit trees is of interest. In Emerald Hill, fruit trees planted in the mid-1850s yielded by 1872 a $600 annual return.)

7.3 Two late 19th century photographs of bungalows set in
their gardens by G.R. Lambert & Company.

Some properties on larger tracts of land evolved into "condominiums" held by individuals for rental or by companies and government departments for staff housing. Examples include White House Park, Ardmore, Chatsworth, John Fraser's Estate at Gallop Road, Adam Park, Goodwood Hill, Bushy Park and Watten Estate (7.4). In these extensive properties, a conscious effort was made to landscape the grounds. No hedges or fences separated the houses, which were built on common ground under single titles. The English owners instinctively applied landscape traditions based on the theories of the Picturesque Movement and landscape practitioners such as William Kent (building and landscape architect, 1685–1748) who "leapt the fence and saw all nature was a garden." The undulating hills of Tanglin sometimes provided for Charles Bridgeman's "ha-ha", a sunken fence along boundaries which was then not visible, thereby visually enlarging a landscaped park. Trees were planted in isolated clumps between green swards in a manner

that Capability Brown (landscape gardener, 1716–1783) would have approved. These traditions survive today in parts of Tanglin, as well as in the Botanic Gardens and the grounds of the Istana.

The informal layout was also adopted in the smaller gardens of individual European homes, although the extent of the grounds offered less scope for landscaping on a large scale. Trees were closely planted along boundaries to some depth and undergrowth allowed to flourish to provide a screen that ensured privacy. Between the house and the main road was a broad expanse of land with a driveway winding its way to the house. When tennis became popular after the turn of the century, a court sometimes faced the garden verandah. If the grounds were large enough, more trees were planted, inevitably in groups and informally arranged to provide interesting vistas. The most widely planted tree in Tanglin was the Tembusu (*Fagraea fragrans*). Nearer to the house, close by the verandahs and garden terraces, were beds of Cannas, Ixoras, and other flowering shrubs. A gazebo or garden pavilion was sometimes erected on the lawn.

The gardens of Chinese homes (7.1 and 7.9) were more formal due to the preference for symmetry. Often a straight driveway lined with potted plants in regimented rows ended in a roundabout that looped under the carriage proch. Sometimes the driveway circled round the front of the grounds as in Magenta Cottage (page 176) where the slight rise towards the house was demarcated by a balustrade. At Mandalay Villa (page 124), the entrance gate was at the side of the house and the driveway terminated beyond the house at a roundabout, at the centre of which was a sculpture. A paved pathway ran in a straight line, at a right angle to the driveway, from the front verandah through the garden to the pier that led to a sea pavilion. Potted plants on pedestals lined the

7.4 Watten estate (above) circa 1965. The houses were owned
by a single company and the grounds without fences.

7.5 19th century houses and their settings — framed by foliage and shaded by palm trees (top).

pathways on either side. There were few plants on the four-acre site except for fruit trees at the rear and two magnificent Angsana trees (*Pterocarpus indicus*).

Most Chinese houses were fenced or walled in with one entrance gate in the centre or one gate at each end of the road frontage. (Asians, particularly wealthier Chinese, tended to wall in their homes.) Gates were usually of timber and hung on timber posts or brick piers. In grander homes, wrought iron or cast-iron gates were hung on cast-iron gate posts or brick piers decorated in relief plaster. The piers were often surmounted by ornamental vases or statuettes of elephants, lions, eagles or dragons, serpents, and other mythological animals in the manner of the entrance gates of English country houses. In more modest homes, particularly those in the suburban areas, hedges were grown in lieu of boundary fences or walls, the most popular being of Bunga Raya (*Hibiscus rosa-sinensis*).

In the suburbs of Serangoon, Tampines, Ponggol and particularly Geylang, Katong and Siglap, gar-

7.6 A contemporary view of the grounds of a group of black-and-white houses on Nassim Road (above).

dens assumed a different character because of the flatness of the land and the sandy soil. Here the fine "Serangoon" and "Siglap" grass grew profusely while the coarser "buffalo" thrived better in the clay soil of Tanglin. Whereas the Tembusu dominated Tanglin, the coconut palm, the Ketapang (*Terminalia*) and the Rhu (*Casuarina equisetifolia*) were found in abundance in these areas. The coconut groves that fringed the shores of the island survived until recent years.

By the 1920s, the coastline was dotted with seaside houses and holiday bungalows. The East Coast offered the best prospect and as early as the 1840s the government had erected a bungalow described as a "sanitaria" at Changi. Felix Henry Gottlieb, a barrister who was in government service from 1846 to 1882, owned Elfin Cottage at Fairy Point, Changi in the 1860s. Dunman, Little and d'Almeida were probably among the first to build seaside bungalows at Katong and Siglap. Lee Cheng Yan, the owner of most of the land at Kampong Amber, had three holiday bungalows fronting the sea at Amber Road (7.13) in addition to one at Tanah Merah, known as Ayer Manis, and another at Changi Point. Tan Soo Guan acquired a large tract of land that was part of John Armstrong's coconut estate and built a seaside bungalow for his family in 1914. By then, there were already three houses on Armstrong's land. Judging by their Scottish-sounding names — Ben Ledi, Benzoline and Belmont — they were probably built by Mathew Little between 1868 and 1886, the period he owned the property.

The seaside houses were generally set back from the shore, particularly those along the southern coast where tides inched to the top of seawalls and the ground swells during the December monsoons cascaded onto lawns. The Foreshore Ordinance later required that houses be built at least 50 feet from the shoreline. Where seawalls were needed,

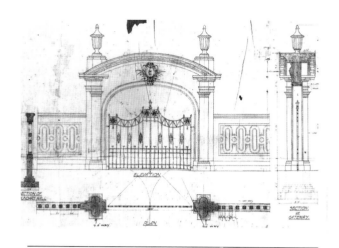

7.7 Gate for a house on Tanjong Rhu Road, 1929.

steps were constructed leading down to the beach from the garden, which was usually cleared of trees to ensure a panoramic view. Gazebos or shelters were sometimes built close to the seawall or shore.

Swimming enclosures and outhouses (7.11 to 7.15) built over the sea on piles were a common feature of the seaside houses — from Tanjong Rhu to Bedok, along the west coast at Pasir Panjang and at Pasir Ris, Punggol, Sembawang, Lim Chu Kang, Pasir Laba and Tanjong Penjuru where J.B. David had a bungalow which was acquired by the Singapore Anti-Tuberculosis Association in the 1950s. The enclosures were necessary particularly between Tanjong Rhu and Tanjong Katong, where the waters were notorious for sharks. Originally in timber, they were replaced by more solid concrete and brick structures by the 1920s.

Outhouses varied from simple open pavilions to fully furnished chalets which were used for picnics and house parties. Many of the swimming enclosures were demolished during World War Two and virtually all of the remaining ones disappeared when land was reclaimed along the coast in the 1970s. By the mid-1980s, only one outhouse in Lim Chu Kang owned by the Cashin family survived.

One of the most outstanding gardens in all of Singapore's history was that of Whampoa in his house on Serangoon Road and it is fitting to end this chapter with some descriptions of it. No photographs of the garden survive but it has been described in detail in a number of books written by travellers who visited the grounds. J. T. Thomson wrote in *Glimpses into Life in Malayan Lands* (London: 1864):

Here a neglected garden which Whampoa had bought, he soon converted into a tasteful bel-retiro, with its avenues, fruit orchard, hanging gardens, Dutch walks, dwarf

bamboos, and orange trees — its shrubs, stags, and peacocks — its aviary and menagerie, all of which displayed a fine taste, a healthy, robust love of the beautiful in nature, and of the artificial curiosities of horticulture."

Yet another account was given by Ivan Goncharov in his book *The Voyage of the Frigate Pallada* of his visit in 1853. The guests were shown the garden where

... winding footpaths lead to secluded corners and huge trees rise to the sky... The host is not only a lover of gardens, he is actually a great landscapist. He told us the characteristics of each plant. Half of what he said I have forgotten and the other half I couldn't understand. He spoke very fluent English...The description I have given could not express one twentieth of the things I saw in there .... Every tree, every bush has its own colour and charm making you unable to pass them by in haste. Thanks to Whampoa's artistic mind and skilful planning, the plants were arranged in such a way that they looked like attractive paintings in a gallery.

The visitors also saw birds and animals in special enclosures in the garden, and some lambs and deer were seen wandering in the woods. Finally, their host showed them a "beautiful Arab horse, which was silvery white throughout."

7.8 A young woman poses next to a typical flower pot and stand.

110

7.9 Houses on spacious grounds occasionally had a gazebo or
pavilion such as the one that provided a backdrop to this group
photograph circa 1910 (top). The bungalow of a Chinese family
with the pot-lined roundabout (above) was probably built
between the two wars on a large compound. The circular
driveway fronting the house conforms to the Chinese
love of symmetry.

7.10 Life along the coast. The house at Pasir Panjang is dated
1926 and belonged to the Alkaff family. The interior view
shows a family member relaxing on the enclosed verandah.

7.11 The Katong Pier (top) and a house at Upper East Coast
Road capture some of the flavour of life along the East Coast
before the Pacific War.

7.11 The sea pavilion (above) at Lim Chu Kang belonged to A.W. Cashin.
Photographed circa 1920, it no longer exists.

7.13 The seafront at Amber Road (top) photographed by Wearnes Airways in 1938.
The second house from the left belonged to Lee Choon Guan. The one on the
extreme right was designed by Bidwell.

7.14 Seaside bungalows, such as this one in Katong framed by
coconut trees, were used as weekend retreats or for longer
holidays away from the town.

7.15 Sea pavilions were once a common feature along the coast. They often had bedrooms as well. Leisure activities included fishing and boating.

8.1 Karikal Mahal was built by Moona Kader Sultan shortly
after he bought the land in Katong in 1917. It is a good
example of the coarsened classicism so typical of that period.
The house still stands, and the original windows have been
replaced. 8.2 Elevation of a house in the Modern International
style in Holland Park estate, 1934.

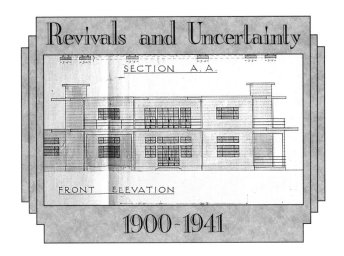

Revivals and Uncertainty

SECTION A.A.

FRONT ELEVATION

1900-1941

The turn of the century saw the further expansion of Singapore's suburbs, particularly in Geylang, which expanded rapidly after World War One, and Katong, which developed gradually into a residential area following the fragmentation of the large coconut plantations. The expansion was due mainly to population growth caused by the influx of immigrants attracted by the growing prosperity of Malaya and Singapore following the proven success of the rubber industry after 1900. In 1901, Singapore's population was 228,555; by 1921 it had risen to 418,358. An inevitable consequence was the expansion of the suburbs across the Rochor River towards upper Serangoon, and especially into Geylang and Katong. At the same time, the advent of motorised transport made living further from town more attractive and practical. In 1914, there were about 200 motor cars on the island, and by 1925 the number had increased to 3,248. An electric tram service initiated in 1902 had, by 1905, extended to Geylang, Pasir Panjang, and Serangoon as far as Bidadari.

In Geylang, the completion of Sims Avenue in 1921 accelerated urbanisation along the main Geylang Road and in the many *lorongs* formed on both sides of the road. In 1921, the municipal architect, William Campbell Oman, noted that "Great activity was noticible in the building of residences in the Tanglin district and small bungalows and shophouses in the Geylang district." In Katong, between Dunman Road and Grove Road, to the west of Tanjong Katong Road, new roads were laid and building lots formed from about 1913 on land that had been Thomas Dunman's estate; but the area did not develop until around 1918, when the first of the detached houses in the enclave between Bournemouth and Swanage Roads was built.

From 1919 to 1930, the Katong residential suburbs crept steadily eastwards to cover the whole of Armstrong's original plantation and part of Little's Siglap estate. After World War Two and into the early 1950s, the Credit Foncier d'Extreme Orient company cut down the coconut trees in Dr Little's estate when it built the Siglap and Opera housing estates. Credit Foncier purchased the land from the Frankel brothers who had acquired it around the turn of the century. The brothers were furniture manufacturers and household names in the period between the two world wars. By 1926 the area had its first school, the Telok Ayer English School, and by 1928 Katong had grown to the extent that the Inspector-General of police, H. Fairburn, remarked: "The development of the area from Katong to Joo Chiat, which has been so rapid in the past two years, promises to continue, and from every point of view one sees the necessity of providing for a subdivisional station in that suburb. The suburb at present possesses no police station."

Thus, when the Pacific War broke out in 1941, many of the main residential areas as we know them today were well-established. The town and suburbs, as defined by the municipal limits, included Telok Blangah, Tanglin, Bukit Timah as far as the Chinese High School, Lornie Road, Serangoon, Paya Lebar, Geylang, Siglap, Joo Chiat and Katong. In Geylang and Katong, the residential areas had reached Telok Kurau. In Tanglin, where they had already reached Swiss Cottage and Mount Rosie by 1900, they now expanded as far as Coronation Road where Messrs Palmer and Turner, architects, built their "Spanish style" houses in 1939. In the Thomson Road area, houses were built up to the junction with Braddell Road. At Bukit Timah, the suburbs reached the junction of Clementi Road, where the first two houses in

8.3 The turn of the century saw the expansion of suburban areas. An electric tram service (top) initiated in 1902 had extended to Geylang, Pasir Panjang and Serangoon as far as Bidadari by 1905. The face of the town was also changing with new buildings along Collyer Quay (middle left) and Stamford Road (above left). The Hotel de L'Europe (middle right) and the Orchard Road market (above right) were also built in the early years of the century and photographed circa 1914.

8.4 By 1914, there were about 200 motor cars (top) on the island. The onion domes in the office building at Finlayson Green (above) reflect late Victorian architectural tastes and recall the domes of the Royal Pavilion at Brighton by John Nash.

H 224   The Victoria Memorial Hall, Singapore.

8.5 An early example of Edwardian Baroque architecture in
Singapore is Victoria Memorial Hall.

King Albert Park were built in 1940, the same year in which Braddell Road was completed.

During these years, the town area underwent great physical changes, particularly along Collyer Quay in the post-war years from 1919. A string of new commercial buildings rose along the stretch from Fullerton Square to Finlayson Green. In Fullerton Square itself, Battery Road and Raffles Place, new buildings replaced existing ones that were in many cases a mere 20 to 30 years old. The Esplanade finally shed what remained of its original residential character when the remaining two of the three houses attributed to G.D. Coleman, Dr Montgomerie's and Thomas Church's, were demolished to make way for the Municipal Offices (City Hall), which was constructed from 1926 to 1929. The adjacent Supreme Court building was built in 1939 on the site of the Hotel de L'Europe.

In the 50 years preceeding World War Two, architecture in Singapore continued to be influenced by successive trends in Britain, Europe and America, where there had been a steady increase in the pace of architectural change. Until the late 1920s, the main trends were the Edwardian Baroque and other classical revivals, including the stylistic influence of the Ecole des Beaux-Arts, and the late Arts and Crafts Movement. In the late 1920s and the 1930s, Singapore saw the arrival of the Modern Movement, Art Deco, and a mutant form of classicism.

The Gothic Revival had never succeeded in totally subverting the influence of the grand classical manner, particularly for civic architecture, and throughout the Victorian period classical buildings continued to be constructed. Towards the end of the century, however, there was a renewed interest in classicism in reaction to the Gothic and the eclecticism of the Arts and Crafts Movement. This revival embraced all manner of classical styles. Before about 1906 it was characterised by bold baroque forms developed from early 18th century English Renaissance architecture — thus the term "Edwardian Baroque". Thereafter, in the words of Alastair Ser-

8.6 The Royal Naval College in Dartmouth was designed by
Aston Webb and built between 1899 and 1903.

ARIEL VIEW OF EU TONG SENG'S HOUSE S PORE.

8.7 Eu Villa was planned in the grand manner with a double-storey entrance hall. The post card is circa 1940.

vice in *Edwardian Architecture* (London: 1977), "Edwardian Baroque was gradually replaced by other forms of the Grand Manner ... sometimes in the elegant French Beaux-Arts style, sometimes in styles that attempted to adapt classicism to the new steel and concrete frame structures." London's Ritz Hotel is one example, a French Beaux-Arts style building by Mewes and Davis completed in 1906 and thought to have been the first steel-framed building in Britain; the technique was first used in an office building for the Home Insurance Company in Chicago by William Le Baron Jenney in 1883–1885. In the 1905 redesign of the Picadilly Hotel, Richard Norman Shaw, the Arts and Crafts architect turned classicist, used the baroque freely, creating the huge, heavy, overwhelming facades in Portland stone to a grandiose, almost Pirenesian, scale. In the next two decades, it became the predominant style of civic architecture in Britain and throughout the Empire, and its influence extended to domestic architecture, as we shall see.

The late Arts and Crafts Movement was initially advocated by Charles Voysey (1857–1941), who influenced Frank Lloyd Wright as well as the Singapore-based architect Frank Wilmin Brewer. Voysey had a distinctive style, and, according to John Betjeman in *Pictorial History of English Architecture*, invented a new style of Arts and Crafts cottages in which the wall surfaces were "dematerialised" by being coated uniformly in soft plaster. Such roughcast walls were also a feature of Brewer's houses.

The early years of the century also saw the beginnings of the Modern Movement when a handful of architects in Europe and America began to question the relevance of the classical styles. The debate widened to question what aspect should dominate the design process, form or function. In the beginning, the changes initiated by them resulted only in the exclusion of some ornament on buildings which continued to retain their classical character with simplified details. The free plan and plastic forms that are the hallmark of the Modern Movement were made possible by new construction methods. Auguste Perret built the first reinforced concrete frame building in 1903, a block of flats in Paris. By the 1920s, the Modern Movement had been firmly established in Europe, although it was not universally accepted, under the influence of architects such as Walter Gropius (1883–1969), Le Corbusier (1887–1965) and Mies van der Rohe (1886–1969). The 1920s saw a growing number of buildings with the signature flat roofs, curved balconies, horizontal ribbon windows and a white-washed cubist look. The Modern Movement, in turn, spawned the Art Deco style, which replaced old decorative practices with new geometric patterns, and a mutant or "stripped" classicism with Classical details entirely omitted or simplified on essentially classical facades.

All of these new developments reached Singapore even as Victorian classicism and eclecticism continued to flourish well into the present century.

123

8.8 Mandalay Villa. The richly embellished facade was characterised by an uncontrolled application of the Classical Orders and free use of decorative motifs.

The Edwardian Baroque was particularly important, as it exerted a strong influence on the Coarsened Classical architectural style that had evolved particularly in domestic and shophouse architecture. An early example of Edwardian Baroque is Victoria Memorial Hall, a conversion of and addition to Bennett's Town Hall by Swan & Maclaren (1902–1906). The centre portion bears a remarkable resemblance to that of the Royal Naval College in Dartmouth (8.6), designed by Aston Webb and built between 1899 and 1903. Other early examples of buildings influenced by the Baroque Revival were the Boustead Institute building, 1892 (page 59), and the Chartered Bank building of 1896–1897. The style reached its peak after the introduction of steel and reinforced concrete frame structures in about 1912. Two of the larger buildings which resulted (hither-to buildings had not exceeded three storeys) from the new technology which emulated the grandiloquent style of the Edwardian era were the Banque de l'Indochine designed by D.M. Craik circa 1913, and the Chartered Bank building by Swan & Maclaren in 1914.

In domestic architecture, the Edwardian Baroque style was used in three larger houses whose fashionable owners were eager to imitate the dominant style in public buildings: E.S. Manasseh's house at Ladyhill (1903), Mount Echo (1911), and Eu Villa (1915). All were designed by Swan & Maclaren and planned in the Grand Manner with double-storey entrance halls placed along a central axis. Although basically symmetrical, the three houses had greater depth than was typical of the three-bay arrangement. Mount Echo, the smallest, had five bedrooms, Manasseh's had nine and Eu Villa more than ten. The scale of the houses called for giant classical columns raised on tall plinths. Mount Echo (page 204) and Manasseh's house (page 200) had open colonnaded verandahs and French Renaissance roofs reminiscent of Government House, the Exchange Building and General Post Office and revived under the influence of the Beaux-Arts. Eu Villa (8.7 and page 208) was less symmetrical in plan and elevation. Decidedly more eclectic, it had a Renaissance dome over the entrance hall and steeples over first floor dressing rooms. It was probably the first partially in reinforced concrete, which was being used more frequently by 1915; the large column-free areas were made possible by steel joists and reinforced concrete floors.

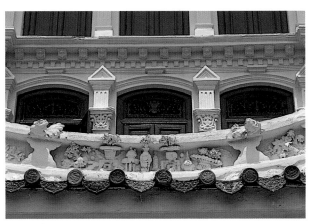

8.9 The origin of coarsened classicism lies in the evolution of shophouse architecture.
Here details on an Emerald Hill terrace house.

The Edwardian Baroque style in public buildings and larger houses influenced the development and popularity of the coarsened classicism which had begun to emerge in the 19th century. The style flourished throughout the first quarter of the present century, particularly in terraced houses, and can be readily identified on buildings with richly embellished and textured facades characterised by a free use of classical details and decorative motifs, both Eastern and Western. The evolution of an ornate and decorative style can be seen by contrasting the simple elevations of G.D. Coleman's Georgian houses, the early Anglo-Indian bungalows and the typical three-bay-across-the-front colonial houses with the eclectic Bonnygrass, Mandalay Villa and even the earlier and less ornate Magenta Cottage. Whereas Coleman's houses were a conscious and studied exercise in Regency classicism, Magenta Cottage was untutored in its application of classical features and belonged more to the Straits. Its architecture was spontaneous, unsophisticated and hybrid, and in turn spawned the decorative style of Bonnygrass and Mandalay Villa.

Mandalay Villa (8.8), built in Katong in 1902 for Lee Cheng Yan, was less refined and quite different in character from Tyersall, Mount Echo or Eu Villa. Its facades were characterised by the uncontrolled application of classical features and the free use of decorative motifs — plaster reliefs were applied to wall surfaces, arch spandrels, parapets, solid balustrades and roof gables like icing on a cake. The first floor verandah columns were short, fat and thick, and stood on classical plinths. The verandah was supported by an elaborate arrangement of arches and Corinthian pilasters while its semi-octagonal form was repeated at the wings. Dentils strung around the building marked the first floor. Window openings were flanked by Corinthian pilasters, and simulated stone quoins were rendered in plaster at the corner of the rear wings. On plan, the house was basically a traditional three-bay design and more modest in scale than Mount Echo and Tyersall.

The origin of the Coarsened Classical style, typified by Mandalay Villa, lies perhaps in the evolution of shophouse architecture. Certainly Cameron's remark in 1864 that the style of Chinese shophouses "is a sort of compromise between English and Chinese" proves beyond doubt that eclecticism was widespread

8.10 The house of Nah Kim Seng at Kampong Java Road (left)
and the house of Lee Kia Soon at Cairnhill Road (right).

by the 1860s, and it may have made its first appearance in the 1840s. It is conceivable that the eclectic mix of European and Chinese styles was initiated by local builders and Chinese property owners. Certainly for private and domestic work mainly Chinese labourers and craftsmen were employed. An important event in regards to public buildings was the withdrawal of Indian convict labour before 1873. It would be too speculative to assume a connection between that event and the assumed emergence of a new trend, but the withdrawal of convict labour did mean that local craftsmen and labourers were used in place of Indian convicts in the construction of public buildings.

The influence of builders and craftsmen who arrived in Singapore from China after the European intervention in that country in the 1840s also cannot be ruled out. These craftsmen would have been exposed to European architecture in the seaports under European occupation. This, and the fact that most private buildings were in fact designed by local men who were untutored in the Classical Orders, must account for the incorrect application of classical features as well as for the eclectic mixture of European and Chinese motifs observed by Cameron on shophouses as early as the 1860s.

Certainly most shophouses were built to the designs of Chinese builders. Two exceptions, almost a century apart, are Ellenborough building, a block of shophouses owned by Tan Tock Seng and designed by J.T. Thomson in the 1840s at South Boat Quay (8.15), and the shophouses at Serangoon Road and Hastings Road designed by D.M. Craik in 1912. The Ellenborough building, demolished in 1987, was, as with Thomson's other buildings, Palladian in style. Craik's shophouses were eclectic without any trace of Chinese motifs or influence; the Tuscan columns were Palladian in their simplicity, in contrast to his

treatment of the corner pediments topped by decorative Renaissance pots.

Thomson's and Craik's preference for an unadulterated European style and Cameron's remarks suggest that a mixture of Asian and European architectural elements had little appeal to Europeans. This may account for the fact that a Coarsened Classical style was rarely adopted by European architects with the notable exception of Frank Brewer. If such building plans were submitted by European architects for approval, they were almost certainly the work of the offices' local draughtsmen.

As the shophouses and terraced houses began to shed their Chinese elements, an exuberant and highly decorative style evolved that further coarsened the Classical Orders and other European ornamentation (8.15). The facades of the terraced houses on Emerald Hill Road and Amoy Street provide clear evidence of the changes. The older ones, dating from the late 19th and early 20th century, have more

8.11 The pargetting is from Nah Kim Seng's house.

8.12 A house in Chapel Road (left) and the house of Sim Cheng Neo (right) at Mountbatten Road.

Chinese features. These include the solid granite bases to brick piers, the Chinese roof tiles on the overhangs above footways, the friezes decorated with ceramic pieces in floral patterns above the bressumers, and the rounded gable ends. The window treatment of the ground floors is almost entirely Chinese: the main entrance doors panelled in the European style, but often inscribed with Chinese characters in gold; the *pintu pagar*; and the pair of double windows on each side of the front door, the inner pair glazed and the outer timber panels inscribed with floral patterns or Chinese characters in gold. The buildings which date from after World War One, however, have shed their Chinese elements and decorations. Verandah piers are entirely of brick, and bressumers above the footway and around airwells are in reinforced concrete. Overhangs above footways and decorated friezes are absent, and gable roof ends are pointed. As the house fronts assumed a more "Western" appearance, the lone Asian element to survive was the *pintu pagar*.

C. Northcote Parkinson, writing in the journal of the Institute of Architects of Malaya in the 1950s, referred to the style of the Emerald Hill houses as "Chinese Baroque Mannerism". On the shophouse designs in general he remarked that "there emerged a style which we might define as Roman Chinese with classical pilasters boldly added to shophouses not otherwise reminiscent of the Ancient World." As most of the details on the buildings were executed by Chinese craftsmen, and probably even designed by them, Parkinson's observations perhaps point to the truth that the shophouse style was a Chinese interpretation of European classical architecture in the widest sense, regardless of whether seen as classical, renaissance, mannerist or baroque. It is interesting to note that a parallel architectural development took

place in Hong Kong where Anglo-Chinese influences resulted in buildings with facades similar to those in Singapore. The office of Messrs Cheun Kwong Yuen (8.13), built in 1912, is a striking example.

It is thus not surprising that the elevational treatment of some of the detached houses owned by Chinese made use of stylistic elements that originated with the shophouses. In fact, having adopted and adapted the European-style house for their own use, Chinese owners freely added the Chinese elements common to terraced and shophouses to facades and interiors. Examples of houses with coarsened classical elements but strong Chinese influence as well are Madam Teo Hong Beng's house, Seah Song Seah's house and Bonnygrass. Photographs of Bonnygrass (page 159) reveal Chinese doors and

8.13 Coarsened classicism was not limited to Singapore as the Hong Kong premises of Cheung Kwong Yuen illustrate.

windows while the interior had built-in Chinese cupboards (which were salvaged by antique dealers when the house was demolished circa 1960).

The decorative style of Mandalay Villa had great appeal and persisted into the 1920s. Other fine examples include the house of Frederick d'Almeida built in 1910 at Lloyd Road and still standing (page 49, second row left); a pair of identical houses at 57 and 59 Cairnhill Road built in 1907 for Lee Kia Soon (8.10); the house of Nah Kim Seng built in 1913 at Kampong Java Road (8.10); and three identical houses still to be seen at Mountbatten Road built in 1927 for Madam Sim Cheng Neo (8.11). The decorative tendency can also be seen in a number of bungalows including George d'Almeida's house at Cuppage Road which he designed in 1898 (page 71); Lee Sian Teck's bungalow at 13 Amber Road built in 1901; and the house of P.N. Mohammed Miskin Sahib built in 1920 at Geylang Road.

There were houses built during the same period that were less baroque and with little discernable Chinese influence, although they were most certainly erected by mainly Chinese contractors and workmen. In these, which can possibly be viewed as belonging to the earlier type represented by Magenta Cottage, plaster relief decorations and ornamentation were minimal. Typical examples are the house at Mount Elizabeth designed in 1894 for C. Hodge (page 190); W. Wolber's house at Napier Road designed in 1903 by Lermit & Westerhout (page 196); and the house of Miss J. Motion (8.16), also designed by Lermit & Westerhout in 1900. Hodge's house was on the whole plain despite the pediments over the ground floor windows, the decorative plasterwork on the pilasters and spandrels of the arches. Wolber's house had much the same character as Hodges' despite its heavier appearance. The only decorative features of Motion's house were the eaves boards and jack-roof.

Simple or elaborate, the hotch-potch of elements do not seem to have been applied according to any architectural theory or principle. Architectural developments in Britain and elsewhere never led to a coherent movement in Singapore. The British architects and engineers who innovated copied from England and their local counterparts, in turn, indiscriminately emulated them.

Many houses were characterised, as previously mentioned, by European-inspired designs, motifs and patterns in exuberant plasterwork. The skill of external decorative plaster relief, or pargetting, was introduced by Italian plasterers during Tudor times to England where it became extremely popular. The plasterers used a stucco mixture of lime, fine marble dust, with the occasional addition of fine sand and

hair. Although there are no known examples of plaster reliefs extensively applied externally in early Singapore, some was done on mouldings, cornices and columns. It is possible, therefore, that pargetting was introduced earlier than we are aware of, became popular around the 1870s, and persisted until the late 1920s.

Another popular decorative element was the verandah balustrade. Bottle-shaped balusters appeared in northern Italy about 1480. In Singapore, the early timber balusters were replaced by concrete and brick or green glazed earthenware vase-shaped balusters. Examples may be seen at 23 Amber Road, designed by R.A.J. Bidwell in 1912 (page 211), Lee Kia Soon's houses at Cairnhill and Nah Kim Seng's residence. Iron balusters were sometimes used, as at Tan Soo Guan's house at St Patrick's Road and W.M. Allen's house at 74 Meyer Road.

The plain eaves boards of the early houses gave way to elaborate ones (8.14), a feature that originated with the Gothic Revival in Victorian England (see chapter three). Originally called valences, (defined as "a short curtain, round frame or canopy of bedstead") these hung like lace along the roof eaves of British railway stations. Over time all pretence that the valence fulfilled a useful function disappeared and eventually fancy ironwork replaced wood. Valences were widely adopted in India and elsewhere and suited the tropical climate well for they also functioned efficiently as drips. The local version differed from other countries' and designs were possibly of Anglo-Malay origin (although decorative eaves boards were not found on early Malay houses).

Timber lattice screens were often used, especially in more modest houses, to protect staircases in open verandahs, the earliest known example being Meyer's house at Oxley Rise, circa 1870. Lattice screens, also

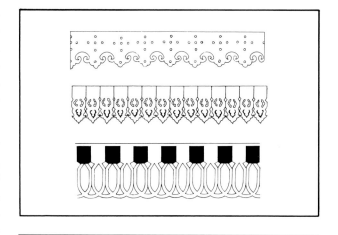

8.14 Examples of decorative eaves boards, or valences.

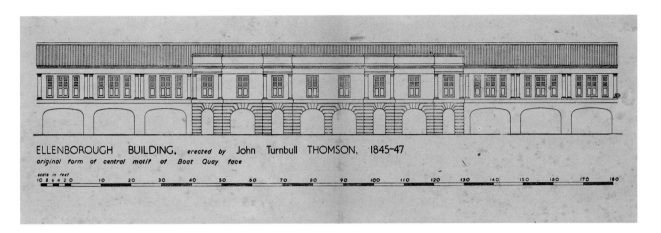

ELLENBOROUGH BUILDING, *erected by* John Turnbull THOMSON, 1845–47
original form of central motif of Boat Quay face

scale in feet
10 8 6 4 2 0   10   20   30   40   50   60   70   80   90   100   110   120   130   140   150   160   170   180

8.15 The evolution of shophouse architecture. The Stanley Street house, circa 1885 (middle left) is the earliest and most Chinese. The later examples, (middle left, and above), are circa 1928 to 1935. The Ellenborough building (top) is European classical

129

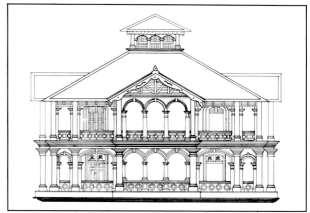

8.16 Jack-roofs ventilated interiors and gave light, as in the houses of Miss Motion at St Thomas Walk, (left) and the Sultan of Siak at Chancery Lane.

common in India, were, however, probably used in Singapore from the earliest days of the settlement. They were fixed above carriage porches as added weather protection and served admirably as ventilation and security screens when fitted into the spaces between walls and eaves soffits, as in Verappa Chitty's bungalow (page 218). In some instances, fixed louvres were used instead of lattice screens.

There was also greater variety in the roof forms during this period. Most of the early houses, two-storey and bungalow, had roofs hipped on all four sides as can be seen from the photograph on pages 44–45, Caldwell's and Coleman's houses being virtually the only exceptions. Economy alone, inevitable during the early years, must account for the choice of this simpler roof form. The jack-roof, or lantern roof, was later frequently adopted to ventilate interiors or roof spaces, such as in Cashin's house at Rochalie Drive built in 1916 and the Sultan of Siak's house at Chancery Lane built in 1907. The clerestorey above the dining room in the Cashin house was somewhat unusual. Gambrels were equally popular and in later years the jerkin-head, or hipped gable roof, was often used. The mansard was confined to very large residences.

Gable roofs, impractical for the main body of houses, were often regarded purely as a design element and confined to small projections such as carriage porches, front verandahs, bathrooms, bay windows and outhouses. Generally, gable ends extended beyond the faces of the end walls and where they formed a feature or decorative element they were sometimes framed in timber as in the Mock Tudor or Renaissance manner. A variation was the "Dutch gable", the deliberate extension of a part of or the entire gable end wall surmounted by a pediment, as in Puey Yeun Chan's house at Grange Road de-

signed by J.B. Westerhout in 1916 (8.17) which bears a striking resemblance to the house occupied by the Indian High Commission, also at Grange Road. A.W. Cashin's house at Rochalie Drive, designed by Westerhout in the same year (page 210), had a modified Dutch gable with straight sides and a semi-circular pediment. His Dutch origins could account for his choice of the Dutch gable, although a similar one can be seen at Stiven's house by Swan & Maclaren built in 1901.

The vogue for adopting different elements from various historical periods led to an innovative use of the Gothic steeple, or fleche, in domestic buildings. The earliest known example is Ang Seah Im's house at Seah Im Road designed by George d'Almeida in 1911. The steeple in its many proportions continued to be used on countless houses in the 1920s, (see page 216). Domes also enjoyed some popularity. There are no records of classical domes being used in the early years. The dome over the corner bedroom at Golden Bell (8.17), built in 1909, resembled a Buddhist stupa which was very likely deliberate considering that the owner, Tan Boo Liat, had long and close business connections with Thailand. The bell-shaped dome perhaps suggested the name given to the house. The earliest known dome complete with drum and lantern was at Eu Villa. Other versions could be seen in Low Teng Lin's house at Kampong Bahru Road built in 1920 and in Teo Hoo Lye's house built in 1913 in Dhoby Ghaut. Domes over open colonnaded towers, as in Tan Kah Kee's house at Cairnhill Road (8.19), became much more common in the 1920s.

The post-World War One years up to the onset of the Great Depression in 1929 saw a building boom in Singapore which attracted a new generation of expatriate

8.17 Puey Yuen Chan's house (left) and Golden Bell (right). 8.18 Following pages:
Singapore in the 1920s and 1930s.

architects who brought with them the latest stylistic trends prevalent in Britain. Among the most successful were P.H. Keys and F. Dowdeswell, the latter an engineer. They were especially engaged by the Public Works Department in 1921 to design Fullerton Building (8.18), completed in 1928. F.D. Ward, who was in the municipal service from 1923 to 1939, designed City Hall. After 1928, Keys and Dowdeswell continued in private practice until the outbreak of the Pacific War. Their versatility was reflected in three buildings of different character designed in 1929: the KPM Building, the Overseas Chinese Banking Corporation Building, both demolished, and the Heeren Building (8.23) which is still standing on Orchard Road.

Around the same time, Swan & Maclaren, the most active and largest practice since its founding in 1892, employed three expatriate architects who remained with the firm during its most prolific years — F.G. Lundon in 1919, and Denis Santry and Frank Brewer in 1921. The three were most likely involved in the important buildings the firm designed in the 1920s, including the Hong Kong and Shanghai Bank Building of 1922; Union Building in Collyer Quay, 1923; Ocean Building, 1923; the College of Medicine, 1927; Meyer Chambers, 1930; and the Mercantile Bank Building at Raffles Place, 1929.

All of the buildings designed by the two firms were steel framed structures and, except for the College of Medicine, over five storeys in height, the longer spans and the larger scale made possible by the new construction techniques. The controlled application of the Classical Orders in the grand manner of the Beaux-Arts style and the wall finishes mark the difference of the buildings from their Baroque predecessors such as the Victoria Memorial Hall; all but two, the Heeren Building and the College

of Medicine, were clad in reconstructed stone or in brick rendered in Shanghai or granolithic plaster and grooved to simulate masonry, lending the neo-classical facades a solid and enduring appearance that echoed the confidence of the colonial empire.

Fewer examples of Beaux-Arts classicism can be found in domestic architecture. An early one is the house designed by Ralph Booty, a British architect, in 1922 for J.B. David at 7 Oxley Rise (page 221) which had a stately portico in the Roman Doric Order. Not since the days of Coleman and Thomson had the Orders been so conscientiously applied. Whereas Coleman's architecture had the delicate touch of feminine grace akin to the Romantic Classicism of the Regency, Booty's house was masculine and Roman in character. It's precision was due principally to its construction in reinforced concrete, and it bears comparison with Keys and Dowdeswell's Fullerton Building.

Booty, who practised in Singapore for a brief period before moving to Kuala Lumpur to form Booty & Edwards, could well have been the first to introduce Beaux-Arts classicism in domestic architecture. He was soon followed by others, especially the architectural firm of Chung & Wong. Chung Hong Woot, reputed to have been the firm's designer, can be credited with many fine houses, including three in the same classical mode as the David house. Two of them, Tan Kah Kee's at Cairnhill Road and Aw Boon Haw's at Nassim Road, were built in 1926 (8.19). The third, and possibly the best, was built a year later for Dr. S.C. Yin at Gilstead Road (page 214). All are still standing. Tan Kah Kee's house was, even before the 1930 additions by Seah Eck Jim, inexplicably eclectic in the use of a mansard roof, the treatment of the windows and the inclusion of the tower, elements that did not appear to be quite in

Hongkong & Shanghai Bank Singapore

Fullerton Building, Singapore

TELEGRAPH OFFICE
SINGAPORE

NORTH BRIDGE ROAD
SINGAPORE

Battery Road, Singapore.

Municipal Building, Singapore.

SUPREME COURT AND MUNICIPAL BUILDING, SINGAPORE.

8.19 The houses built for Aw Boon Haw at Nassim Road (left) and for Tan Kah Kee at Cairnhill (right) in 1926 were influenced by the Ecole des Beaux Arts.

character, particularly with the portico and the rear verandah. Except for the steeple on the corner tower, Aw Boon Haw's house at Nassim Road is in the same mode as the David house.

While Ralph Booty and Chung Hong Woot were designing their Beaux-Arts houses, Frank Brewer was employing a distinctive style that was mildly inspired by the works of the late Arts and Crafts architects. Brewer (1886–1971) was born in Suffield House, Richmond, Surrey and was the son of Frank J. Brewer, FRIBA. He was educated at King's College School and graduated in architecture at King's College, University of London. He was a partner in his father's London firm, Brewer, Smith and Brewer, from 1908 to 1919. (The firm still exists.) During World War One, he was a captain in the Royal Engineers. He arrived in Singapore in 1920 to join Swan & Maclaren, and in 1930 started his own practice. Just before Singapore fell to the Japanese Army, Brewer escaped in a ship which was sunk by Japanese planes off Pompong Island. He survived the ordeal, landed in Sumatra and eventually reached Colombo in another vessel. He returned to Singapore after the war and re-established his practice. He retired in 1957 and died in Jersey aged 84.

While working in Swan & Maclaren, Brewer may have been influenced by the architect Dennis Santry, who was also an adherent of the Arts and Crafts Movement. Santry was born in Cork, Ireland in 1879 and was a graduate of the Royal College of Art, London. He worked in South Africa for several years and was described as a pioneer of the Arts and Crafts Movement in South Africa. Santry came to Singapore in 1918, became a partner in Swan & Maclaren in 1924 and retired in 1935. It is not known what happened to him after that.

Brewer spent 30 years in Singapore, and designed countless private homes, which are still to be seen, from Katong to Tanglin. His 1921 design of the Tanjong Katong Exchange for the Oriental Telephone & Electric Company (8.20) already showed elements of his distinctive style, and his houses can be readily identified by his consistent use of several features: brick buttresses, a steeply-pitched roof upturned at the hips, oriel windows, and rough-cast plaster rendering of external wall surfaces, which were textured by combed decoration and other patterns (8.21 and 8.22). It should be noted that all of these were common features of late Arts and Crafts houses; the exposed brickwork on arches and buttresses recall Folly Farm and Deanery Garden, two English houses designed by Sir Edwin Lutyens, who had a great influence on Brewer. Brewer later splayed the top corners of windows, haunched bressumers, and arranged the glazing beads and security bars of window openings in geometric patterns. His heavy and robust style was in keeping with his physical build. W.I. Watson, a retired partner of Swan & Maclaren, said Brewer was "a very large man physically". He was reputed to have been amateur heavy-weight boxing champion of Britain.

Brewer also applied these features to non-domestic buildings, such as the St Andrew's School at Woodsville (circa 1939), the Tamil Sports Club at Norfolk Road (1933), and the Anglo-Chinese Secondary School at Cairnhill (circa 1928). In some of his non-domestic buildings, the English cottage mood gave way to Spanish Moorish, as in St Andrew's School, or to a Chinese, as in the Anglo-Chinese School at Cairnhill, where he turned his cottage roof a little further at the corners to effect a Chinese roofline. Versatile and always a man of his time, he abandoned his buttresses and plunged into the

134

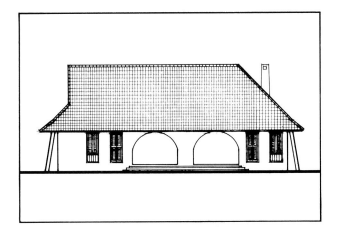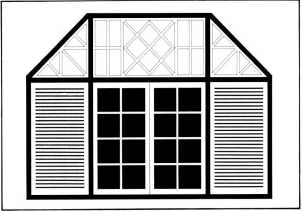

8.20 The Katong Telephone Exchange, 1921 (left), had buttresses and roof with upturned hips. Windows with splayed corners (right) were another Brewer trademark.

Modern Movement in two of his major projects in the 1930s: the Singapore Swimming Club (1936) and the Cathay Building (1939). In the Swimming Club (8.24), the circular balcony with its horizontal iron pipe balustrade at the corner of the building was reminiscent of the De La Warr Pavilion at Bexhill, Sussex, designed by Mendelsohn and Chermayeff in 1934, which without doubt must have also influenced the design of the Kallang Airport building, completed by the Public Works Department in mid-1937 (8.24). But in his domestic architecture the Arts and Crafts spirit never left him, and all his houses from the 1920s through to the post-war years were designed with corner buttresses and deep overhanging roofs curved gently at the corners.

I n the 1930s the Modern Movement gained ground in Singapore. The circular motif was copied in balconies, verandahs, stair-halls, bay windows and flat roof terraces. The house at Holland Park Estate built in 1934 by Credit Foncier D'Extreme Orient, a Belgium property investment company (8.2 and page 140), is one of the earliest examples. The influence of the Modern Movement can be seen in the reinforced concrete flat roof and the strong horizontal emphasis carried through in the window glazing bars, the balustrade, the continuation of the projecting eaves of the outhouses, and the link round the main building. The entrance hall was omitted so that one entered directly into the lounge. The ground floor had an open plan, except for the partition between the lounge and the dining room. Old habits die hard, however, and the main house was linked to an outhouse.

In retrospect, the 1930s can be regarded as a period of uncertainty. In a number of houses, the more decorative Art Deco and the Modern International vied for supremacy; the result was a style similar to that of old Miami Beach, which has been dubbed "Tropical Deco" (8.24). At the same time, a mutant form of classicism, already fashionable in Britain and Europe for some time, came into vogue in Singapore. Buildings sprang up with facades that were basically classical in character but with traditional details and decorations omitted or simplified. The earliest known example in the Straits Settlements is the Empire Cinema in Penang, built in 1914. Other non-domestic examples include the Phoenix Building (1920) by Seah & Le Cain; Heeren Building by Keys & Dowdeswell, mentioned earlier; Shaw's Building, including the Capitol Cinema (circa 1927); and Meyer Flats at North Bridge Road, designed by Swan & Maclaren.

The interest in mutant classicism (8.23) extended to domestic architecture as well, and examples of the use of the idiom are the houses of Lim Boon Thin at Tanjong Katong Road, designed by Ho Kwong Yew in 1934, and Manasseh Meyer's at Meyer Road, designed by Swan & Maclaren in 1930 and still standing. Meyer's house has a formal and classical symmetry akin to Mount Echo and Government House but is bare of ornamentation and decoration, the walls being finished in roughcast granite rendering. The arches and piers along the ground floor loggias are without mouldings, string courses or bases. The columns on the first floor verandahs have simplified capitals and bases.

Lim Boon Thin's, on the other hand, was basically a three-bay colonial house. The shallow projecting porch was roofed over by a terraced verandah, cantilevered beyond the square piers of the porch. The reinforced concrete cantilevered beams were in the

8.21 House by Frank Brewer at Dalvey Road. The buttresses, roughcast plaster rendering and roof upturned at the hips are typical of his designs.

form of simplified classical brackets; the mouldings to the pier bases, capitals and cornices were reduced to simple profiles of stepped fillets. Simplified or reduced mouldings can also be seen on the piers of 44 Wilkinson Road (8.23) and the columns supporting the arches on the verandah of 56 Dalvey Road, both built in the 1930s. At 82 Branksome Road (8.23), the capitals of the pilasters are stylised.

Throughout the 1930s, bungalow design continued along a well-trodden path despite the introduction concrete beams and lintels. Three identical bungalows at Ramsgate Road (8.23) built for Lim Bock Kee in 1927, a senior staff officer of the Overseas Chinese Banking Corporation in the 1930s and after World War Two the compradore of the Hongkong Shanghai Bank, are typical examples. The outhouses were retained and the original timber-framed gables were almost Mock Tudor. The Arts and Crafts cottage influence was apparent in a number of other bungalows where the gable was partially hipped, such as the houses numbered 33 to 45 Goodman Road. The hipped-gable, or jerkin-head, roof graced the fronts of many bungalows built in the late 1930s and early 1940s. The elevations of Lau Chung Kui's bungalow at

4 Poole Road (page 219) are stark and severe with a touch of the mutant classic.

Yet the uncertainty of the decade was apparent in bungalow floor plans. The plan of the Ramsgate Road houses departed from the standard three-bay plan. There were no verandahs, and the sitting room and one bedroom faced the front directly without an intervening verandah space. In contrast, Seow Sam Whatt's house at Lorong K Telok Kurau, built in 1934, adhered rigidly to the three-bay colonial bungalow plan, with two bedrooms at each side and a hall and dining area in the centre. The front verandah hall extended forward with steps at the sides. Built obviously for a less affluent client, the house was served by only one bathroom and toilet. There were no servants' rooms or syce's quarters, although a garage was provided. The house was supported by a framework of brick piers and concrete beams. The external walls were a half-brick in thickness but the internal partitions were timber, which suggests that the bungalow was built on a low budget. This could partly account for its stark and unpretentious elevations. The walls and the brick piers on the verandah were stripped of all decorations and mouldings.

8.22 The Dalvey Road house. The use of exposed brickwork is another frequent element in Brewer's designs. The entrance under the projecting porch is above right.

number of political, social and economic changes beginning with the Pacific War ushered in a new era in housing in Singapore. At the end of the war the housing shortage and growing population encouraged the development of large housing estates, both public and private.(Housing development, as we have seen, had been on a modest scale.) The earliest, and possibly the first large private housing estate, had been Siong Lim Park, designed by Chung & Wong and built in 1926. Credit Foncier developed Queen Astrid Park in 1939/40. An estate planned in 1935 on the site of the old Alkaff Gardens was abandoned; Sennett Estate was built on the site around 1950, the first post-war housing estate. Quite often, however, developers merely built the infrastructure and retailed the subdivided building lots; in this manner King Albert Park in 1940, and some post-war estates such as Siglap Estate, Binjai Park and Bintong Park, were developed.

Apartments, or flats, were first introduced into Singapore in 1909 when Manasseh Meyer built Crescent Flats at Katong. It remained the only one until 1921 when three blocks were built: St Nicholas Flats at River Valley Road, Meyer's Flats at North Bridge

Road and Amber Mansions at Penang Road. Before the end of the decade more were built — Capitol Flats, Heeren Building and Loke Yew's flats at Loke Yew Street. With the formation of the Singapore Improvement Trust in 1927, flats were built for lower income families to meet the housing shortage.

The influence of the Modern Movement intensified after the war, while the novel approach of Bidwell, Craik, Brewer and others also continued into the immediate post-war years, a short period of little change. Brewer returned to the colony and continued to build houses with buttresses and splayed window corners. Some expatriate architects retired in the 1950s as overseas-trained local architects, bringing fresh ideas and developing the open plan, returned to a Singapore on the verge of self-government. By 1960, these men formed the majority of architects and the colonial house had slipped into history.

It was the period from 1945 to 1950 which saw the demise of the colonial house. For more than a century it had changed very little even after construction in reinforced concrete. Born of a stable community, it thrived blissfully under stern colonial rule until the outbreak of the Pacific War.

8.23 Examples of mutant classicism — buildings with
basically classical facades but with the details simplified or
omitted, and popular in the late 1920s and 1930s — are
clockwise from top left: the house of Lim Bock Kee at Ramsgate
Road, 1927; house of Lim Boon Thin at Tanjong Katong Road,
1934; 82 Branksome Road, circa 1930 and the Heeren Building
on Orchard Road. The two details are from 44 Wilkinson Road
(right) and Lim Boon Thin's house (left).

8.24 Examples of the Modern International are clockwise from top: Kallang Airport, 1937; house at Bukit Timah Road, circa 1935; house at Brizay Park, circa 1940; De La Warr Pavilion, Bexhill, Sussex, England, 1934; Singapore Swimming Club, 1935/36; and a house at Holland Park circa 1935 which is an eclectic mix of Modern International and Tropical Deco.

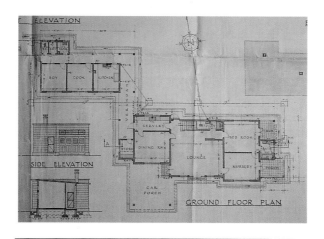

Plan for a house in the Modern International style built in
Holland Park estate, 1934. Note the retention of the outhouse.

Before the introduction of structural steel, some industrial and commercial buildings were framed in wrought iron sections which supported timber floors, brick walls and partitions. A composite system of load-bearing brick walls, cast iron columns, and wrought iron beams was also often adopted. The first structural steel-framed building in the world was built in Chicago in 1883–1885; in Britain, the first was Mewes & Davis' Ritz Hotel in London in 1906. The system was introduced into Singapore a decade later in commercial buildings. Steel beams supported by brick walls were used in some houses, but there are no records of steel-framed houses before World War Two as the costs were comparatively expensive.

The greatest impact on building came about with the introduction of reinforced concrete. The first reinforced concrete building was built in 1903 in Paris by Auguste Perrett. It is uncertain when reinforced concrete was introduced to Singapore but probably the first reinforced concrete frame building was the Banque de l'Indochine built in 1913. The structural and reinforced concrete consultant, Messrs Brossard and Mopin, were in Singapore from 1912 to about 1922, and they probably introduced the new construction method. Reinforced concrete was employed sparingly at first, its use being confined mainly to the casting of the bresummer beams, carried on brick piers and load-bearing brick walls, to support timber floor joists and brick partitions and walls. Concrete roofs were sometimes built over carriage porches and in other small areas. Floors in exposed or wet areas such as verandahs, balconies and bathrooms were also similarly cast in lime or Portland cement concrete reinforced with expanded metal or iron mesh. It was from such experiments using concrete reinforced with expanded metal or iron mesh, first experimented with in Europe in 1850, that modern concrete practice developed when mild steel reinforcement bars were introduced in the 1880s.

An early example of partial concrete construction is E.S. Manasseh's house built in 1903. Eu Villa, built in 1915, was probably one of the earliest houses in which concrete was reinforced with mild steel bars. Interest in the new form of construction, interrupted by World War One, was revived and possibly accelerated by the influx of the new generation of expatriate architects who arrived in Singapore around 1920. In 1921 W. Campbell Oman, the municipal architect, noted that "reinforced concrete has been far more employed this year." He was referring to 18 reinforced concrete buildings comprising offices, warehouses, flats and a school, completed or under construction at the end of that year.

The first reinforced concrete frame houses were built about 1935 and the framing of houses throughout in reinforced concrete became the standard practice only after World War Two. Before then, brick walls continued to be the main supports for reinforced concrete beams and slabs; by the late 1920s this structural support system had become common practice even for smaller houses. After the introduction of reinforced concrete, the raised timber floors in bungalows were carried by concrete beams resting on square brick piers which continued above floor level to support timber roofs and serve as stiffeners to both the internal and external walls. Many bungalows built during the two decades before World War Two adopted the composite framing of brick piers and concrete beams which replaced the wholly timber frame of the Mock-Tudor style and the local timber-framed houses of the 1920s. The transition was complete after 1945 when the reinforced concrete frame predominated.

A Note on Architects

House of L.W Geddes, Ridout Road, 1934 by Frank Brewer.
Note the exposed brickwork on the arches and buttresses.

Until the 1960s, there were few trained architects in Singapore. In the very early years most of the public works, including buildings, were designed by unqualified administrators or military engineers. Foremost among them was Lieutenant Philip Jackson who in 1823 completed the first Raffles Institution building. G.D. Coleman, who arrived in 1827, was the only trained architect until the 1890s. J.T. Thomson, his successor as government surveyor (1841-1853), was a trained surveyor also active in designing buildings including two hospitals on Pearl's Hill and shophouses at New Bridge Road for Tan Tock Seng (page 129). Dennis McSwinney was a building overseer who designed the Cathedral of the Good Shephard, completed in 1846.

Government engineers continued to be involved in architecture until the end of the century. Major Adolphus McNair, colonial engineer 1867–1881, is remembered for his design of St Andrew's Cathedral. His successor, Captain Henry Edward McCallum (1881–1895), designed the present Telok Ayer Market building. James MacRitchie, the municipal engineer 1860s to about 1880, undertook private commissions until about 1890, government employees were allowed to accept private work.

From its founding in 1834, the Royal Institute of British Architects (RIBA) was the controlling authority of the architectural profession throughout the British Commonwealth. Other similar professional bodies were formed, such as the Society of Architects, which was eventually absorbed by the Royal Institute in 1925. If membership of the Insitute was recognition of an architect's professional competence, then there were no "qualified" architects in Singapore until the 1890s. The first RIBA associate was E. Osborne who worked in Crane Brothers from 1893 to 1896. Swan & Maclaren, the firm founded in 1892 by two engineers, Archibald Swan and James W.B. Maclaren, employed its first RIBA associate, E.J. Puller, only in 1902. In the same year, the municipal government employed its first associate, David Macleod Craik.

Between 1907 and 1937 the number of RIBA associates was fairly stable at between two and four in any one year except between 1925 and 1931 when there were five to eight. From 1938 to 1940 the average was eight. All but three were expatriates. There were however, other competent men who were not RIBA associates. Foremost amongst the expatriates was R.A.J. Bidwell who designed many well-known buildings and houses.

Most Asian architects received their training as draughtsmen in private offices or government departments. Among the earliest known, who worked in the 1880s, were Henry Richards, Yeo Hock Siang and Moh Wee Teck or W.T. Moh as he signed his building plans. From the 1890s. The names George D'Almeida, Wan Mohammed Kassim and J.B. Westerhout are seen on building plans. Chye Tian Fook was probably the first local elected a member of a recognised engineering institute. He began his career as an apprentice draughtsman in the municipal engineer's department in 1896 and set up private practice with Sam Tomlinson. Seah Eng Choe and W.J.C. Le Cain were probably the first local engineers to qualify from a tertiary institution, in 1921. Their partnership, under the style of Seah & Le Cain, won first prize in an open competition for three blocks of government flats at Upper Cross Street. It was not until 1938 that Singapore saw her first qualified local architects. They were Koh Cheng Yam, a graduate of the Architectural Association in London, and Ng Keng Siang and Robert Kan, both graduates of the University of London.

THE

ALBUM

〜

VIEW of the COURT HOUSE, SINGAPORE.

An early print of Maxwell's house from *The Malay Peninsula* by
Captain P.J. Begbie published circa 1834.

John Argyle Maxwell came to Singapore in 1822 to establish a branch office of G. Maclaine & Company of Batavia in which he was a partner. He went to Java from England after leaving the Horse Guards in August of 1820 with the rank of ensign. The story of the house he built has been reconstructed from correspondence in the East India Company letter books.

In February of 1822, Maxwell applied through a Donald Macintyre for a piece of land on the north bank of the Singapore River. William Farquhar certified that the application "for such a portion of ground ... (within the space now occupied by His Highness the Toomongong) as may be eventually granted ... is hereby complied, as far as I may be considered vested with due authority for so doing ..." Farquhar's vague and conditional promise was not surprising; he knew that the land was within the area designated by Raffles for government use.

Maxwell was unhappy over the response and applied again in person on August 23, 1822 for a plot of land on which to build godowns. He signified his intention of doing business and settling in Singapore at some future date. (He never did; he was in Singapore intermittently until September 30, 1828 when he left never to return). If Farquhar was cautiously accommodating the first time, he was now far

from encouraging. Since the beginning of 1822 his relationship with Raffles had deteriorated. With the lieutenant-governor's impending visit in a fortnight's time he threw his pride to the wind and admitted three days later, on August 26, "that it is not in my power to make any further allotments of ground at present ..."

Maxwell prudently waited until the completion of the Temenggong's removal to Telok Blangah and Raffles departure for Bencoolen. When it became obvious that Dr John Crawfurd, the new resident councillor, intended to reverse Raffles' ruling on the government reserved land, he made a third application on August 26, 1823. He produced Farquhar's reply to Macintyre to back his plea but conveniently omitted Farquhar's letter of outright refusal. For reasons unknown, Maxwell did not receive a location ticket for his land for two years, until November 1, 1825. An adjacent lot of similar size was granted to George de Hochpied Larpent at the same time which Maxwell subsequently purchased. The two pieces had a total frontage of 240 feet and a depth of about 684 feet.

Maxwell's right to the land was questioned by John Prince, Crawfurd's successor. Anticipating a government ruling, he applied for a permanent grant in December of 1826. Early the following

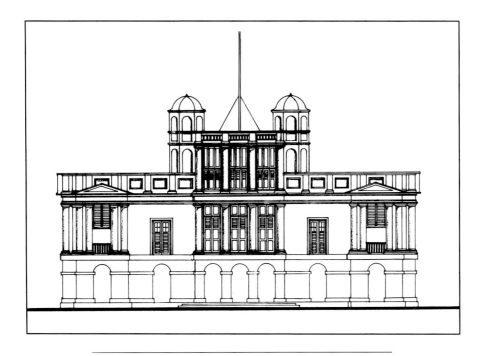

The front elevation of the house.

year he began to build the house and employed G.D. Coleman as architect. Inevitably, in April of 1827, Prince pointed out to the governor that Maxwell's land formed part of an area assigned by Raffles for government stores which had been given away by Crawfurd. Fearing, perhaps, that the house might be requisitioned by the government, Maxwell offered it for use as "...a Government House or Court House and Recorder's Chambers on a three year lease commencing from the date of completion of the house ..."

On receiving a favourable report from Edward Lake, the inspector general, on the adaptation of the house, Governor Fullerton proposed terms of its lease. At the same time he remarked pointedly to Maxwell:

It has been observed that the Location Ticket held by you differs in some respects from all others which have come under notice, in as much as the word entitled to occupy is substituted for permitted and the Residency Seal is not attached to the document in your possession. Upon reference to the proceedings of Sir Stamford Raffles and Mr Crawfurd, it would appear that a large sum (upwards of $5,000 Spanish) was expended in effecting the removal from the ground now occupied by you of the late Tumongoong and his followers, with the

view of appropriating the said ground to Government purposes ... It has also come to the knowledge of Government that Mr Crawfurd refused a previous application from a respectable Merchant of this Settlement upon the plea that the ground was positively set aside for public use.

A tedious exchange of letters on the conditions of the lease and grant ensued. It was finally agreed that the lease would commence on the day of the completion of the house, in March of 1828.

An unexpected problem then developed. On February 7, 1828 Kenneth Murchison, Prince's successor, appealed to Fullerton for a more permanent arrangement regarding his official residence because of "the dilemma in which I am placed in consequence of the difficulty, I must say impossibility, of procuring a suitable dwelling house..." Murchison was then living in a rented house which he expected to vacate within a month and claimed that his rent allowance was insufficient. The few houses available commanded high rents and were "quite unsuitable for the accommodation of the Resident Councillor, where rank and station require that he should have a commodious, permanent and respectable residence." He suggested that either the Institution building (Raffles Institution at Beach

THE SUPREME COURT, SINGAPORE

A postcard circa 1920 of Maxwell's house, after it had been
renovated several times.

Road) or Maxwell's new house be acquired for the resident councillor as a permanent arrangement. Events suggest that Murchison was offered Maxwell's house. Shortly after, the "new Tavern" in Commercial Square was rented and furnished as a temporary court house.

Unexpectedly, a letter from the governor's secretary arrived. Dated March 19, it informed Murchison that the recorder, the official judge for the Straits Settlements, refused to go on his regular circuit to Malacca and Singapore unless his expenses were met by the East India Company. Under the circumstances, the governor would have to preside over the trials scheduled to be held in Singapore in May. Since repairs on Raffles' bungalow on Bukit Larangan, which had been in a state of neglect for some years, could not be completed in time to receive the governor, all the furniture was to be moved to Maxwell's house which the governor intended for himself.

Murchison received these instructions on April 2, just five days after completion of the house. He replied immediately, his disappointment apparent. He adopted a compliant attitude, but between the lines frustration and anger can be detected. He acknowledged that the governor's decision to visit Singapore "will afford the highest satisfaction to

this community" and added that instructions had been given to move the furniture from the old bungalow to the new house. He then attempted a pathetic and futile protest:

This building, which the Honourable Governor was pleased to allot to me as a Residency House ... has in consequence been partly taken possession of, and furnished with all my private furniture, but considering the urgency of the case, I shall not appeal to the Honourable the Governor for a reconsideration of his present purpose, although, I beg to state that I was on the very point of occupying the house and have consequently given up my present residence (which I have not the power of redeeming) and am in a predicament of greater difficulty and embarassment than when I originally brought the subject to the consideration of the Board.

A week later, Murchison received a sharp rebuke from the governor through his secretary. In response, Murchison wrote on May 9, after Fullerton's arrival, that he could not remain silent in the face of such censure. He felt his complaint was not sufficient cause for a reprimand and his "expression of some disappointment was just and natural when I was suddenly deprived of the promised residence..." He ended by noting: "I could not but feel that my fair claims to consideration had been somewhat disregarded... and, although I did complain, I trust that I did so without violating the respect which I sincerely feel for the authority of the Honourable the Governor in Council."

Three days later, Fullerton responded with his own note. He pointed out that he had not expected to visit Singapore for some time, at least not until Raffles' bungalow was repaired. But the recorder's refusal to go on circuit led to his current decision. Referring to Murchison's disappointment the governor retorted:

The Governor does not come here either for pleasure or amusement but for the performance of public duty... From the whole style of Mr Murchison's former letter, and of this Minute as well as another communication of which not being a public one, I have taken no notice; it clearly appears that he expected me to reside to my great inconvenience in the bungalow on the Hill in its present condition infested with rats and vermin of every sort, a dwelling he would not himself occupy or at least thought not worth asking for while he was in lieu of rent of 300 rupees per month to continue to occupy a house which costs the Government 500 rupees per month.

He concluded that Murchison evinced more regard for his own convenience than for the public interest and ended by saying that Maxwell's house was to be used as a court house and Raffles' bungalow, after reconstruction, would be used by himself during future visits.

Fullerton's reply to Murchison's minute of February 7 appealing for a more permanent arrangement regarding his accommodation is missing, but therein could lie the truth of Murchison's assertion that the governnor had agreed to his use of Maxwell's house. Fullerton probably changed his mind, as Murchison implied, when his visit to Singapore suddenly came up. He realised then the awkward situation if his subordinate occupied the grandest and largest house on the island (described by John Prince as a "magnificent brick structure") while he stayed in the dilapidated bungalow on Bukit Larangan. The governor had not anticipated the turn of events and had already issued instructions for repairs to the bungalow which was to be for his own use. Without reference to Lake or anyone else, the governor conveniently assumed that the bungalow would not be ready in time for his visit and this provided the excuse for requesting that all furniture be moved from the bungalow to Maxwell's house.

If the house was ever used as a residence, it was during the brief period in May and June of 1828

when Fullerton was in Singapore, presumably to preside over the court which was held in the temporary court house in Commercial Square. Maxwell certainly never lived in the house; in September of 1828 he left for Europe and three years later sold all of his interests in Java and retired to Scotland.

What happened to the house over the years is not entirely clear. Maxwell sold it on September 1, 1829 to John Cockerell and George Gerard Larpent, according to C.B. Buckley. On September 1, 1841 an advertisement appeared in the newspaper announcing that it was for sale. The building was bought by the government but it is uncertain as to what use it was put since a new court house had been erected in 1839. Apparently that building was found unsuitable due to noise from Hallpike's boatyard next to it and another court house was erected in 1864 which now forms part of the Empress Place building. The court house moved back to Maxwell's house in 1875 and remained there until the present Supreme Court building was completed in 1939. A series of extensions — from 1873 to 1875, in 1901 and in 1909 — have altered the building somewhat.

After housing various government departments, it was decided in 1954 to convert and extensively renovate the entire building as a council chamber for the Legislative Assembly. The work was carried out under the directions of T.H. Hancock, FRIBA, senior architect, Public Works Department. Since self-government in 1959, Maxwell's house has been the seat of Parliament.

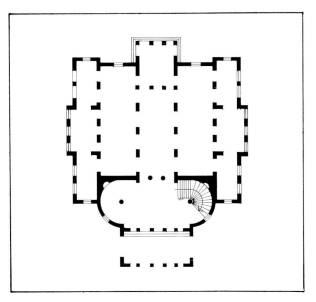

The ground floor plan.

The watercolour sketch by J.T. Thomson is dated 1846. On the left is the Cathedral of the Good Shepherd and on the right is St Andrew's Church. Except for the house of William Renshaw George, on the site of the present Raffles Hotel, none of the other houses can be identified with certainty.

This view of the European residential area around the Esplanade is a detail from a watercolour by J.T. Thomson. There is an air of quiet confidence reflected in the solid form of the houses. Noticeably absent are the encircling open verandahs which later became so common.

The large building in the centre next to the seafront is readily identified as the Institution. G.D. Coleman's St Andrew's church is on the extreme right. To the left of the Institution, standing on the present site of the Raffles Hotel, is the house owned by Robert Scott of Penang and rented to William Renshaw George from the 1830s to 1858. It is the only house that can be identified with certainty. George arrived in Singapore on February 19, 1825. By the end of that year, or in early 1826, he joined Charles Thomas and his brothers in Thomas & Company as a bookkeeper. From 1852 to 1864 he was senior assistant at Jose d'Almeida & Sons and thereafter for four years, from 1864 to 1868, a book-keeper at William Spottiswoode & Company.

According ot Dr C.A. Gibson-Hill, George had an illegitimate daughter, Louisa, born on January 4, 1829. While officially a bachelor, he married Eliza-beth Caroline Burton, the widow of John Campbell Burton on January 9, 1832. She was the daughter of William Farquhar and was born in Malacca in 1800. She probably came to Singapore after Burton's death in Calcutta. By her first marriage, she had one son and three daughters and by George, two sons and a daughter, a large family which may have accounted for the choice of the very large bungalow at Beach Road. The building appears as a square structure with a hipped roof topped by a jack-roof, an uncommon feature for an early house as evident in the picture. There are no verandahs.

George lived there until his wife's death in 1858. In 1861 he moved to Grasslands at St Thomas Walk where he died in 1873, aged 77 years. George is best remembered for his purchase of the *Singapore Chronicle* in 1829. He sold the paper in 1835 and bought the *Singapore Free Press* in 1842, which he sold to Abraham Logan in 1848, having met with fi-nancial trouble the year before. His vast property included 200 acres of orchard land in Tanglin. The 90 acres of coconut plantation at Katong, registered under his wife's name, subsequently became part of Thomas Dunman's Grove Estate.

This 1863 photograph of the Esplanade offers an unusual
view of the three well-known houses attributed to Coleman.
Edward Boustead's portrait is on the left and Alexander
Guthrie's on the right.

The three houses shown along the Esplanade were designed by G.D. Coleman. The house on the right of the picture stood at the High Street corner on the site where Farquhar erected his residency. It was built in 1828 for James Scott Clark, a merchant who joined Alexander Guthrie in 1824 and later embarked on his own business. Edward Boustead lived in the house for some time and in 1844 it was occupied by a Frenchman, Gatson Dutronquoy, who moved his London Hotel from Coleman's house at No. 3 Coleman Street. From 1857 to 1864 the house became the Hotel L'Esperance. The proprietress was Madam Esperanza De Thune. In 1865 the buildings were taken over by the Hotel de l'Europe, and the hotel later expanded to the adjacent house, built by William Montgomerie, the government surgeon who was in Singapore from 1819 to 1843.

Thomas Church, the resident councillor from 1837 to 1856, lived in the house at the Coleman Street corner. It was later used by the Freemasons until about 1880 when they moved to their new headquarters at the upper end of Coleman Street. Around 1890, the municipality took over Montgomerie's house and N.N. Adis demolished Clark's house to build a new Hotel de l'Europe. The hotel was demolished in 1936 when the Supreme Court was built. The City Hall building was built in 1926–1929 on Church's and Montgomerie's properties.

The portrait is of Hoo of Kay, the original owner of the
property. The photograph circa 1908 shows the house when it
was occupied by Seah Liang Seah.

The house shown here was the second built on a large property along Serangoon Road. The first was built around 1840 by the prominent business-man and community leader Hoo Ah Kay, also known as Whampoa (c.1816-1880) and was one of the most well-known residences in 19th-century Singapore. There are no photographs of the house during Whampoa's lifetime, but there are several descriptions of the magnificent and famous grounds, including this one by Mr A.D. Frederickson in 1876:

Mr Whampoa, a rich Chinese merchant, has a large property in the neighbourhood, its gardens laid out after the fashion of the country of his birth, trim hedges, box and myrtle, trained and dipped to shapes of animals, junks, etc, tiny water courses and miniature bridges. A little stream, crowded with gold fish, was made to pass under the central portion of his mansion which formed an open gallery and was supported by a lofty bridge, ad-mitting of a boat passing underneath. A little further on, the water collected in a pond or, rather — begging Mr Whampoa's pardon — into a diminutive lake, full of water lilies... The piggery however, is quite the feature of

the establishment, and one the owner is not a little proud of. There are some enormous beasts — I measured one fully seven feet from spout to tail — tremendously fat and the place they were kept in was wonderfully clean and neat in all its arrangements.

The property was bought by Seah Liang Seah in September of 1894. Whampoa's house was proba-bly demolished and a new structure built that was named Bendemeer. When Liang Seah moved into the house in 1895, Governor Sir Charles Mitchel (governor, 1894 to 1898) performed the ceremony of unlocking the entrance door with a gold key. Seah Liang Seah (1850-1925) was the second son of Seah Eu Chin, one of Singapore's earliest pioneer mer-chants, who arrived in 1823 and by 1830 had set up his own business on Chulia Street. Active in public life, Seah Liang Seah served on the Municipal Board and was a member of the Legislative Council from 1883 to 1890 and again in 1894. After his death, the house continued to be used by the family until it was acquired by the Housing and Development Board. It was demolished in 1962.

The portrait is of Cheang Hong Lim, thought to be the owner
of this house. The photograph shows the house when it was
used as a school circa 1950.

Singapore-born Cheang Hong Lim was an important 19th century figure. His father, Cheang Sam Teo, was a partner in the opium and sireh farm monopolies and Hong Lim continued the business after his father's death. In 1876, he contributed $3,000 for converting an open space into a public garden. Hong Lim Green survives to this day. When he died in 1893 the *Singapore Free Press* wrote:

For many years he has played a prominent part in the affairs of the place. Years ago he was the opium farmer and a public man here. For a long time after he relinquished the Farm he was somewhat nervous and lived a very retired life, fearing perhaps, that he might be attacked, for it is difficult for a man occupying the position he did to avoid making some unfriendly to him. Of late years, however, he has come again into public life and many will remember a splendid wayang he showed for his friends some months ago. He has also assumed a share in the Opium Farm and has been named by the Government as head of the Hokkien Community and a member of the Advisory Board. Mr Cheang Hong Lim will be principally remembered for his acts of charity in the place, always freely coming forward in aid of any useful purpose. The Roman Catholic institutions were particularly the objects of his liberal donations.

When Hong Lim bought the property around 1884 there were several large houses in the vicinity, including Annanbank and Bonnygrass. Annanbank, built by Adam Sykes of Robert Wise & Company, became the home of Dr M.J. Martin from 1843 to 1846. Bonnygrass was the home of Martin's nephew and partner in the medical practice Martin & Little at Raffles Place from around 1845 to 1882 when he left Singapore. The house shown in the photograph was purchased by Wong Ah Fook for his two sons, S.Y. and S.Q. Wong. It became the home of the latter and his family in 1917 until 1925 when they moved to Cairnhill. The house was occupied by the Nan Chiau Marine Institute in the 1940s. Lee Kong Chian, the rubber magnate, bestowed the property on the Nan Chiau Girls' School in 1947. The house was demolished in 1965 and new buildings were completed in 1968 for the present Nan Chiau High School.

The Istana Kampong Glam photographed in 1967.

The Istana Kampong Glam domain as defined in 1821 was more extensive than it is today. It comprised all of the land between Jalan Sultan and Arab Street and stretched from North Bridge Road to the sea. The naturalist George Bennet wrote of his first visit to Singapore in 1830 that: "Being near the village of Kampong Glam, I observed a poor-looking bungalow, surrounded by high walls, exhibiting the effects of age and climate. Over the large gateway which opened into the enclosure surrounding this dwelling were watch-towers." On Bennet's second visit in 1833 he described the house as "the old thatched residence," supporting George Windsor Earl's claim in *The Eastern Seas* (London:1837) that in 1835 the house was an "old thatched residence," and observed:

The buildings of His Highness and followers were now in some degree improved, being surrounded by a neat chunamed wall, and the entrance was by a gateway of brick, which had been only recently completed. Since my last visit His Highness had caused a house to be constructed after the style of the European residents at Singapore, and it was situated exterior to the old boundary of his domain... Besides the new residence and wall, he was erecting a residence and wall for himself, neat and extensive in construction, and in something of a Chinese style of architecture. This building was certainly wanting, for the old thatched palace near it seemed ready to fall about his ears.

It is unlikely that any of the dwellings mentioned above were the present Istana Kampong Glam, which probably stands on the site of the residence "in a Chinese style of architecture." It is generally thought that the three-bay structure was commissioned by Sultan Ali Iskandar Shah, son of the first Sultan of British-ruled Singapore, Sultan

Hussein Mahomed Shah, about 1840 to 1842. The house is thought to have been designed by G.D. Coleman. The plan of the house is symmetrical and there is some similarity in the details around the porch piers with those of the now-demolished Raffles Institution building designed by Coleman that may suggest his involvement. In both, a filleted band encircled the piers below the impost of the supporting arches. The cornice at the first floor level was substituted by another broader but filleted band. The podium of Maxwell's house was treated in a like manner. But there the similarities end. The Kampong Glam house is, in all other respects, a plain and simple edifice without any other evidence of Coleman's handiwork. Even the date of its erection is mere conjecture.

Sultan Hussein, who signed the treaty with Raffles in 1819 granting the British permission to establish a trading factory on the island, died in Malacca in 1835. He was survived by three sons: Tungku Jaffar, Tungku Abdul Jalil and Tungku Mohammed Ali, his successor. Sultan Ali was succeeded by his son, Tungku Allum (or Along) as head of the family. He lived in the Istana for 14 years until his death on August 26, 1891. He left behind his wife, Ungku Mariam, his son Tungku Hussein and two daughters.

A court decision in 1897 declared Tungku Mahmoud, the half-brother of Tungku Allum, heir to the Kampong Glam estate. But Tungku Mahmoud never resided at the Istana. He chose to live in Gedong Kuning (Yellow Mansion) at Sultan Gate on the southwest side of the street adjacent to the Istana grounds. The possibility that Gedong Kuning could be the house "after the style of the European residents" described by Bennet cannot be dismissed.

The Istana Kampong Glam is still standing and is occupied by the descendants of the family.

The watercolour sketch is by Charles Dyce, circa early 1840s.
The photograph shows the Chartered Bank manager's house in
the 1920s.

Cairnhill was built by Charles Carnie who was a partner in W.R. Paterson & Company (forerunner of Borneo & Company and now Inchcape Berhard) before he broke away with the two other partners, George Martin and Alexander Dyce, to form Martin Dyce & Company in 1842 where they were joined by John Cambell.

Carnie remained in Singapore until the mid-1850s when he returned to Scotland. The firm continued until 1885. Carnie is reputed to have been the first European to live permanently in Tanglin. He built the house in about 1840. Broadfields, also in Tanglin, was built much earlier but may not have been occupied on a permanent basis.

The watercolour is by Charles Andrew Dyce, a clerk in his brother's firm, Martin Dyce & Company, who made a series of watercolours of the settlement. Executed only two years after the house was completed, it gives a remarkable impression of the undeveloped state of the area. A later oil painting, reputedly by J.T. Thomson (government surveyor, 1841–1853) and seen on page 37, shows additions made by the extension of the roof eaves along the sides and the addition of a canopy over the windows at the gabled front. The two jungle trees in the Dyce watercolour have been replaced by waringa trees.

In 1884 the Chartered Bank purchased the property, demolished Carnie's house and built the manager's residence. This house, in turn, was sold to a development company in 1958 and a housing estate, Kebun Serai, which includes the apartment building Hilltops, was built in 1961–1963.

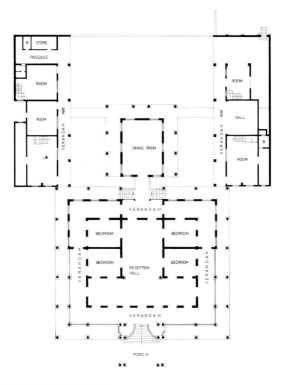

The house as seen circa 1908 and a measured drawing of the plan.

Tan Kim Seng built this bungalow on land purchased from William Renshaw George, a book-keeper and proprietor of the *Singapore Free Press* from 1842 to 1848. He obtained a permanent grant for the property from the East India Company in 1855 and it is likely that a house was built on the site between 1851 and 1855.

The earliest reference to the house is in Jules Moniot's (surveyor-general, 1855 to 1862) map of 1862, although the name "Panglima Prang" appears on an 1824 map. (The Malay name means "military leader" and probably originated from the land having been the burial ground of an officer of the Sultan of Singapore.) Tan Kim Seng's address

The Honourable Tan Jiak Kim, CMG, (top left) and Mr and
Mrs Tan Soo Bin (top right). A view of the front verandah and
carriage porch in 1971 and the rear courtyard the same year.

The front verandah in 1971 (left) and a view of the drawing
room in the same year (above).

from 1848 to 1860, as recorded in the business directory, was "Left bank, Singapore River." From 1861 it was given as "River Valley Road," so the house may have been built in 1860.

In its original form the house formed an almost perfect square. Later additions included a formal dining room which projected into the back court-yard and a pair of two-storey blocks which flanked it. Both the dining room and the two-storey blocks were built before 1888. The two-storey blocks were an unusual way of extending a house and probably replaced the original outhouse. Bathrooms at the sides were added in 1913 by Swan & Maclaren.

Tan Kim Seng (1805–1864) came to Singapore in the early 1820s from Malacca (his father was also Malacca-born) to trade. His business ex-panded and prospered, and he held interests in planting and mining in Malaya as well. He invested in property and at one time held probably the largest single parcel of land in Singapore — 2,859 acres in Pasir Panjang. He is well-known for his offer of $13,000 in 1857 towards the improvement of the town's water supply, a project that started many years later and was completed in 1877,

thirteen years after his death. A fountain to com-memorate his contribution was erected in Fullerton Square in 1882.

At least six generations of the Tan family resided in the bungalow. After Kim Seng's death, his son, Tan Beng Swee (1828–1884), became head of the household. He was followed by his son, Tan Jiak Kim (1859–1917), and Jiak Kim's eldest son, Tan Soo Bin (1882–1940). Tan Soo Bin's family occupied the house until 1982 when the land was sold to a private developer and the house demolished to make way for a condominium.

The interiors of Panglima Prang shown here and elsewhere in the book date back to the time of Tan Jiak Kim and Tan Soo Bin who were both English educated. The interiors reflect the Western influence that was by the 1880s fairly widespread among the upper middle classes. This Western influ-ence was also reflected in the changes in manner of dress. Of the 102 men whose photographs appear in Song Ong Siang's *One Hundred Years' History of the Chinese in Singapore*, all but two of the 56 born before 1860 were in Chinese dress. All of the 46 men born after 1860 were in European dress.

The house photographed circa 1950.

An advertisement dated June 15, 1882 described this house as "That newly erected and desirable residence called Holyrood situated on Mount Victoria Estate." The property was once owned by Jose d'Almeida (1812-1894) who was born in Macao and came to Singapore with his eldest brother, Joaquim, in 1825. He worked for his father and became a partner in Jose d'Almeida & Sons in 1837. He moved from Kampong Glam to Mount Victoria in 1849 when he built the first house on the hill and lived there until the 1860s.

The house has three bays across the front with side verandahs which could have been added later, and was designed by an unknown architect. The last occupants, prior to its demolition in the 1960s, were directors of Boustead & Company who sold the property to a housing development company.

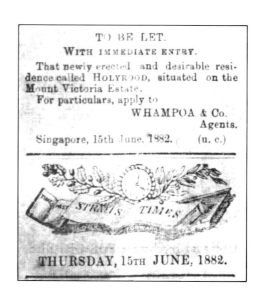

Ong Tiang Soon and family circa 1908. Note the Chinese
interior and the door and windows.

This house, designed by Henry D. Richards and built in 1889 for Ong Ewe Hai, replaced an earlier house built by Adam Sykes of Robert Wise & Company. Sykes purchased the entire area, including Institution Hill, from the Trustees of Raffles Institution in 1844 with Dr Mungo Johnston Martin who lived in the house from 1843 to 1846. Sykes never lived in the house, but close by. Another occcupant was Dr. Robert Little who lived in Bonnygrass from about 1845 until his retirement in 1882; he died in Blackheath in 1888. Dr. Robert Little, the son of an Edinburgh lawyer, had a younger brother, John Martin Little, who with Cursetjee Frommurzee founded Little & Cursetjee in 1845. In 1853 the partnership was dissolved and John Martin with another brother, Mathew Little, established John Little & Company which survives to this day.

Ong Ewe Hai (1830–1889) purchased the property before 1889; plans for the new house were submitted by his architect two months before his death. Born in Singapore, his father, Ong Koon Tian, was an emigrant from China who died when Ewe Hai was seven years of age. Ewe Hai received no education and became a petty trader as a youth to support the family. He went to Sarawak to trade and was so successful that he was able to establish Ewe Hai, Moh & Company in 1856, traders in rice and other produce. The business was continued by his sons, Ong Tiang Soon and Ong Soon Tee. Tiang Soon lived in Bonnygrass, which is an early example of the Coarsened Classical style, which he completed after his father's death. The house was sold to a developer and was replaced by a block of flats, Pacific Mansions, in about 1968.

It is possible that this unusual bungalow dates back to the days of Syed Abdul Rahman Alsagoff, the first member of the well-established Alsagoff family. He was born in Hadramout (now the People's Republic of South Yemen) and was reputed to be the 33rd descendant of the Prophet Mohammed. He came to Singapore in 1824 to trade. His success, marked by the establishment of Alsagoff & Company in 1848, was partly due to the fact that he was a shipowner. He died in 1860 and was succeeded by his son, Syed Ahmad, who was born in Hadramout and arrived in Singapore with his father. Syed Ahmad married Raja Siti, a Celebes Princess and daughter of the Sultana of Gowa, Hajjah Fatimah, who built the mosque which is named after her. Raja Siti was an astute businesswoman from Malacca and the marriage was a fortuitous one.

Syed Ahmad's son, Syed Mohammed (1836–1906), also known as Nong Cik (a Bugis name for the youngest son in a high-born family), was the most successful of the family members. Under his stewardship, the family business prospered even further. In 1878, through his personal efforts, the company was granted the Kukup concession by the Johore government, and even obtained the right to issue their own private currency for use in their estates. By the 1890s, the company was exporting sago, cocoa, coconuts and timber to Europe. In Singapore it owned Perseverance Estate, the Straits Cycle & Motor Company and the Express Saw Mill Company, the largest in the colony. Syed Mohammed was also known for his generous contributions to the Muslim community. He founded the Syed Mohammed bin Ahmad Alsagoff Wokaff Fund, the Muslim Trust Fund and the Alkaff Arab School.

After his death, the management of the company passed into the hands of his nephew, Syed Omar, who died in 1927. The most well-known member of the family today is Syed Ali Redha Alsagoff, grandson of Mohammed by his daughter, Sharifa Bahiyah, and her cousin, Syed Redha Alsagoff.

It was Syed Ahmad who built the large mansion known as Kota Alsagoff, or Kota Nong Cik as it was sometimes called, and several other houses, including probably the unusual bungalow, within the family property at Java Road, said to have been originally about 300 acres in extent. The bungalow, which has been demolished, is the only known early bungalow built on the ground rather than raised. The house was abandoned when photographed in 1967. The interior flooring was marble and the ceilings were alcoved and close boarded.

A view of the Alsagoff compound (left) from the minaret of Haji Fatimah Mosque in 1967. The bungalow (top) is extremely unusual for an early bungalow in Singapore and is the only known example of its type. The other photographs show members of the Alsagoff family. In the middle photograph the house in the background can be clearly identified as the one adjacent to the bungalow on the family property at Java Road.

Government House circa 1890 photographed by G.R.
Lambert & Company.

The official residence of the governors of the Straits Settlements was built on 106 acres of land that were originally part of C. R. Prinsep's nutmeg plantation. When the colonial government purchased the land in 1867, W.H. Read and his cousin R.B. Read lived in a house on the exact site of the building. They moved to Spring Grove soon after. Construction began in 1867 and was completed in two years. The building was designed by the colonial Engineer, Major J.F.A. McNair of the Royal Engineers and is essentially Palladian in character with eclectic touches in the mansard roof and the ornate cornices. McNair's choice of the classical style showed his versatility as his other important work, St Andrew's Cathedral, is Gothic.

The high open verandahs on the upper levels are protected from the weather by fixed louvres and pivoted louvred windows, all in timber, below which rattan chicks were hung.

The total expenditure for the project amounted to $161,451.94 — $109,000 for the building, $42,800 for the land and $9,000 for furniture and fittings. The workforce was primarily Indian convict labourers. Workers such as masons, carpenters, stone-cutters, painters and plumbers who worked on the building were paid 20 cents per day while local coolies were paid from three to seven cents per day.

Since independence, the building has been called the Istana and is the official residence of the President of Singapore.

On the grounds of Government House an auspicious event is
celebrated in 1918. Mrs Lee Choon Guan is conferred a
Member of the British Empire by Governor Sir Arthur
Henderson Young, the first Chinese woman to receive the
award. The postcard (above) shows the grounds of
Government House circa 1910 and illustrates British tastes in
landscape design.

The house photographed in 1972. The glazed windows have replaced the original louvred ones. Portraits of Mr and Mrs Hans Becker (opposite) complement interior views.

Spring Grove stands on land that once formed part of a large estate of "19 acres, three rods and 33 poles," bounded by Grange Road, Irwell Bank Road and River Valley Road granted to Hoo Ah Kay by the East India Company on May 7, 1845. Hoo Ah Kay sold the property to William Wemyss Ker in 1849. John Harvey, the first managing director of Borneo & Company was the next owner and he was followed in 1858 by Edward Boustead who founded Boustead & Company in 1827. In 1883 Boustead sold the property to ship chandler Tan Keng Cheow, best known as the founder of the Singapore Steam Laundry in 1880. The property continued to change hands over the years and among the subsequent owners were Herman Muhlinghaus in 1894, Wee Kay Poh, and Adolf Laspe, a partner of Behn Meyer & Company, in 1901. From 1904 the house was lived in by various partners of Behn Meyer & Company and it was conveyed to the firm itself in 1906.

When war broke out between Germany and Britain in 1914 the house was seized as enemy property. In 1916 it was sold to J.A. Elias, a well-known Jewish millionaire, who in turn sold it to the Straits Trading Company, a move which renewed the company's association with the house as former resident Muhlinghaus was a founder of the company in 1886. Since 1936 the house has been the residence of the representative of the United States government; the property was purchased by the United States in 1950.

It is not known when Hoo Ah Kay's original land holding was parcelled out. By 1862 there were three houses on the property — Spring Grove, Dovecot and Irwell Bank — which could have been built by Boustead, Ker or possibly Harvey. William Henry Mcleod Read and his cousin Robert Barclay Read (son of Christopher Ridout Read, one of the founders of A.L. Johnston & Company) were recorded as residents of Spring Grove from 1868 until William Read left Singapore in 1885, his cousin having died in Yokohama the previous year.

Originally a modest structure of three bays across the front, Spring Grove was initially bachelor quarters. The house was probably erected before 1868 and could have been built by Ker sometime

between 1849 and 1857 since, as mentioned, there was a Spring Grove in 1862. Rebuilding by the Reads was unlikely as they were in continuous occupation and reconstruction of the roof in 1891 indicates that the house was by then old. The roof reconstruction was done in conjunction with the addition of the two side bays. The architects were Crane Brothers who carried out the work for W. E. Hooper, a junior civil servant and possibly part-owner of the house. Hooper lived there with the Read cousins from 1882 to 1885. Another short-term resident was author John Cameron who lived with the Reads in 1875.

After the renovations, the house became a family home for successive directors of Behn Meyer & Co. This description of the house appeared in *Twentieth Century Impressions of British Malaya*:

The suburbs of Singapore furnish many examples of beautiful bungalows, and 'Spring Grove' is among the most charming of these. As one enters the gate an extensive garden greets the eye, rich in various kinds of tropical verdure. Here on Wednesday afternoons large numbers of the German community meet together without ceremony at the invitation of the genial host and hostess, Mr and Mrs Hans Becker, and the scene is one of life and colour. Some engage in tennis, while others chat together across the tea-table at the head of the lawn, which is fringed with palms, shrubs, bushes, plants and flowers. In the background is a typical Eastern bungalow, solidly built for coolness and comfort, which was bought by Messrs. Behn, Meyer & Company Limited, in 1894, and has been the residence of the senior partners of the firm ever since. It contains a handsome saloon, spacious dining, drawing and billiard rooms, and is lighted throughout by incandescent gas, and is furnished with taste. The weekly reunions, at which the employees of Messrs. Behn, Meyer & Company Limited, can meet Mr Becker, the managing director of the firm, and his wife on terms of friendship, are very popular, and it may be justly said of Mr Becker that during his nineteen years residence in Singapore he has done much to cement in bonds of friendship the members of the German community.

A view of the house circa 1875.

The Castle was owned by the Braddell family whose connection with Singapore began in 1862 when Thomas Braddell came to Singapore to join Abraham Logan as partner in the law firm Logan and Braddell. Braddell (1823–1891) was born in Rahingrany, County Wicklow, Ireland and went to the West Indies to learn sugar planting in 1840. He moved to Penang in 1844 to work in Brown & Company's sugar plantation at Ayer Hitam. Called to the Bar at Grey's Inn in 1859, he was attorney general from 1867 to 1882 while concurrently in private practice. He was forced to retire after a serious carriage accident and died in London.

The Castle was probably built by Thomas Braddell about 1870. His eldest son, Sir Thomas de Multan Lee Braddell, was born in Province Wellesley in 1856 and returned to Singapore in 1879 after obtaining a law degree from Oxford University. He joined his father and served in government for a brief period as attorney general from 1911 to 1913. He left Singapore to work in Malaya in 1914, retiring to England in 1917.

Roland St. John Braddell, grandson of Thomas and eldest son of Sir Thomas, was born in Singapore on October 20, 1880. He graduated from Oxford University in 1904 and practised law in Singapore until the outbreak of World War Two. He returned to Singapore after the war and it is believed that he

A view of the drawing room.

retired to Malaysia where he died in about 1970. He wrote *Lights of Singapore*, published in 1934. The photographs of the house were inscribed by Roland Braddell with the following remarks:

TO BE LET.
WITH IMMEDIATE ENTRY.
THE CASTLE, situated on Cavenagh Road near the Government House, and lately occupied by T BRADDELL, Esq.
Also,
WOODSVILLE situated on the Sirangoon Road, one of the most charming country residences in Singapore. Apply to
H. ABRAMS,
Horse Repository, Brass Bassa Road.
Singapore, 21st Feb., 1883.

The Castle, Cavanagh Road, which belonged to my grandfather Thomas Braddell: shows his peon, his palanqueen and his (illegible) and (illegible) all servants. These were Madrasees. The photos of the Castle must have been taken between 1879 and 1883, certainly not earlier and not later. My mother came out as a bride in 1879 and took over the house; keeping at the Castle, assisted (by) my father's eldest sister Honor (Lady Merewhether) who was not married to E.M. Merewhether until 1883. The Castle was sold by my father soon after my grandfather retired in 1882. The general period is thus fixed: It is my belief that the photos were in fact taken before my birth in 20 December 1880. I would therefore date them as circa 1880.

Another view of the drawing room.
Few interior views from this period
have survived

The house photographed in 1914.

Balaclava was built around 1880. The architect is unknown. The photographs shown here were taken around 1914 when the house was occupied by William George Hennings. According to his daughter, Mrs Helen Bell, Hennings arrived in Singapore in April of 1895 and "married Gertrude Owen in 1908 and probably then moved into Balaclava. My brother Richard was born in England in 1911. I was born in the house in December 1913. We returned to England when my father retired in 1922. He was then head of Mansfields."

The house had a deep verandah that surrounded the building completely on the ground floor, the ceiling height of which was much greater than that of the first floor. The drawing room was on the first floor behind the two side windows nearer the front and the dining room, complete with pungkahs, was probably on the ground floor. The exterior view of the house was probably photographed later than the interior views, as the projecting verandah is screened in by louvred windows in the exterior picture while the interior ones show an open verandah with rattan chicks.

The house was demolished many years ago but the gatepost can still be seen along Dalvey Road.

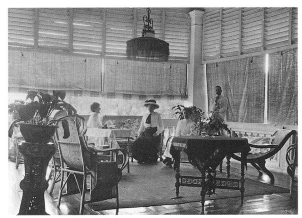

The photographs on these two pages, taken in 1914, offer a remarkable record of early 20th century interiors. Note the use of rattan furniture, indoor plants, chick blinds and the pungkah in the dining room. The gate pier which announced the entrance to the grounds, opposite, can still be seen along Dalvey Road although the house was demolished long ago.

The house photographed in December of 1968.

Botan House was built by Tan Kim Tian and was connected with four generations of the Tan family until it was sold in 1978. Designed by an unknown architect, it stood at the corner of Craig Road and Neil Road on land that was among the earliest cleared and settled in Singapore.

The first owner of the land was Charles Ryan, the first civilian postmaster. When Ryan left Singapore in March of 1827 he sold the plot of land known as Ryan's Hill, which he had cleared and planted with nutmegs, to Syme & Company who renamed it Duxton Hill. Three partners of the company, Hugh Syme, Robert Dingle and Gilbert McMicking, lived there successively until 1836 when the land was sold to Dr Montgomerie, the government surgeon. In 1856 the land, described as "belonging to the Estate of the late Dr. Montgomerie," was advertised for sale by auction. Archibald Spottiswoode, a partner of William Spottiswoode & Company, was the owner of Duxton Estate in the early 1860s. The land, as with most plantations, was eventually subdivided and sold in lots, probably from the 1870s.

When Tan Kim Tian, who made the family fortune and built the house, arrived in Singapore from Malacca in 1847 he was 15 years old. He worked as an office boy in Paterson Simons & Company where he attracted the attention of William Paterson who arranged for him to learn English. He was promoted to storekeeper in the produce department, which traded in gutta percha, cloves and rattan, and retired at the age of 33 to form a shipping company of his own with the assurance of cargo support from his previous employers. With his son, Tan Beng Wan (1850–1890), he founded Tan Kim Tian & Son Steamship Company Limited, the first local Chinese shipping company to build and purchase steamships. By the turn of the century the firm owned 11 ships with a total gross tonnage of over 8,000 tons.

After the death of Kim Tian and Beng Wan, the company was inherited by Beng Wan's only son, Tan Cheng Siong, who was seven years old at the time. The company, which by then was partly owned by Straits Steamship, was taken over by

The reception hall photographed in 1968. In the centre of the family photograph below, and wearing Chinese dress, is Tan Cheng Siong who was born in the house in 1883. He is surrounded by several generations of family members.

two of Cheng Siong's young and inexperienced uncles, Tan Hup Seng, 23 years old, and Tan Hup Leong, still in his teens. Disagreements arose and Straits Steamship sold their interest in the company to Oei Tiong Ham, the Indonesian sugar king, from whom the Tans had borrowed money. To raise more cash, the uncles persuaded Tan Cheng Siong to sell the properties of his father's estate. The company met with further difficulties and was finally bought over completely by Oei Tiong Ham and became part of his shipping company, Heap Eng Moh Steamship

Company, founded in 1912.

Tan Cheng Siong then set up his own stevedoring business. The Singapore Harbour Board (now the Port of Singapore Authority) was one of his clients. He was born in the house in 1883 and died there in June of 1977, aged 94 years. Shortly after, the family sold the house and it was demolished in the early 1980s.

Built about the same time as Magenta Cottage, the house was slightly more decorative and more in the style of late Victorian Classicism, evident in the fluted column shafts on the first floor and finely detailed mouldings of the ground floor piers and arches. It was heavy in appearance despite the open verandahs on the ground floor and generally in the same character as Bonnygrass. The interior, as with most Chinese houses, was quite Chinese and had built-in cupboards with finely carved doors of Chinese design. The house had a carriage porch, which Margenta Cottage does not, and the approach to the house, as seen in the photograph, was through the semi-circular driveway fronting the house.

Two views of Tyersall shortly after its completion in 1892 by
G.R. Lambert & Company.

The 67 acres land on which Tyersall was built was originally the property of William Napier, a lawyer and the younger brother of David Skene Napier. Together with G.D. Coleman and others, William Napier founded the *Singapore Free Press* in 1835. He married Coleman's widow in 1844 and built a house, Tyersall, in 1854. The property was bought by Sultan Abu Bakar of Johore (1831–1895) around 1860 and Napier's house was demolished when the palace was built. This long account appeared in the *Singapore Free Press* when it was completed in 1892 under the headline "H.H. The Sultan of Johore, "At Home" at new Tyersall":

Seldom has a more numerous gathering of Singapore Society been seen in this place than that which assembled on Saturday last in response to the invitations issued by H.H. the Sultan of Johore to celebrate the opening of the New Tyersall, a fine house built by the Sultan as a Singapore Residence.

Among the guests were Sir Cecil, Lady Clementi Smith and the Misses Clementi Smith, the Sultan of Lingga, the Yam Tuan of Rhio, Tengku Mahmoud and Tengku Ali of Pahang and all the most prominent citizens of Singapore. The Johore contigent of visitors was naturally a large one and included the Tengku Makhota, Datos Abdul Rahman, C.M.G., Mentri, Yahya, Bintara Dalam, Bintara Luar, Hakim, Stia, Timor, Barat, Endau, Meldrum, Bentley, and Ungku Sleiman.

On arrival the guests were greeted at the main entrance by H.H. the Sultan, who looked very well in health and was resplendent in diamonds. In immediate attendance upon him was Dato Abdul Rahman, Sri Amar di Rajah. There was some waiting as it was expected that the Sultan of Pahang would be present. That

monarch, however, did not appear, and shortly before six o'clock the Sultan delivered an address in Malay of which the following is the translation, read by Dato Abdul Rahman:

"Your Excellency, Your Highnesses, Ladies and Gentlemen. It affords me much pleasure to welcome you here today to assist me in opening this new house which stands on the same site where many of you often did me the honour of visiting me in days gone by. The plans of the building were drawn to the approval of my late wife, but the house is on a larger scale than was originally intended."

The Building
The New Palace at Tyersall, for Palace it is, stands in a commanding position on the summit of a hill, the upper slopes of which have been already terraced, and are now being laid out. When this work is accomplished and the roads completed, Tyersall will be one of the most charmingly situated residences in the island. The front of

the building is towards the southeast, looking towards the Town that is, the drive winding round the hill and opening to the Grand Terrace.

The building is rectangular in shape, being 210 feet long by 174 feet deep, with a central courtyard. It is in the Corinthian style of architecture, freely treated, with a red tiled roof and a tower nearly seventy feet high in the centre, above which floated yesterday the well-known crescent and star of H.H. the Sultan. The large portico is seventy feet long and there is ample accommodation for carriages on the Grand Terrace. The Entrance Hall is well proportioned with a broad flight of steps leading to the first floor. To the right of the Entrance Hall are waiting rooms and offices, and to the left the spacious Dining Hall, seventy feet by twenty eight, but looking perhaps by reason of its size, rather out of proportion as regards the height.

The wings, including the double verandahs, are each 56 feet wide and are appropriated for various purposes, the billiard room being in the right wing. Passing up the Grand Staircase, with its ornamental iron balustrades, access is gained to the first floor. Over the Portico is the Drawing Room, a handsome and well lit room beautifully furnished. From its verandah, or better still from the terraced roof, a fine view of the island is obtained.

The greater portion of the main building is occupied by the Grand Reception Room, like the Drawing Room beautifully furnished, with a large lounge in the centre. A suite of rooms at the eastern end is set apart for H.H.'s own use, the ladies of the household having rooms in either wing. The Ball Room is another very handsome room 98 feet by 34, with a floor that made some of the ladies on Saturday wistfully stroke it with their toes. Around the Ball Room, in the interspaces, are settees, upholstered in handsome figured yellow satin, the leading note of colour however, being given by the crimson hangings at the doors and windows.

Such is a brief glance at the New Tyersall. As to the construction, as the Sultan said in his opening speech, it was built to plans approved by the late Sultana. The Architect, Datoh Yahya, modestly disclaims having done more than submit plans and carry out the designs of Her Royal Highness, but during the period of building, nearly three years, much of the responsibility must have been his. Most of the iron-work has been carried out by Messrs. Howarth Erskine, and the designs are of a pleasing character and in unison with the general tone of the building. The fanlights, Arabesque in design, and bearing the crescent and star, and the ornamental carving of the doors of the cabinets inset into the walls, of which there are many, follow the same style. The wood-work has had special care bestowed upon it, none but the best and hardest woods being accepted throughout, teak and ironwood entering largely into the construction. The

magnitude of this branch of the contract may be guessed from the fact that there are no less than 420 doors in the building. Wong Ah Fook (the father of Dato S.Q. Wong) of Johore was the Contractor. We have already said that Messrs. Howarth Erskine executed most of the iron-work, but Mr H.C. Hogan is also responsible for some portion of it. The upholstering has been in the hands of Messrs. John Little & Co.

The Electric Light

The installation of Electric Light — which forms a chief element of attraction in the opening ceremony of H. H. the Sultan of Johore's new Tyersall Palace — may be regarded as a distinct acquisition to the improvements of domestic civilisation and a marked step in the industrial progress of the Colony.

The generating station is 400 yards away from the Palace, where the power is obtained from two compound Robey Engines, running two Crompton's compound wound dynamos, each capable of sustaining 400 lamps separately, but also arranged to run in parallel with the engines coupled, and each engine to run the dynamo of the other in case of necessity. The main cables branch leads and all wires, which aggregate a total of 7 miles, are insulated with Fowler-Waring patent composition, said to have a resistance of 1,700 ohms and to be especially suitable for the climate, and lead coated. It may have been noticed that little or nothing of them is visible in the building, the wires being brought to the lamps within the walls, where they are encased in plaster of Paris thus avoiding unsightly casings. The general effect of the light was by no means glaring, but pleasantly mellow, which is due to the lamps being of frosted glass, and nearly all placed on the ceilings of the spacious rooms and corridors. Some of the clusters have as many as 9 lamps each, and many of the brackets and electroliers are of handsome and artistic design, and it is only a pity that in many places their effect is spoilt and their beauty wasted by being placed under bare floor joists.

The whole installation does great credit to Mr Macbean, M.I.M.E., who designed it and selected every detail of the fittings, and to Mr W. A. Foster, the Electrical Engineer, who executed the work and now superintends the operation of the plant.

Unfortunately, the house was destroyed by fire reported at 2:45 a.m. on September 10, 1905. By the time the fire was put out, the centre portion of the main back wing, which consisted of billiard and supper rooms on the ground floor and the ballroom on the first floor, was completely gutted. The cause of the fire was defective electric light wiring. Damage was estimated at $75,000. Unoccupied for some time, it was never rebuilt.

An oil painting by A.L. Watson circa 1904.

Magenta Cottage stands at the corner of Killiney and River Valley Roads on land that once was part of Thomas Oxley's Killiney estate. William Willans Willans, a civil servant, sold it to George Tod Wright, a sea captain, within a month of purchasing it in 1863. In 1851 Wright was given command of the *Hooghly*, in succession of Jonas Daniel Vaughan (master attendant, 1856–1862) and had an unsuccessful encounter in 1859 with Chinese pirates off the Trengganu coast. He was well-connected for he married a daughter of Governor E. A. Blundell (governor, 1855–1861). Magenta Cottage was sold to Lee Cheng Yan on September 29, 1882.

The date of the construction of the main house shown in the painting is a matter of conjecture. Moniot's map of 1862 shows a Magenta Cottage on the site with an entrance at River Valley Road, which it faced, while the present house is entered by Killiney Road. Therefore an earlier building, probably erected by Oxley, was most likely demolished and a new house built by Wright which he called Edrington. It is uncertain whether Lee Cheng Yan retained Edrington after purchasing the property. It is more likely that he demolished the house and built the present building in 1882 and 1983, keeping the old name.

Lee Cheng Yan and family members photographed at Magenta Cottage circa 1910.

Additions or alterations to the house, carried out from time to time, included the enclosure of the open verandah by top-hung louvred windows. The second house, next to the main house, was built before 1891, most probably by Cheng Yan to accommodate his extended family.

Lee Cheng Yan (1841–1911) was born in Malacca and came to Singapore at an early age. He founded Chop Chin Joo in 1858 at 143 Telok Ayer Street. In 1891 the firm moved to 10 Malacca Street, and after Lee Cheng Yan's death it was managed by his son, Lee Choon Guan. Cheng Yan lived in town, initially at Telok Ayer Street and

later at Stanley Street where he maintained two houses. Magenta Cottage was used as a holiday home in what was then the countryside. The family moved permanently to the house around 1890.

A.L. Watson, the artist, was a friend of the family, according to Mrs. Trixie Eu, the granddaughter of Lee Cheng Yan. Watson became acquainted with the family through a Miss Moss, the children's private tutor. No less than eleven of Watson's paintings executed between 1904 and 1912 once hung in the front hall of the house. Little is known of Watson except that he lived on Orchard Road near the Scott's Road junction.

View of the house in the 1920s. Only one gate post has survived to this day.

White House Park was originally a 54-acre estate granted to Gilbert Angus (1815–1887) by conveyance in 1852. Angus came to Singapore after some years in Bencoolen and worked for various firms as a bookkeeper, including Whampoa's, before venturing into his own business as an auctioneer. He also owned property including nutmeg plantations in the Tanglin district. By 1862 he had sold White House Park to Reme Leveson & Company, a firm of insurance agents founded in 1858 by George Adolph Reme.

The next known proprietor was John Fraser who was called "Bill-Broker" or the "Jolly Octopus" because of his involvement in numerous businesses. Fraser came to Singapore in 1865 and worked in the Chartered Mercantile Bank. He left the bank soon after joining it, spent a few years in Shanghai and returned to Singapore to join Alex Gentle in business as brokers and accountants. He purchased the Mission Press in 1875 after the death of the wife of its founder, Mrs Keasbury (nee Charlotte Parker of Boston, Massachusetts). David Chalmers Neave was a partner and the name of the Press was changed to Fraser & Neave. They also founded

the Singapore & Straits Aerated Water Company in 1883 and in 1898 it became part of Fraser & Neave Limited. Fraser was also in the property and building business. Together with James Cumming they formed Fraser & Cumming, property developers and brick manufacturers. Fraser retired to England in 1897 and died in February of 1907.

Four houses were built on the original estate. White House was possibly erected by Gilbert Angus and was certainly there in 1862. Fraser built Glencaird in 1897 and possibly also Cree Hall and Sentosa. Mansfield & Company purchased the estate in 1908 and in the 1920s erected a few more houses as staff quarters. The photographs shown here date from the 1920s when the house was occupied by the Hennings family.

Of the four original houses only Glencaird has survived. Designed by Regent Bidwell of Swan & Maclaren, it is the residence of the Australian High Commissioner. It is not known when White House and Sentosa were demolished. Cree Hall was still standing in 1967 when the land was acquired by the Housing and Development Board and it was demolished sometime after that.

What made Glencaird unusual in its day was its asymmetry.
The entrance to the house, designed by Bidwell of Swan &
Maclaren, was placed at a corner instead of centre front while
the placement of the sitting room broke with long-held
conventional planning to take advantage of pleasant views.
The photographs here show the sitting room and dining room
as well as the carriage porch.

The house photographed in 1985.

Designed by Regent Bidwell of Swan & Maclaren and built in 1898 for John Burkinshaw, this house was unusual at the time. Departing completely from the conventional bungalow form, the main building is L-shaped with an external verandah access plan. A covered way between the two arms connects the main house to the outhouses. The drawing room is located at the junction of the arms, next to the dining room which is served by a pantry at the rear. Beyond are the bedrooms with bathrooms below which are accessible directly by separate stairs. The bungalow is raised one floor height and has a colon-nade of unusual design. The arches are English deco-rated while the round piers are of Norman propor-tions. The trusses over the carriage porch are also unusual. Here Bidwell used mediaeval bearer trusses but added crucks or arch braces.

Burkinshaw, a barrister, was called to the bar at Westminster in 1863 and to the local bar in 1874 when he became one of the three partners of Aitken, Donaldson & Burkinshaw. He retired in 1902 and died in England in 1909. The house is owned by the Straits Trading Company and is rented to the French government.

A view of the house from the garden probably taken in the
early years of this century. Below is a detail of a cast-iron post
from the original building plan.

This eclectic house was probably designed by the
firm of Crane Brothers and followed the traditional
three-bay plan. The narrow central bay formed a
corridor and stairhall which led to four bedrooms
upstairs and the ground floor dining and billiard
rooms. The drawing room was above the carriage
porch. The four towers at each corner of the main
building enclosed the dressing rooms and each was
connected to a bathroom directly below by a staircase. A jack-roof crowned the main roof, giving
more light to the interior. The main structural supports, as shown in the original building plan, were
load-bearing nine-inch brick walls. The verandahs
were supported by cast-iron columns bearing iron
girders and beams which in turn supported timber
joists and planked floors. The iron columns were
bolted to plinths of lime concrete. The roof was
formed of timber trusses and covered with imported
English slate tiles. It is not known when the house
was demolished.

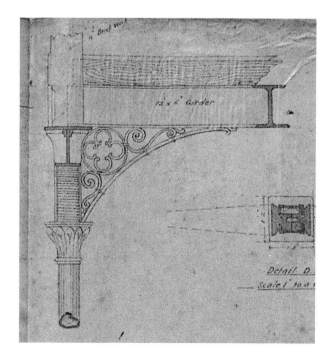

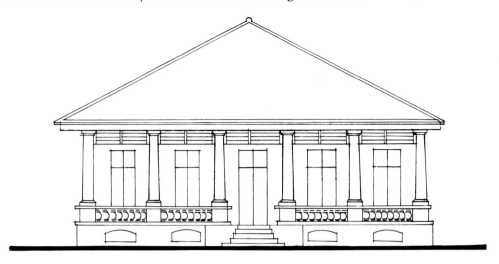

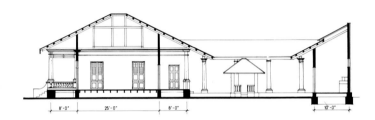

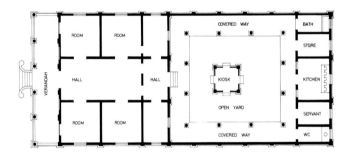

Measured drawings of the front elevation, section and plan of the house. The photograph below shows Syed Omar Alsagoff and the office and staff of Alsagoff & Company circa 1908.

This bungalow on Green Hill with an unusual enclosed courtyard at the back was built by Syed Mohammed Alsagoff, the grandson of Abdulrahman Alsagoff who founded the family business in the 1830s. It was entered through a private driveway that led to a few houses and continued to join Thomson Road. The driveway was later taken over as a public street and named Chancery Lane. Green Hill was sited on the high ground at the end of the present Chancery Hill Road. The Alsagoff family owned much of the land around Chancery Lane, including Bukit Tunggal on the other side.

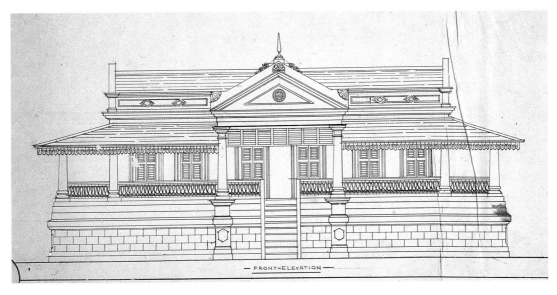

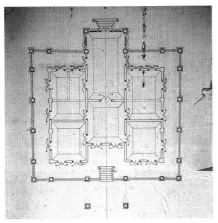 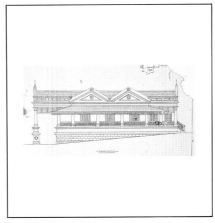

Front elevation, floor plan and side elevation of the house.

The name of the owner is given in the original plans for an extension to the house as "Mr. Norris" and must refer to either Richard Owen Norris or his brother George Norris, sons of an Indian Army officer. Buckley mentions R. O. Norris as a clerk in Maclaine Fraser & Company in 1848. From 1859 until his death in 1905, he worked for the Netherlands Trading Society.

The brothers owned a large tract of land at Serangoon, part of which Norris Road runs through today, and where there once stood a granite memorial erected in 1935 with the following inscription: "Erected to the Memory of Richard Owens Norris who originally owned an estate here extending from Serangoon Road to Jalan Besar from 1853 to 1897, and who was born in Singapore during the reign of King William IV on the 18th April 1832, and died in his Paya Lebar Estate during the reign of King Edward VII on the 2nd October 1905."

The opposite side of the slab was inscribed:

"This memorial was erected by the third and only surviving son of the said Richard Owen Norris, namely Harry Hugh Norris, who was born on this orchard on 3rd of August 1870."

Harry Hugh Norris was a lawyer. He served in the British Army in World War One in Italy and France and died a bachelor in Johore in 1940. The memorial was destroyed during an air raid in 1941/42.

George Norris is remembered for his account of old Singapore reproduced in *The Straits Times* in 1883 entitled, "Singapore 30 years ago". His grandson, Dr. Victor Norris, remembered in the Norris Block of Singapore General Hospital, died in a bombing raid at Kandang Kerbau Hospital, not far from the old family orchard.

The additions to the house appear to follow the style of the older part and involved the extention of the rear of the bungalow. The house, which has been demolished, was raised on solid perimeter walls rather than the more common arched ones.

The front elevation of the house, above, is a measured drawing while the watercolour sketch, opposite, was executed by a pre-war occupant of the house, Air Marshall Lord Tedder, circa 1938.

The land on which Inverturret was built originally formed part of the Cluny estate first granted to John Burkinshaw in 1883. The house was built by Charles McArthur who bought the property, including Atbara, in 1903. In 1916 he sold Inverturret to Adamson Gilfillan & Company and Atbara to W. Lowther Kemp, an accountant and principal of F.W. Barker & Company. Straits Trading Company bought the two houses in 1923 along with the adjacent land and built three more houses, numbers 15, 17 and 19 Gallop Road.

The house was the home of Lord Tedder, (Commander-in-Chief Far East Air Force, November of 1936–1938) during the period from April 1937 until his departure from Singapore. Lord Tedder, who executed the sketch shown opposite, was Deputy Commander to General Eisenhower in 1944 and was elevated to the peerage in 1946. The house is now rented to the French government.

Inverturret was one of the earliest houses to break away from the symmetrical three-bay plan. It has, however, retained the character of the earlier houses in the encircling verandahs. The house has a compact square-shaped plan with rooms off a passage that cuts diagonally across the centre and turns to meet the rear verandah. The drawing and dining rooms are on the east and north sides while the bathrooms on both floors are on the west.

The asymmetrical plan of the house has much in common with Meyer's at Oxley Rise, Galloway's, and Namazie's house at Nathan Road, which are discussed in chapter three. All are compact and square with entrance halls placed at the corner of the buildings. The entrance hall of Inverturret, which pre-dates the other three houses by a decade or so, is not however diagonally placed. The asymmetrical plan, introduced by Regent Bidwell of Swan & Maclaren in Glencaird in the 1890s, was very much accepted by 1916.

The large piece of ground on which the house stands was not fenced round until recent years; it was originally part of a "condominium" landscaped and planted with groves of Tembusu trees. A driveway winds its way to the house which is on the crest of a hill. One of the finest old houses to have survived, it has been well maintained by the present owner.

A view of Carrington House from Mount Emily circa 1880 by
an unknown photographer.

This house on Mount Sophia stood on a site of over two acres purchased from C.R. Prinsep's estate on June 23, 1873. It was built by W.T. Carrington under his own supervision; the architect is unknown. With wide encircling verandahs, it is typical of the period.

Little is known of Carrington who was the municipal engineer from about 1876 until his death in 1878 when the house was advertised for sale. The owner from the time of Carrington's death until it was bought by N.N. Adis in 1903 is a mystery. For a time it was occupied by Alfred Walter Vaughn Cousins who was in government service from about 1870. Cousins was appointed coroner on September 18, 1874 and second magistrate on August 1, 1881, the same time he moved into Carrington house. *The Straits Times* of December 28, 1883 reported an unwelcome guest in his residence; the Mr Drummond mentioned in the report was a partner of Gaggino & Company and lived in another house on Mount Sophia:

A panther measuring six feet and one-and-a-half inches from tip of nose to end of tail was shot yesterday evening at Carrington House, Mount Sophia. A pack of dogs chased the animal into the house, where it took refuge at the top of the bathroom stairs, the cover of which was fortunately closed. Mr Drummond put three revolver balls into the brute, and gave him the coup de grace with a Japanese spear. We understand he intends to present the skin to the Raffles Museum.

Adis demolished the house and built Adis Lodge. The photograph was taken from the grounds of Osborne, a house on nearby Mount Emily.

A view of the house and interiors circa 1908.

Nissim Nissim Adis, owner of Adis Lodge, was the son of a Calcutta merchant. He was born in Howrah in 1857. A trained barrister turned businessman and stockbroker, he came to Singapore in 1893 after working in Hong Kong. He invested in property, accummulated great wealth and became the sole proprietor of the Hotel de L'Europe when he bought it from a syndicate in the late 1890s.

Adis purchased Carrington House in 1903 and demolished it to build Adis Lodge. The Adis family did not stay there long and in 1912 it was bought by Eu Tong Sen who demolished it in 1915 when he built Eu Villa. Undoubtedly one of the most impressive residences in its day, this detailed description of the house appeared in *Twentieth Century Impressions of British Malaya*:

Mr and Mrs Adis reside at Adis Lodge, Adis Road, which is, without doubt, one of the most magnificent mansions east of Suez. The house, which was completed in the early part of 1907, is situated on Mount Sophia and commands an unrivalled view of Singapore Harbour and its surroundings. It is constructed mainly of steel and concrete... An airy verandah encircles the building on the ground floor, which embraces a large and homely dining room, a well-appointed billiard room, and two large bedrooms. The first floor contains a spacious front verandah, breakfast room, a beautiful drawing room, and six bedrooms. Every bedroom has a bath and dressing room adjoining it, fitted with hot and cold water and lined with white glazed bricks, and they are all fitted with Bostwick collapsible gates, such as are used on elevators, and these give a maximum amount of fresh air while securing absolute safety from the nocturnal raids of would-be burglars. The ground floor is paved with black and white mosaic marble, and the first floor with Mallin's tiles in fancy patterns. Uralite, panelled in various designs, is used mainly for the ceilings, but in the drawing room stelconite is employed.

The water supply is from a specially constructed tower, as the house is on the same level as the reservoir from which the town supply is run. The general colour scheme throughout the house is pale green with white and gold ceilings, and the furnishing, which is both luxurious and comfortable, is in excellent taste. The architects were Messrs Tomlinson & Lermit; the constructional steel-work was supplied by Messrs. Riley Hargreaves, Limited; the ornamental iron-work by Messrs. Howarth Erskine, Limited; the uralite and stelconite by Messrs. Huttenbach; and the tiles by Messrs. Mallins.

A photograph of the house circa 1908.

Photographed about 1907, the house was probably built around the turn of the century. A.M.S. Angullia belonged to a fourth generation Indian family. His great-grandfather, Eramje Mohammed Salleh Angullia, came to Singapore from Surat, India in 1837 and started an import and export business dealing in Indian and local produce. His business prospered and was continued by his son, Mohamed Salleh Essofjee Angullia, the father of A.M.S. Angullia. A.M.S. Angullia was born in 1873 and became a partner in 1897, seven years before his father died in 1904. The style of the house is similar to that of Mandalay Villa. The house is still standing, easily recognisable by its classical details.

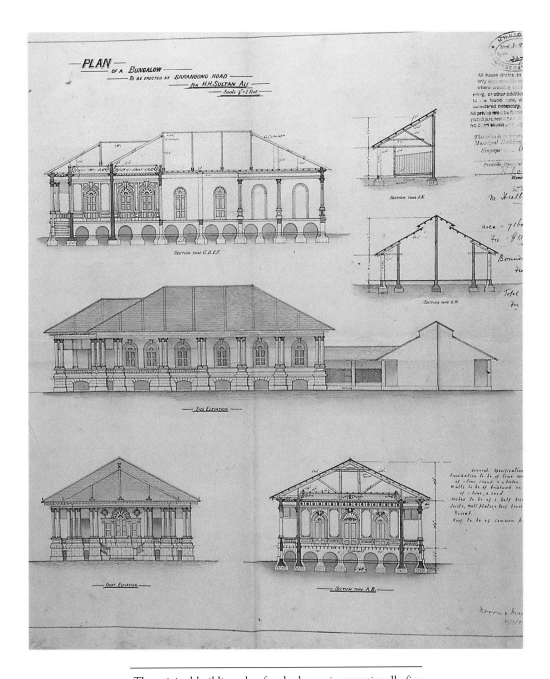

The original building plan for the house is exceptionally fine.

Sultan Ali was the son of Sultan Hussein who ceded Singapore to the British. He held jurisdiction of the Muar district and came into continual dispute with Sultan Abu Bakar over the control of Johore. It was only after his death in 1877 that Johore was united under a single sovereign.

The rear portion of the bungalow, designed by Norris and Macdougall, was in two sections. One part was connected to the ladies' parlour and the other contained the male servants' quarters and a second kitchen which were linked directly to the dining room, an arrangement that conformed with Islamic customs.

The house has been demolished.

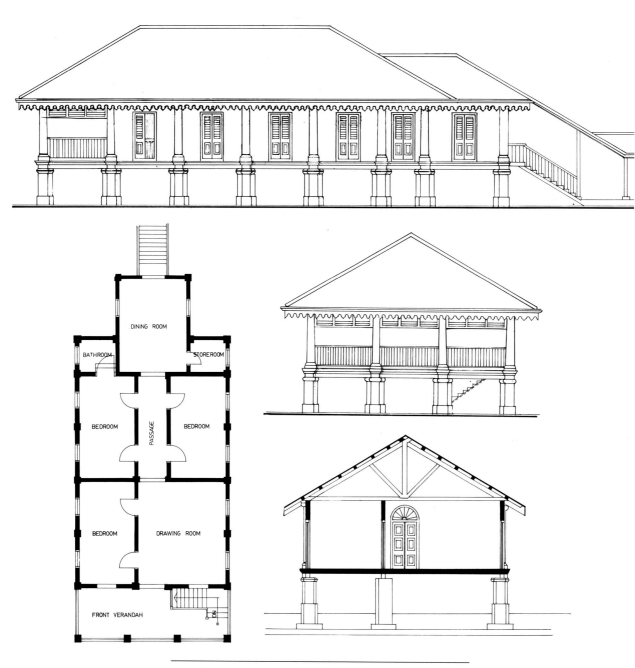

The original building plan is by Swan & Maclaren and is
typical of the small bungalows built on narrow sites.

This house for for Colin Hodge is the earliest known building designed by Archibald A. Swan, a New Zealand engineer who established Singapore's oldest architectural firm, Swan & Maclaren, with J.W.B. Maclaren in 1892. He had earlier been in partnership with Alfred Lermit in Swan & Lermit from 1888 to 1890 and was on his own for about a year in 1891 before he joined Maclaren. Little is known of Colin Hodge who was a sail-maker for McAlister & Company from 1886 until about 1900.

The house was typical of small bungalows built on narrow sites. The absence of a carriage porch suggests that he did not own one. Entrance was by stairs located under the bungalow which were raised to allow sufficient headroom below. Quite often space such as this was used as a sitting area or it was sometimes partitioned for stores or bathrooms.

The bungalow belongs to a type without encircling verandahs, due most likely to the narrow site. The elevations are simple: the front verandah is protected from the weather by overhanging eaves and fixed timber louvres. French windows, louvred on the upper half and panelled below, fenestrate the sides between the pilasters.

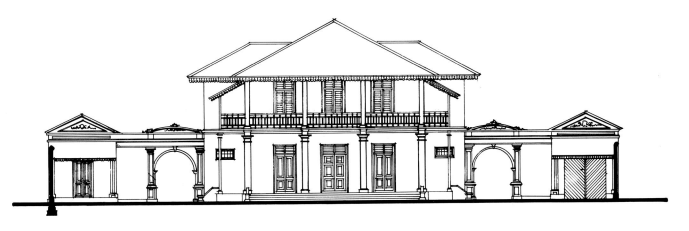

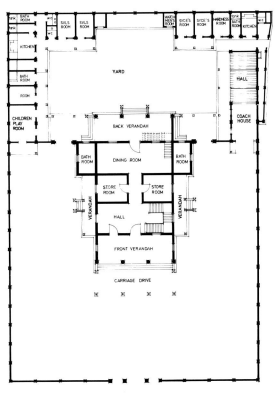

It is the plan which makes this otherwise conventional house of
interest. The rear yard was enclosed on three sides by
outhouses to create a fully enclosed courtyard.

The plan of Liem Ie Ging's house, designed by Lermit & Westerhout, was a variant of the standard colonial house plan of three bays across the front with an internal central hall. The side verandah posts were cast iron while the Tuscan columns of the front and rear verandahs were brick. The most interesting feature of the house was the yard at the rear which was enclosed on three sides by outhouses built up to the boundary lines of the property, the fourth side being enclosed by the rear of the main house. Side gates separated the outhouses and the main building. One side of the outhouses accom-modated quarters for the syce, with its own separate kitchen, harness room and coach house; the other side had the domestic servants' quarters and the household kitchen.

Lim Ie Ging was born in Rembang, Java and died in Singapore around 1840 at the age of about 80 years. He was married to the eldest daughter of Oei Tiong Ham, the multi-millionaire sugar king of Java. Two of his sons, Dr Albert Lim and Dr Harold Lim (born in Java in 1893), were well-known medical practitioners in Singapore.

It is not known when the house was demolished.

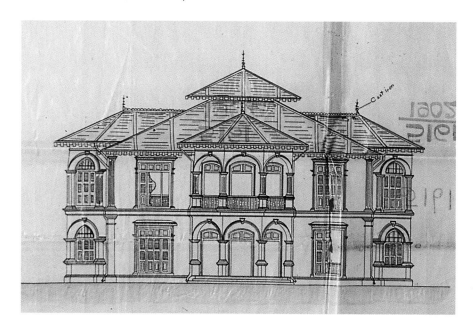

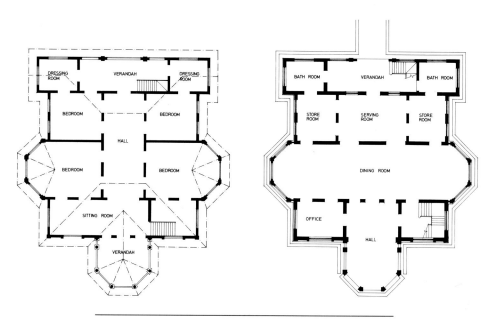

The front elevation is from the original building plan while the
plans are measured drawings.

Designed by Lermit & Westerhout and built by Lee Cheng Yan as a holiday house, Mandalay Villa became the residence of his son, Lee Choon Guan, who moved there from the family house at Stanley Street. Lee Choon Guan (1868-1924) was born in Singapore and began his career as his father's assistant in the family business, which he inherited on his father's death in 1911. He married Tan Teck Neo, the third daughter of Tan Keong Saik, in 1900 after the death of his first wife. Tan Keong Saik was a well-known Malacca millionaire who together with T.C. Bogaardt, lawyer John Burkinshaw, Tan Jiak Kim, Lee Cheng Yan and others founded the Straits Steamship Company.

Tile detail photographed in 1969.

Lee Cheng Yan, top left, and Lee Choon Guan, top right. The interior views taken circa 1950 include a birthday celebration for Mrs Lee Choon Guan, bottom left.

After Lee Choon Guan's death, his widow and family continued to live in the house until her death in 1974 at the age of 101 years. The home of a wealthy and influential family, it was the scene of many social events, particularly during the period before the outbreak of the Pacific War in 1941. By far the most important event was the birthday of Mrs Lee Choon Guan, when the fishermen of Kampong Amber held their annual parade in her honour as a gesture of appreciation of the family's kindness in allowing them to live free of rent in the kampong which they owned.

The property was sold by the family and the house demolished in 1983.

Tile detail photographed in 1969.

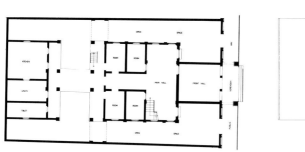

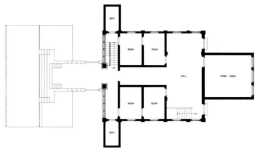

The photograph was taken in 1982 while the plans are
measured drawings. The house was acquired by the government
and has been preserved.

This house was originally built on a simple rectangular plan of three bays across the front with a main hall at the front and four rooms at the sides on both levels, providing eight bedrooms in all. The unusual projecting front built up to the public footway was a later addition. It comprised the front hall on the ground floor and the front room on the first floor. The bathrooms were also later additions.

Madam Teo, whose name appears on the building plans, married into the Tan family. Her husband was a businessman with Indonesian connections. Among their children was Tan Sim Boh, a well-known barrister of his time. He was born in the Kerbau Road house and received his early education at the Anglo-Chinese School. He graduated in law from Cambridge University in 1922 and worked for the legal firm of Donaldson & Burkinshaw from 1924 to 1936, the year he was appointed the general manager of Lee Rubber Company Limited.

Tan Sim Boh was active in public life. He served in the Municipal Board and was a captain in the Singapore Volunteer Corps. He was also active in raising funds for the war effort in China and agitated vigorously for the boycott of Japanese goods in Singapore. He evacuated Singapore on February 11, 1942, four days before Singapore fell to the invading Japanese army, and died when his ship was sunk by Japanese planes off Pompong Island in Rhio. He was survived by his wife, the daughter of the police commisioner of Shanghai. According to C.C. Tan, a contemporary of Tan Sim Boh and now a senior member of the bar, Sim Boh was a brilliant lawyer and was the second Chinese advocate to appear in the Supreme Court, the first being Wee Thiam Tew (1866–1918).

A portrait of Pang Teck Joon and a view of the house in 1967.
Note the *ji-ho* above the front entrance and the typical
detailing of the front verandah.

Pang Teck Joon, born in Malacca, came to Singapore as a child with his mother after his father's death. According to his grandaughter, Madam Pang Siew Peck, Pang Teck Joon never received a formal education. A Baba Chinese, he was fluent in Malay and learnt Chinese from a neighbour who accepted chicken eggs in payment. He became so proficient in that language that he translated Chinese mythology, including the legend of Madam White Snake, into Peranakan Malay; the books became bestsellers. He worked as a store-keeper for Getz Brothers and later for Henry Waugh & Company until his retirement. He invested wisely in property and eventually became a successful property developer. He died in this house at Scotts Road in 1927, aged 84 years. He fathered three daughters and a son, Pang Cheng Kiat, who was a second cousin of Pang Cheng Yan, father-in-law of Lim Kim San, who was a minister in the Singapore government in the 1960s and 1970s.

The house is typical of the period, the influence of the eclecticism of the 1890s being evident. The Chineseness of the entrance doors and windows was typical of the houses designed by its architect, Moh Wee Teck, who was also responsible for Madam Teo Hong Beng's House at Kerbau Road (c. 1905), and Seah Song Seah's at River Valley Road (1896).

The house was demolished in 1980 to make way for the Sheraton Hotel. Before then, it had been partly used as a ballet studio.

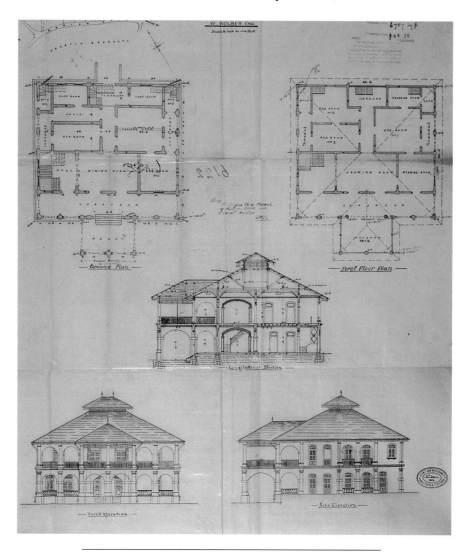

The original building plans of the house.

It is possible, as often happened, that G.C. Wolber built the house on land leased from someone else: For the house was later the home of Dr Noel L. Clarke whose father-in-law, a Captain Daly, had another house also built in 1903 at Napier Road although by a different architect. Wolber was a partner of Hugo Brauss of H. Brauss & Company from 1888 to about 1908 and thereafter until 1915 was assistant manager (export) in Katz Brothers, a German firm that continued into the 1920s. Wolber was not heard of again after 1915. The house is a conventional three-bay example.

Noel Clarke moved into the house about 1930. He was educated at Raffles Institution and received the Queens Scholarship in 1905. He went to Cambridge University from where he graduated in medicine and returned to Singapore in 1909. He was in private practice and was later joined by his younger brother, Farlie, at Raffles Dispensary in Hill Street. He retired in 1938 and settled in Britain where his children were educated. The house, named Harvestehude by Wolber, was changed to Enibertoan by Clarke after his three children, Enid, Bertrand and Joan. Bertrand was head boy at Eton but died tragically in his youth in 1939 of leukemia. He is commemorated on one of the pew seats in St Andrew's Cathedral. Joan Clarke lives in retirement in London and is the only surviving member of the Clarke family.

After the Clarkes left, the house became the Gleneagles Boarding House owned by two European ladies. In 1946 it was purchased by Foo Ah Nam who added a new building on the grounds to establish Gleneagles Hotel in 1956. The British-European Association bought the property and used the new building as a nursing home and the house as staff quarters, naming it Macaulay House in 1959. The home eventually became part of Gleneagles Hospital. The hospital has since changed ownership and is now run by a public company.

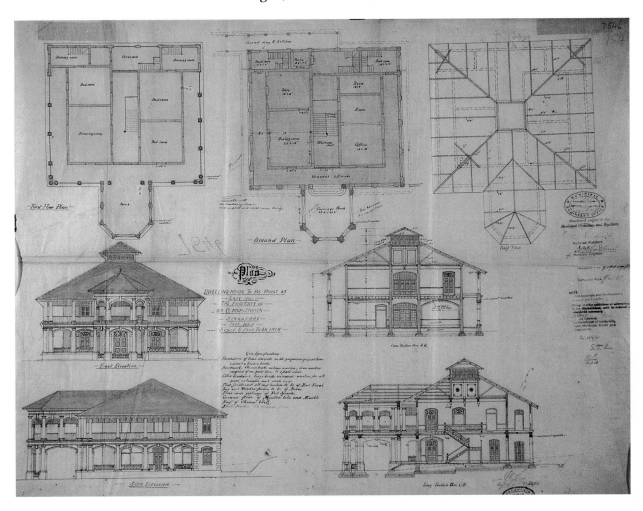

The building plan and an original stained glass window.

The land on which this house was built formed part of the Lady Hill estate owned by Gilbert Angus. From 1856, it was succesively owned by the various partners of Ratenburg, Schmidt & Company until the estate was finally subdivided into building lots from about 1900. Three of the houses built on the lower slopes fronting Nassim Road can be identified — Eden Hall at number. 28, built by E. S. Manasseh in 1909; Fairlie at number. 20, built by T. C. B. Miller in 1903; and Bangor at number. 24. Bangor was built by O. Muhlenbien, a partner in Hartwig & Company (founded circa 1864) since 1900, who purchased the land from Otto Jaegar in 1903. The name of the architect given on the plan is Tan Chin Hin. Cheang Jim Chuan, a son of Cheang Hong Lim, lived in the house for some years. In 1931 he sold the house to the Scheut Mission who still occupy it.

The house has a conventional three-bay plan with a projecting carriage porch and is quite similar to Wolber's house, shown opposite. The dining room is on the ground floor and the drawing room on the the first floor. Open verandahs run continuously along three sides of the house on both levels. The jack-roof, an attractive feature of the house, lights the interior. The variation in column spacing along the side verandahs is the result of the varying room widths.

The front of the house as originally designed.

The career of Teo Hoo Lye was typical of the Chinese immigrants who came to Singapore and Malaya to seek a fortune for themselves. His obituary, published in November 1933, tells the story of his life:

The story of how a man commenced life on a miserable pittance of $2 a month and rose to be the owner of sago factories and steamers describes in a nutshell the life of Mr Teo Hoo Lye who died this morning at his palatial residence in Dhoby Ghaut.

Mr Teo Hoo Lye was 81 years of age and was ailing for about a month. He leaves behind three sons and two daughters, and a host of grandchildren and great-grand children. His wife pre-deceased him about two weeks ago.

Mr Teo Hoo Lye was born in China and came to Singapore 63 years ago and commenced work on $2 a month. Possessing the acumen of a shrewd businessman, he soon saw an opening for his talent. He went to the Anamba and Natuna Islands where he established Chops (a term for Chinese-owned businesses).

Success crowned his efforts from the very outset and he enlarged his business, opening sago factories in Cebu and Sarawak. Singapore was the base of his operations and he had a Chop here in Beach Road, under the style of Chop Soon Bee.

A little over 5 years ago, Mr Teo extended the scope of his business and ran a steamer, the Little Banka. This effort met with disaster for the steamer was subsequently lost. Undaunted by this setback, he continued to press this branch of his activities forward and at the date of his death he owned no fewer than 14 steamers.

In 1929 Mr Teo Hoo Lye commenced the educational institute which bears his name and which to-day has 400 boys. He was one of the founders of the Chinese Chamber of Commerce and remained a member of the Committee until 15 years ago. He was also one of the founders of the Sze Hai Tong Bank (now the Four Seas Communication Bank), in which he owns several shares.

The reserved man that he was, Mr Teo Hoo Lye chose to live a simple life and refrained whole-heartedly from entering the realms of politics. His bungalow at Dhoby Ghaut took three years to construct and cost him over $300,000. He was a naturalised British subject.

The house shown here was originally built as a simple building of five bays with front and rear verandahs and a pair of semi-octagonal sitting verandahs at the front corners that were topped by a pair of Renaissance domes. The architects were Swan & Maclaren.

Extensive additions were carried out later at the front and sides. The postcards, of circa 1915 and 1920, show the building after the extensions had been completed. The front portion was then occupied by Louis Molteni who had worked as a confectioner for M. Gorsky at number. 1 Stamford Road (The Sailors' Home in the 1880s and the site of the present Capital cinema). He started on his own at 387 Victoria Street and moved to Teo Hoo Lye's house in 1917. He seems to have vanished after 1921.

The Teo Hoo Lye Institute mentioned in the obituary occupied part of the house for a time. Before then, according to a member of the family, there was another school in the building, the Royal English School. The house was demolished in 1939 when the present Cathay Cinema and flats were built by Loke Wan Tho. The flats became the headquarters of Lord Louis Mountbatten, Commander in Chief, Southeast Asia Command, in 1945.

Two views of Mr Teo's house in postcards circa 1920 (top) and 1915 (above). The house was extensively renovated over time and became commercial premises. It was demolished in 1939 to build Cathay Cinema. The portrait of Mr Teo is circa 1918.

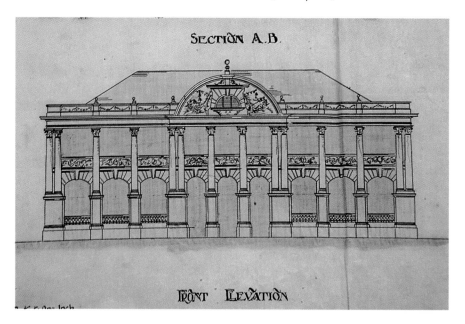

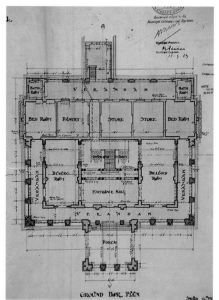
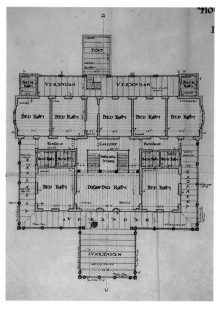

The front elevation and floor plans from the original building plans.

Ezekial Saleh Manasseh was the proprietor of S. Manasseh & Company "Gunny Rice and Opium Merchants", founded by S. Manasseh of Calcutta prior to 1883. Some Manasseh family members were partners of the firm between 1896 and 1921 while a non-relative, Saul Jacob Nathan, was a partner from 1885 to 1912. From 1922 until his death around 1945, E. S. Manasseh was sole proprietor.

The land on which the house stood was part of the original land grant No. 17 issued in 1848 to Gilbert Angus who was to acquire White House Park four years later. In 1856 Angus sold the land, subsequently known as Lady Hill estate, to Frederick George Schmidt, one of the founders in 1849 of Ratenburg, Schmidt & Company. The prevalence of German names in the subsequent title deeds connected with the property is intriguing. Most, such as Adolphe Emil Schmidt, Franz Kusterman and Conrad Sturzenegger, were directors of Ratenburg, Schmidt & Company.

Manasseh built this house before he bought the land. Soon after he built another house close by,

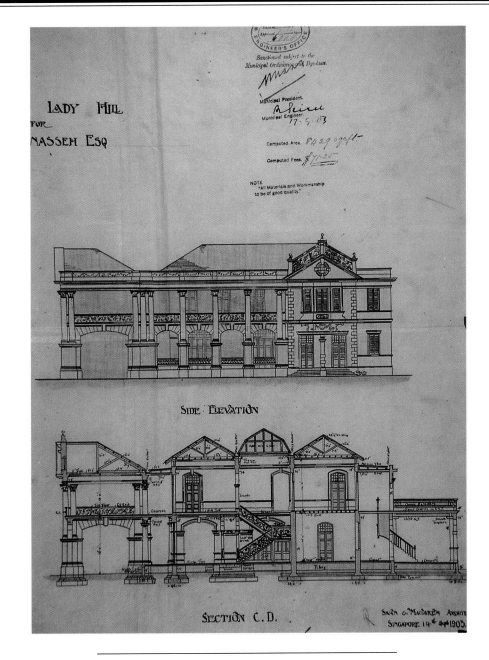

The side elevation and section are also from the original
building plans.

Eden Hall, now the residence of the British High Commissioner, on land that was owned by his partner Saul Jacob Nathan. Nathan had bought the land in 1903 and sold it to Manasseh in 1912.

It is possible that Manasseh lived in the Ladyhill house after its completion, for Eden Hall was let to a Mrs. Cambell immediately after its completion. Mrs. Cambell, who ran a boarding house, remained in occupation until the Manassehs moved in about 1917 or 1918, presumably from the house at Ladyhill which is no longer standing.

The house was designed in the Grand Manner as was Mount Echo nine years later by the same architects, Swan & Maclaren. It is an early example of the influence of Edwardian Classical Revival in domestic architecture. The symmetry and high curved pediment of the entrance elevation and the use of double-storey columns on tall pedestals enhanced the formal dignity of the building. The elevational treatment is highly decorative with simulated stonework and plaster relief on the walls, roof parapets and the pediment of the front elevation.

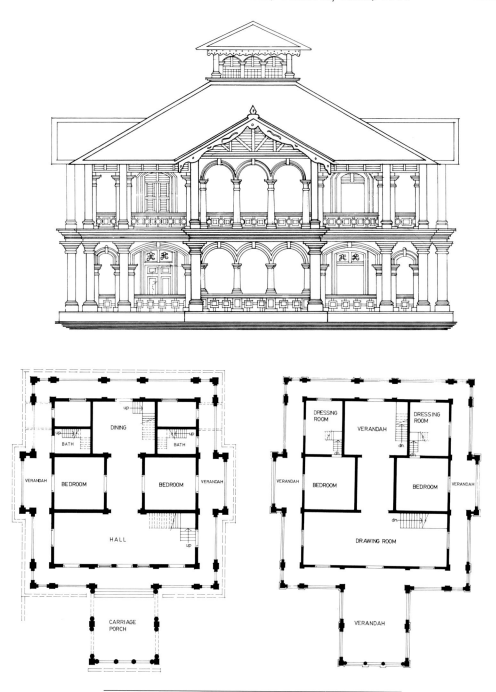

Measured drawings of the elevation and plans of the house.

The Siak royal family had business connections with Singapore that dated back to the 1850s and owned property in Singapore as well. Their house, designed by Wan Mohammed Kassim, architect, was conventional in its three bay plan and symmetry.

Verandahs entirely surrounded the house on both levels. The ground floor of the main house contained a front hall connected to a dining room at the rear by a corridor with bedrooms on either side. Bathrooms at the rear were situated immediately below the dressing rooms. The first floor drawing room and front verandah were above the ground floor hall and carriage porch. The front verandah gable was originally adorned with decorative eaves boards or valances.

The house was demolished in 1985.

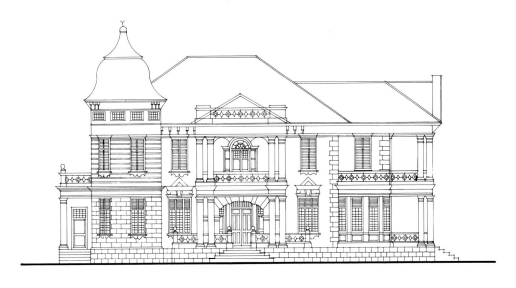

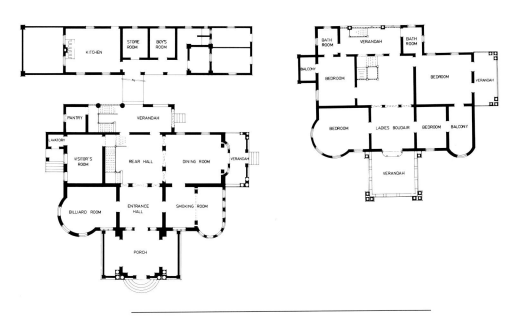

Measured drawings of the elevation and plans of the house.

This house still stands on a hill, once known as Mount Washington, which commands a magnificent view of the sea at Pasir Panjang. It was built by Tan Boo Liat, grandson of Tan Kim Ching and great-grandson of Tan Tock Seng, the well-known founder of the hospital that still bears his name. The family had business connections with Thailand that date back to Tan Kim Ching when he first established rice mills in Thailand, Vietnam and elsewhere. He was appointed consul and special commissioner for Siam and held a title conferred upon him by the King of Siam. He built a family house, Siam House, that stood at the corner of North Bridge Road and Coleman Street on the same site as Miss Takoyee Manuk's house which he demolished. Tan Boo Liat continued to live in Siam House after his grandfather's death in 1892 (his father, Tan Soon Toh, pre-deceased his own father), for his house at Pender Road was not built until about 1909.

The house is a simple three-bay structure in plan but unusual in the asymmetrical elevation treatment and absence of a carriage porch. The projecting verandahs to the dining room and bedroom above face the best view. The architect was Moh Wee Teck. Sun Yat Sen, according to Song Ong Siang, spent a night in the house during a visit to Singapore. The house was sold after Tan Boo Liat's death in Shanghai in 1934, aged 60 years. The house is now owned by a building contractor.

The front of the house photographed in 1971.

The house in the photograph above is the second to stand on the site. It was built in 1911 by the Hongkong and Shanghai Bank who bought the property in 1882 from the estate of John Fraser. The history of the property, however, goes back to the 1830s. The first Mount Echo and its grounds were described in an advertisement in April of 1863 in glowing terms:

That magnificent and spacious Dwelling House in Tanglin district, lately occupied by Joacquim d'Almeida, Esq. The house is situated on a Hill commanding a fine view of the Country around and likewise of the Harbour. It is only about 20 minutes drive to Commercial Square, and is particularly cool from its construction and elevation.

The property possesses excellent outhouses and stabling and has a variety of exquisite flowers and plants in the Gardens in front and on both sides of the house, with a lawn neatly laid out in front with shrubs and trees.

The whole of the ground, which contains an area of about 30 acres, is planted out with a variety of fruit trees and some nutmeg trees...

As mentioned, the house belonged to Joaquim d'Almeida, son of the well-known Dr Jose d'Almeida and father of George d'Almeida, an architect and engineer. It was advertised for sale a year before Jose d'Almeida & Sons failed as a result of a world trade depression that began in 1858 and continued into the 1860s.

This house, which can be seen in the background of the photograph on the far right bottom of the facing page, was a typical colonial bungalow possibly built in the 1840s. It had an open verandah with balustrades spanning the front. The centre bay was projected to form a carriage porch with a flight of steps leading up to the house. The house was raised on brick pedestals with Tuscan columns that supported the roof at the outer edge of the verandah.

The original house was demolished by the Hongkong and Shanghai Bank who built a new Mount Echo, designed by Swan & Maclaren, a building of formal symmetry. The porch, entrance hall and the main central hall and staircase were along the central axis. On the ground floor, the study, billiard room and service area were on one side and the dining room, ante-room and drawing room on the other. Verandahs and loggias flanked the building. On the first floor were four large bedrooms. The house departed from the traditional arrangement of placing the drawing room on the upper level.

The facade was essentially Renaissance inspired. The rusticated base combined with the Ionic columns lent a measure of dignity to the building. The property was sold to a development company in 1974 and demolished in 1986.

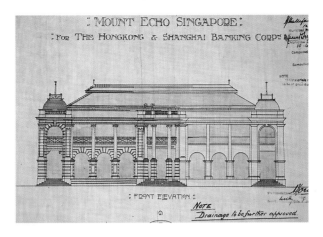

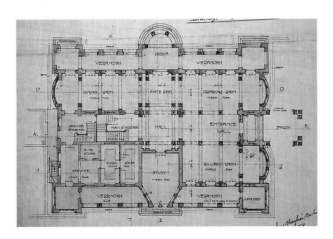

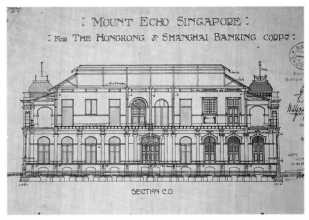

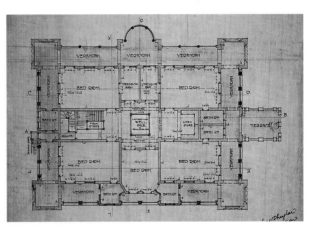

The elevations and floor plans are from the original building plans. The two photographs show Hong Kong & Shanghai Bank staff posing in front of the house.

The exterior of the house photographed circa 1950 and the
upstairs sitting room photographed in 1927.

This house was probably built soon after Thomas Oxley began disposing of the lands within his estate. Henry Heweton, chief clerk of the land department and later municipal secretary, was the owner and occupier of the house in about 1860 and could have built it as well. He moved to Orchard Road and William Renshaw George occupied the house from 1861 until his death in 1873. The next known tenant was Bennett Pell who introduced the telephone to Singapore. When Chia Keng Chin purchased the house in 1917, it was occupied by the Russian Consulate.

Chia Keng Chin (1887–1975) worked for the Mercantile Bank like his father, Chia Hood Thiam, who was head shroff, or chief cashier, throughout his working life. Keng Chin raised a family of nine children, including two sons, Boon Ho and Boon Swee. The family sold the house in 1962 and a block of flats stands now on the site.

The house was rectangular in form with open verandahs along the sides and projecting at the front and rear. The timber posts supporting the roof eaves at the front, seen in the photograph, were a later addition and were repeated at the rear. This was unusual as most such extensions were along the sides, as at Cairnhill and Broadfields.

A view of the house in the 1930s is complemented by
photographs from the Chia family albums.

Rosedale was the house of Chia Hood Thiam, eldest son of Chia Leong Chuan who was head shroff, or chief cashier, of the Mercantile Bank for many years. Hood Thiam attended Raffles Institution, joined the Mercantile Bank, and later succeeded his father as head shroff. Two of his four sons, Chia Keng Chin, who lived at Grasslands, and Keng Tye, became the third generation to work for the bank. Keng Tye, who stayed in Rosedale after his father's death, was a good tennis player and skilled violinist, rare accomplishments in his day.

The architect of the house is not known and the date of the house is uncertain. Its appearance and the projecting carriage porch, seen in the photograph, suggest that the house had a conventional three-bay plan. Conventional, too, was the treatment of the front elevation where the ground floor had open verandahs. The projecting verandahs was enclosed by timber louvred windows that continued on the sides. The side bays have timber louvred windows with fanlights. The house was demolished in 1972 when a housing estate, Devonshire Court, was built by Hong Leong Holdings. Dr. Chia Chin Tiong, the eldest son of Chia Keng Tye, and his family were the last occupants of the house. The photographs are from family albums.

The house photographed circa 1919 and elevations from the
original building plans.

The house known as Eu Villa stood on a hill in one of the earliest residential areas. We have only William Flint's word that he obtained permission in 1819 from his brother-in-law Sir Stamford Raffles to occupy Mount Sophia where in 1822 he built a house. In the sketch of the waterfront drawn in 1823 (page 16), Philip Jackson referred to the hill as Mount Sophia and from this, the earliest known reference, there can be little doubt that the hill was named after Lady Sophia Raffles and not Sophia Cook or Sophia Blackmore as some believe. Flint continued to live on Mount Sophia until he left Singapore on September 20, 1828 on long leave. Just 13 days later, on October 3, he died at sea off the China coast.

Mount Sophia was later sold to Charles Robert Prinsep who had earlier bought the adjacent hill, Bukit Cawa (now Mount Emily), from William Farquhar in 1831. Prinsep's 217 acres estate was advertised for sale in 1859 and by the 1860s the estate had been broken up and the land parcelled out — including Mount Sophia and the large grounds of Government House, now the Istana — to the various purchasers.

It is not known how long Flint's house survived but by 1880 there were already a number of houses on the hill and the most prominent of them all was

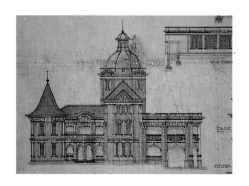

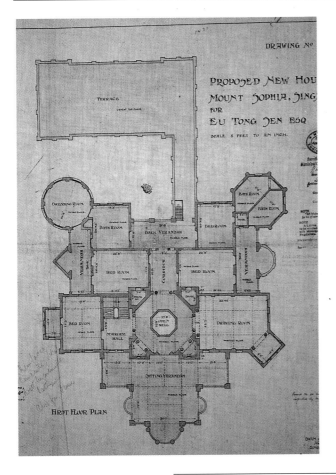

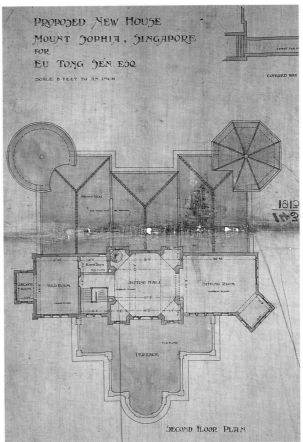

The floor plans and an elevation from the original building plans.

Carrington House. It was demolished in 1904, after N.N. Adis purchased it, to build Adis Lodge. Eu Tong Sen purchased Adis Lodge in 1912. By that time it had become a lodging house. Eu lived in the house until 1914 when he demolished it to build Eu Villa which remained the residence of the Eu family until 1973. It was sold to a development company and demolished in the early 1980s.

Eu Tong Sen was born in Penang in 1877. His father, Eu Kong, was a prominent tin miner in Perak, Malaysia. He founded Eu Yan Sang, a company dealing in Chinese medicine which is in business today. Eu Tong Sen was sent to China for his education but returned to Malaya in 1891, shortly after the sudden and unexpected death of his father. He expanded the family business and by the time he was 30 years old had become one of the richest merchants in the region. He died in 1940.

The house, designed by Swan & Maclaren, was one of the largest in the colony. The five-storey building included a sub-basement which accommodated the kitchen and a wine cellar. The floors of the house were in reinforced concrete supported on concrete beams that were carried on load-bearing brick piers and walls. The main living areas were in the front of the building and had a magnificent view of the harbour and town. Bedrooms were at the rear.

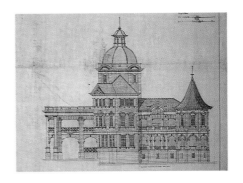

The Cashin house in Pongol, J.W. Cashin, and the side
elevation of a house built for A. W. Cashin at Rochalie Drive
in 1916. Note the Dutch gable and gambrel roof under which is
the clerestorey above the dining area.

The name Cashin goes back to the early 1840s when Charles Cashin was a special constable with the Singapore Police Force. His son, Joseph William Cashin (1843-1907), started his career as a lawyer's clerk in 1867. During his long career he worked for some of the best known barristers of the time, including A.G. Baumgarten, Alexander Gotlieb, Edwin Keok and J.P. Joachim. He also invested in property and in 1880 made his first large investment in a coconut estate of 100 acres that bordered Tanjong Katong Road, Geylang Road and East Coast Road. In 1887, he purchased 40 acres of land at Grange Road and by 1901 he had acquired another 100 acres at Bukit Timah Road, 50 acres at Serangoon and 64 acres at Ponggol.

Cashin retired in 1897 and in 1905 became a

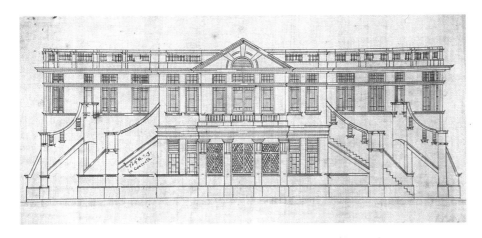

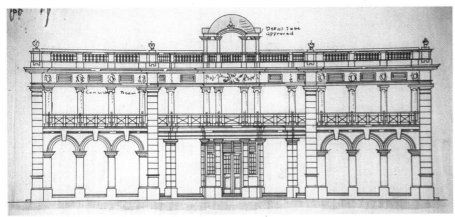

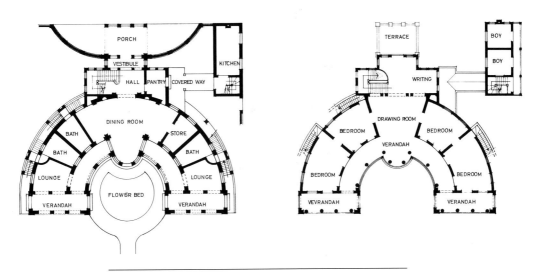

Elevations and plans of the house lived in by D. Kitowitz. It is
the only known house based on the "butterfly plan".

partner in an opium and spirit farm. He lived in his Geylang estate where in 1880 he built a house that was to be the family home until the outbreak of the war in 1941. His son A.W. Cashin, (1876-1947) continued to look after the estates while managing the opium and spirit farm. He increased his property holdings and extended the Ponggol and Serangoon estates to over 400 acres by further purchases. His

two sons, Howard and Joseph, are well-known lawyers in Singapore.

The Cashin family owned a number of houses. The Pongol residence, opposite top, was used to film the BBC television serial "Tangko". It was acquired by the government in the mid-1980s. The house above was given by A.W. Cashin to his brother-in-law D. Kitowitz and is still standing at Amber Road.

Tan Soon Guan photographed circa 1919. The house shown
above, built in 1925, was the second on the property. The first,
below, has a roof parapet and faced the seafront.

Tan Soo Guan was the son of Tan Jiak Chuan
(1858–1909) and the grandson of Tan Beng Gum,
who was himself one of the sons of Tan Kim Seng
who built Panglima Prang. The house on the right
was built in about 1914 and the two-storey house
above in 1925. The grounds of the estate originally
extended from the sea to the East Coast Road. The
houses are still standing and are still occupied by
family members.

The house from the front garden, the banister, and the
front verandah, all photographed in 1967.

A plan submitted for the erection of a fence wall
in 1914 suggests that the house was built before then.
Although the plans were signed by Regent Bidwell,
it is doubtful if he designed the house as well. The
Allen family occupied the house until about 1970.
According to Mrs. Allen, the house was originally
owned by a Chinese towkay. If Bidwell had a hand in
the design it was only the staircase.

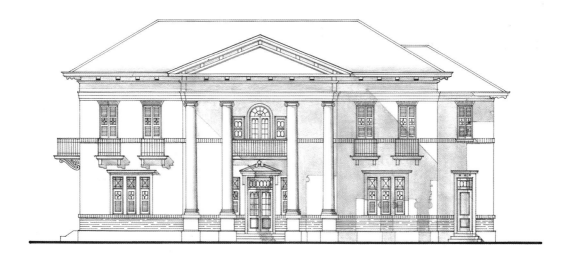

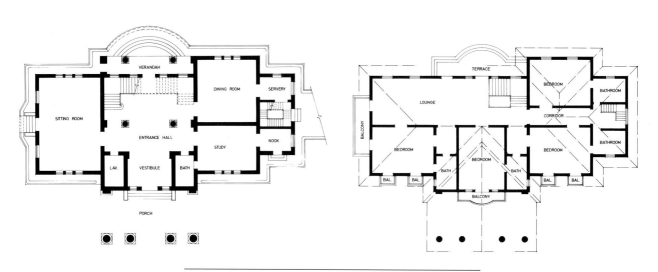

The elevation and plans of the house are measured drawings.

Dr. Yin Suat Chuan was born in Amoy, China in 1877. He received his schooling at the Anglo-Chinese College, Foochow and came to Singapore in 1898 to work as a court interpreter. In the following year he left on a private scholarship for the University of Michigan in the United States to study medicine, but completed his training at Toronto University, Canada. He obtained his post-graduate degree at University College, London in 1904. After working in London he returned to Singapore to join his brother-in-law, Dr. Lim Boon Keng, in private practice. He married Lydia Bowyer of London in 1905 and among his children are Canon Roy Yin of St. Andrew's Cathedral and Leslie Chartaris, the well-known novelist.

The front of the building is symmetrical but for the location of the bathrooms, servery and stairs at the side. The lounge on the first floor could have been used as a drawing room or family room. The outhouse is located to the side and the view of the rear garden from the main house is not obstructed.

The house has an imposing double storey portico in the Roman Ionic Order arranged tetrastyle prostyle. The glazing beads of the windows are cross patterned. The balusters of the balconies are cast iron uprights. The Ionic entablature is without decoration except for the mutules and guttae on the underside of the corona. The house bears some resemblance to John Jay Chapman's residence at Barrytown, New York built in 1914. Both could have been inspired by the White House in Washington D.C. completed in 1800.

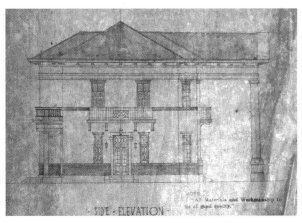

Dr S.C. Yin circa 1919, a side elevation from the original
building plans and a photograph of the house taken in 1986.

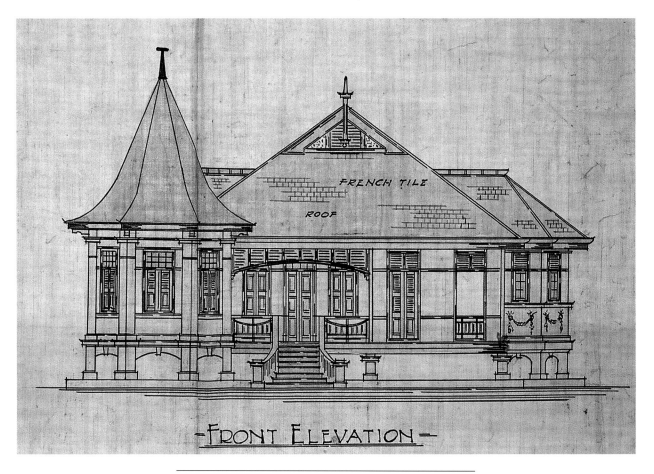

— FRONT ELEVATION —

FRENCH TILE

ROOF

A variety of houses with turrets. The earliest (opposite bottom right) is dated 1909 and the latest (opposite left, second from top) is dated 1929. Chee Soon Keng's house (opposite right, second from top) is a typical example.

The steeple became popular in the 1920s and continued to be adopted in the 1930s. In the house above the steeple lent emphasis to the asymmetrical front. The house was raised on brick piers and was constructed partly of load-bearing brick walls and partly of timber framing with half-brick infill. Other examples of houses with steeples of varying proportions are shown on the opposite page. The earliest known example, far right bottom, was designed by George d'Almeida in 1911. One of particular interest, second row right, belonged Chee Soon Keng.

Chee Soon Keng, a businessman and land proprietor, was a well-known racing figure involved in the Singapore Turf Club in the days before the Pacific War. He built two identical houses at Tanglin Road, living in one and renting the other to Vivian Ignatius Evan Wong, chartered accountant, from 1935 until 1944. Wong was born in 1901 in British Guiana. He was educated at Queen's College, British Guiana, New York University and Cambridge Unviersity. He arrived in Singapore in 1927 and practised under the style of Evan Wong & Company which is now managed by his son, Cecil. Chee Soon Keng's own residence was demolished when his sons developed Tangling Shopping Centre in the 1970s and Evan Wong's a few years later.

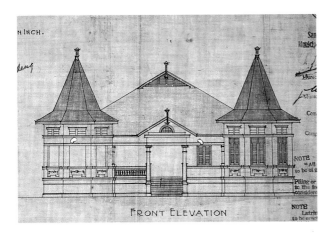

N INCH.

FRONT ELEVATION

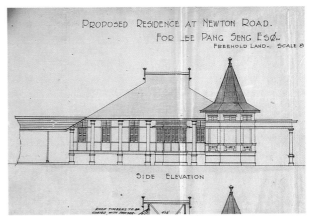

PROPOSED RESIDENCE AT NEWTON ROAD.
FOR LEE PANG SENG ESQ.
FREEHOLD LAND. SCALE 8

SIDE ELEVATION

ROOF TIMBERS TO BE
COATED WITH PRESER-

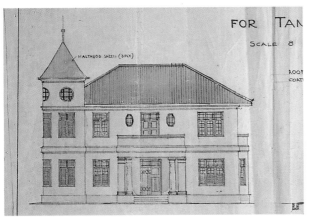

FOR TAN
SCALE 8

MALTHOID SHEETS (3PLY)

ROOF
COAT

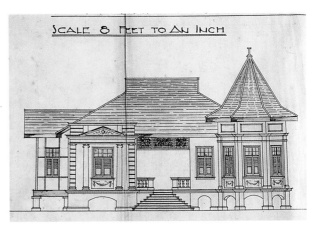

SCALE 8 FEET TO AN INCH

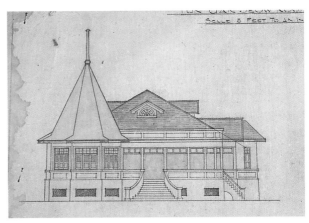

SCALE 8 FEET TO AN IN

ALL ROO
COATED

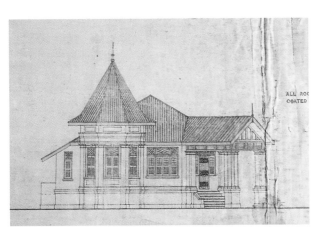

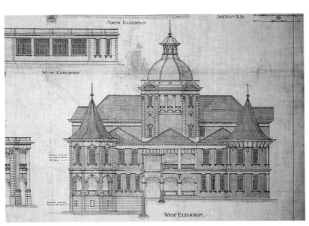

NORTH ELEVATION
SECTION R.B.

WEST ELEVATION

WEST ELEVATION.

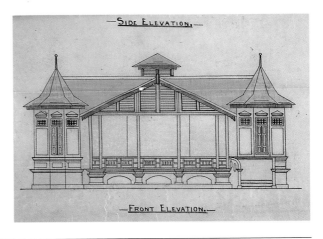

SIDE ELEVATION.

FRONT ELEVATION.

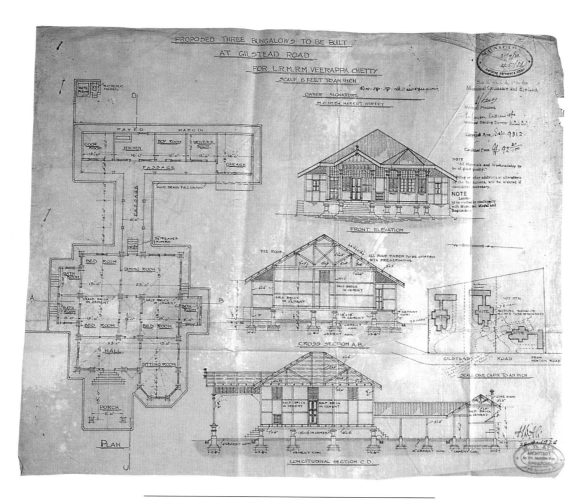

The original building plan for Veerapa Chitty's house.

Here is a 1920s bungalow typical of the kind that proliferated particularly in the suburbs or Katong, Geylang and Serangoon. Built on brick piers, the bungalow walls are entirely timber-framed with half-brick infill. The front hall roof was extended over the carriage porch. Timber lattice screens and open timber rail guards above the windows provide additional ventilation.

H.D. Ali, the architect of the house, was in practice from 1921 until the 1950s, according to Lee Fei Hoong. Like most of his contemporaries, he probably received his training while working as a draughtsman in an architect's office.

The house has been demolished.

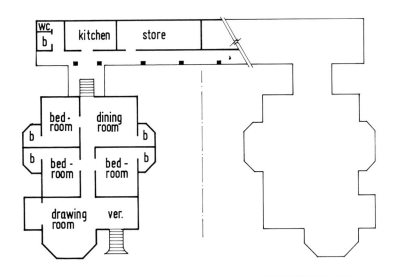

A photograph of one of the Poole Road houses and a
measured drawing of the plan

These modest houses are somewhat unusual because their outhouses are joined. In other respects the plans are conventional. The two units are identical and sited with one entrance verandah facing the other. The plan and elevations are symmetrical but for the steps placed at the side and the projection of the enclosed verandah at the front and one side.

The houses were built by Lau Chung Kui, a building contractor, who also built and owned three other houses and one pair of semi-detached houses at Poole Road. His family still occupies the houses. The architect was Kwan Yow Luen.

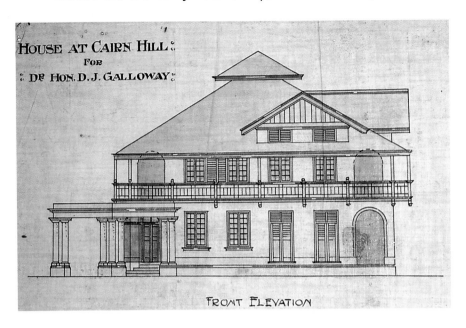

The front elevation from the original building plans. Dr D.J. Galloway , and S.Q. Wong. Photographed below at the 1939 St Andrew's Ball are S.Q Wong, Mrs Lee Choon Guan and Lee Chin Hak, the author's father.

This is one of three identical houses built for David James Galloway, who was born in 1858 in Edinburgh. He graduated from Edinburgh University in 1884, came to Singapore in 1895 and worked at the Dispensary under Dr. John Hutchinson Robertson. In 1897 he started his own clinic, the British Dispensary. A well-known figure, he served in the Legislative Council from 1907 to 1911 and from 1922 to 1923. Knighted by the British government for his public service, he retired in the mid-1930s.

It is not known if Galloway ever lived in any of the three houses. One was bought by the late Dato Wong Siew Quee (1888–1980). S. Q. Wong, as he was known, was one of the five sons of Wong Ah Fook. Born in Singapore, he was educated at Raffles Institution and at Blundell's School, Devonshire, and Jesus College, University of Cambridge. He was called to the Bar from Middle Temple, London in 1910 and was appointed Attorney General of Kwangtung Province in China but returned to Singapore in about 1913. Dato Wong served on the Municipal Board in the 1930s and was director of many public companies including the Overseas Chinese Banking Corporation, the largest Singapore bank. He received his title, Dato, for services to the Johore state government where he served on the State Council for many years. He moved to this house in 1925 where he raised six sons and six daughters. The house was demolished in 1988.

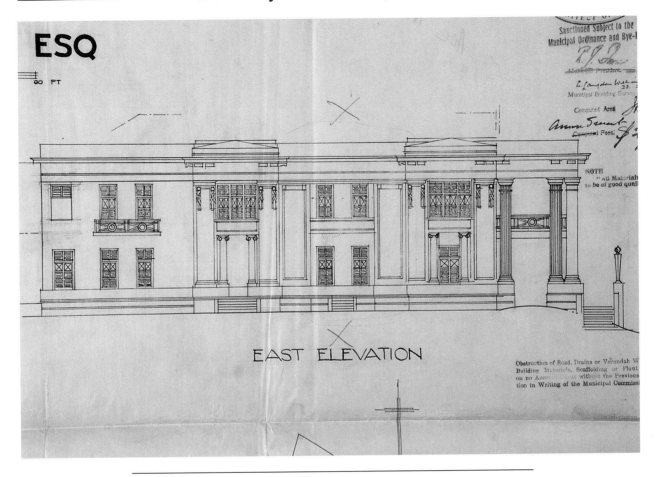

ESQ

EAST ELEVATION

The elevations of the house are from the original building plans.

J. B. David was a local-born Jewish businessman. According to his nephew, A. M. Gareh, David was working for a British engineering firm in 1914, selling mining equipment and machinery. Though short, his good-looks, European features and obvious talents, gave him a decided advantage in dealing with European customers. Soon after, he established his own agency business. He ventured into prospecting in Malaya and Thailand and eventually owned mines as well as becoming a rubber planter. He was adversely affected by the Great Depression but survived. During World War Two he was interned by the Japanese and died in 1946 in Calcutta while on his way to the United Kingdom for medical treatment. He was a bachelor and was survived by two brothers and two sisters.

The front portico columns are two storeys in height and arranged tetrastyle in antis between two corner piers along the front. Triglyphs are absent from the freize. The entablature was, on the whole, plain and without ornamentation. The balusters on the upper storey verandahs were of cast iron or bronze and crossed diagonally, a motif repeated in the glazing beads of the windows. The double-storey arrangement of the portico columns was also used in the verandah adjoining the billiard room. Wall surfaces were in white stucco; the pilasters had pairs of fasces below the capitals. The house once formed part of the Cockpit Hotel.

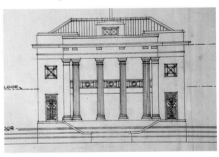

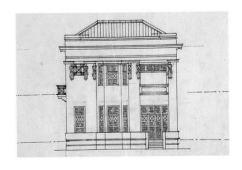

A variety of east coast bungalows. All are symmetrical with front verandahs except the larger house on the top which has a car porch.

Katong, Geylang and Siglap developed into residential suburbs in the first four decades of this century, and especially after World War One. Many modest houses were built on small plots of land in the lorongs off Geylang Road, around Joo Chiat. and Tanjong Katong Roads, and further east. Larger homes lined Mountbatten and East Coast Roads while comfortable holiday bungalows dotted the coast. The houses built in these areas are not characterised by any particular style. Those built in the 1930s are in concrete. Decorative elements applied were those fashionable at the time.

More modest bungalows and an elaborate gate to the Villa
Dolce. All are on the east coast except the house dated 1918
(middle left) which is in Pasir Panjang.

An early black-and-white house in Nassim Road (above). Access to the first floor
is by a staircase behind the lattice screen on the right. The other houses, built
between 1910 and the 1930s, include a Tropical Art Deco pair (opposite bottom).

The Mock Tudor or "Black-and-White" style was popular with government architects in the first four decades of the century. Early examples, such as the one above, are symmetrical in plan with three bays across the front. There is a carriage porch below a projecting first floor verandah. Some of the later houses are technically bungalows although two storeys in height. Long, narrow and of single room depth, the houses were built on sloping ground. The ground floor contains an entrance hall with a stairway. On the first floor, the rooms are arranged between continuous verandahs along both the front and the back of the house. The main house is linked to an outhouse on top of the slope. In the 1930s, the Mock Tudor gave way to the so-called Tropical Art Deco style, with a streamlined appearance and flat roofs.

Many black-and-white houses are still standing. Owned by the government, they are rented out.

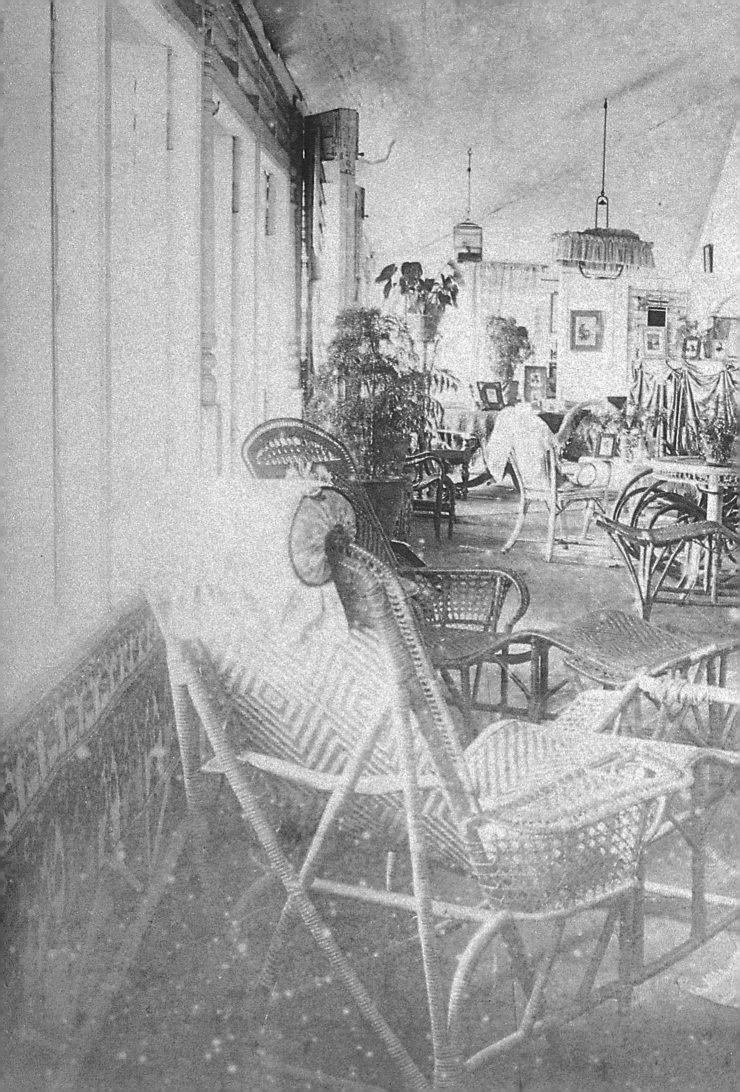

THE

APPENDICES

SELECTED BIBLIOGRAPHY

Official Documents
Straits Settlement Records
Building Plans, 1884-1941, in the National Archives collection

Newspapers
The Daily Times
The Malaya Tribune
The Singapore Chronicle
The Singapore Free Press
The Straits Times

Periodicals
Journal of the Malayan Branch of the Royal Asiatic Society
The Malayan Architect, Journal of the Institute of Architects of Malaya
The Straits Times Annual

Books and Articles
ASLET, Clive and Powers, Alan, *The National Trust Book of the English House*, Penguin (U.K., 1985).
BUCKLEY,Charles B., *An Anecdotal History of Old Times in Singapore*, (F&N 2 vol. 1902, reprinted Kuala Lumpur 1965).
CAMERON, John, *Our Tropical Possessions in Malayan India*, Elder Smith (U.K., 1865).
CRAWFURD, John, *Journal of an Embassy to Siam*, Henry Colburn (U.K.,1828).
DAVEY, Peter, *Arts and Crafts Architecture*, The Architectural Press (U.K.,1980).
DAVIDSON, G.F., *Trade and Travel in the Far East*, Madden & Malcolm (U.K.,1846).
DIXON, Roger and Muthesius, Stephen, *Victorian Architecture*, Oxford University Press, (U.K., 1978).
DOGGETT, Marjorie, *Characters of Light*, Donald Moore (Singapore, 1957).
FELDWICK, W. (ed.), *Present Day Impressions of the Far East*, The Globe Encyclopedia Company, (U.K.,1917).
MACMILLAN, W.H. and Collingridge, L. (eds.),*Seaports of the Far East*, (U.K.,1923).
FLETCHER, Sir Banister, *A History of Architecture*, The Athelone Press (U.K.,1961).
HITCHCOCK, Henry Russell, *The Pelican History of Art*, Penguin Books (U.K.,1982).
JACKSON, James C., *Planters and Speculators*, University of Malaya Press (Kuala Lumpur, 1968).
LAVIENT, Michael (ed.), *The Cree Journals*, Webb & Bower (U.K.,1981).
LIANG, Ssu-Cheng, (ed. Wilma Fairbank), *A Pictorial History of Chinese Architecture*, Massachusetts Institute of Technology (Boston, 1984).
LLOYD, Nathaniel, *History of the English House*, The Architectural Press (U.K.,1975).
MAKEPEACE, Walter, *One Hundred Years of Singapore*, J. Murray (U.K.,1921).
NORRIS, George, "Singapore Thirty Years Ago", *The Straits Times*, Straits Times Press (Singapore, 1878).
PEARSON,H.F., *A History of Singapore*, University of London Press (London,1956).
RAFFLES, Lady Sophia, *Memoir of the Life and Public Services of Sir Stamford Raffles*, J. Murray (U.K.,1830).
RASMUSSEN, Steen Eiler, *London the Unique City*, Jonathan Cape (U.K.,1948).
SERVICE, Alastair, *Edwardian Architecture*, Thames and Hudson (U.K.,1977).
SHERRY, Norman, *Conrad's Eastern World*, Cambridge University Press (Cambridge,1966).
SIM, Victor, *Biographies of Prominent Chinese in Singapore*, Nan Kok Publication Company (Singapore, date unknown).
SIMPSON, Duncan, *C.F.A. Voysey: An Architect of Individuality*, Watson-Guptill Publications (New York,1979).
SONG Ong Siang, *One Hundred Years' History of the Chinese in Singapore*, John Murray (U.K., 1923).
THOMSON, J.T., *Glimpses into Life in Malayan Lands*, Richardson & Co. (U.K.,1864).
TYRES, R.K., *Singapore Then and Now*, University Education Press (Singapore, 1976).
WATKIN, David, *The Buildings of Britain*, Regency, Barrie & Jenkins Ltd (U.K., 1982).
WITTKOWER, Rudolph, *Palladio and English Palladianism*, Thames & Hudson (U.K.,1980).
WRIGHT, A. and Cartwright, H.A. (eds.), *Twentieth Century Impressions of British Malaya*, Lloyds Greater Britain Publishing Co.(U.K.,1908).
WURTZBURG,C.E., *Raffles of the Eastern Isles*, Hodder & Stoughton (U.K., 1954).

Cover and frontispiece Lee Kip Lin
Endpapers, 8-9 Lee Kip Lin
10-11 The Choa family
12-13 The Chia family
14-15 The Chia family
16-18 Lee Kip Lin
19 National Library
20-21 Lee Kip Lin
22 Keng Ah Wong (top, middle and bottom right)/Frank Marciano (middle left)/Dr Teoh (bottom left)
23 Lee Hin Ming (top)/the Tan family (middle left)/Frank Marciano (bottom left)/ *Twentieth Century Impressions*
24-25 Lee Kip Lin
26-29 National Museum
30 Dr John Hall-Jones
31 National Museum
32-36 Lee Kip Lin
37 Lee Kip Lin (top)/second row from *One Hundred Years of Singapore* and *Twentieth Century Impressions of British Malaya*/ third row Lee Kip Lin and National Museum
38 Top from *Towns and Buildings* by Steen Eiler Rasmussen (London:1951)/bottom from *History of the English House* by Nathanial Lloyd (London:1931)
39 Second row from *History of the English House*/ third row reproduced from *A History of Architecture* by Sir Banister Fletcher, Athelone Press (London:1961)/Lee Kip Lin (bottom)
40 National Museum
41 National Museum (top)/Popperfoto
42 Reproduced from *Old Bungalows in Bangalore* by Janet Potts (London: 1977)
43 National Archives (top left)/Lee Kip Lin (top right)/National Library (bottom)
44-45 Lee Kip Lin
46-47 Top reproduced from *History of the English House*/ middle Lee Kip Lin/portrait reproduced from *Twentieth Century Impressions*
48-49 National Archives
50 Lee Kip Lin (top)/ National Museum
51 National University of Singapore Library
52 Lee Kip Lin
53 Private collection
54 Royal Commonweath Society Library
56-57 National Archives (postcards)/Lee Kip Lin (maps)
58 National Museum (top)/Private collection, UK
59-61 National Archives
62 Top from *One Hundred Years of Singapore*/ Ray Tyres collection (middle)/Lee Kip Lin (bottom)
63-70 National Archives
71 National Archives (top)/ Lee Kip Lin
72-73 National Archives
74 Marjorie Doggett collection
75 Keng Ah Wong
76-77 Lee Kip Lin
78 From *One Hundred Years' of the Chinese in Singapore* (top)/National University of Singapore Library
79 Ho Yue Weng
80-82 Lee Kip Lin
83 *Twentieth Century Impressions*
84-85 National Archives
86 Dr John Hall-Jones
87 National Library
88 National Archives
89 Private collection, UK
90 Lee Kip Lin

91 Reproduced from "Traditional Malay House Forms in Trengganu and Kelantan" by Haji Mubin Shepherd, *Journal of the Malayan Branch of the Royal Asiatic Society*, vol XLII, part 2 (Dec. 1969)
92-93 Ho Yue Weng
94 Private collection
95 Keng Ah Wong
96-97 Lee Kip Lin/Keng Ah Wong (catalogue)
98 Lee Kip Lin
99 The Chia family (middle)/Private collection
100 The Pang family
101 Lee Kip Lin
102 Private collection
103-104 Keng Ah Wong
105 Lee Kip Lin
106 The Pang family
107 Lee Kip Lin
108 Private collection, UK (top)/Lee Kip Lin
109 Popperfoto (top left)/Private collection, Singapore (top right)/Lee Kip Lin (bottom)
110 National Archives (top)/ Private Collection
111 National Archives (top)/Keng Ah Wong
112 The Alkaff family
113 Lee Hin Ming (top)/Lee Kip Lin
114-115 The Chia family
116-117 Lee Kip Lin (top)/the Cashin family
118 Lee Kip Lin
119 National Archives
120-121 Lee Hin Ming/National Archives (top left)
122 National Archives (top)/bottom reproduced from *Edwardian Architecture* by Alistair Street (Thames and Hudson: 1977)
123 Lee Kip Lin
124 National Museum
125 Ho Yue Weng
126-127 Lee Kip Lin/bottom right reproduced from *Present Day Impressions of the Far East* (London, 1917)
129-131 Lee Kip Lin
132-133 National Archives
134-135 Lee Kip Lin
136-137 Ho Yue Weng
138 Lee Kip Lin
139 Lee Kip Lin/ Marjorie Doggett (top left)/ Royal Institute of British Architects, UK (bottom right)
140-141 National Archives
142-143 The Chia family
144 Reproduced from *The Malay Peninsula* by Captain P.J. Begbie
145 Measured drawing by Chang Hong Kam and Lionel de Rozario
146 National Archives
147 Measured drawing by Chang Hong Kam and Lionel de Rozario
148 Dr John Hall-Jones
149 Lee Kip Lin
150 Portrait from *One Hundred Years' of the Chinese in Singapore*/ house from *Twentieth Century Impressions*
151 Portrait from *One Hundred Years' of the Chinese in Singapore*/Nan Chiau School (house)
152 Lee Kip Lin
153 National Museum (watercolour)/ Standard Chartered Bank (photograph)
154 Photograph of house from *Twentieth*

Century Impressions/Lee Kip Lin (floor plan)
155 Portraits from *One Hundred Years' of the Chinese in Singapore*/house Lee Kip Lin, photographed by Chew Studios.
156-157 Lee Kip Lin
158 Lee Kip Lin, photograph taken by Dr C.A. Gibson-Hill
159 *Twentieth Century Impressions*
160 Lee Kip Lin
161 Lee Kip Lin (top)/Ronnie Pinsler (centre)/ the Alsagoff family (bottom)
162 Private collection, Singapore
163 Ronnie Pinsler (top)/National Archives
164 Lee Kip Lin
165 *Twentieth Century Impressions*
166-169 National Museum
170-171 Mrs Helen Bell
172 Lee Kip Lin
173 Lee Kip Lin (top)/the Tan family (bottom)
174 Lee Kip Lin
176 Dr D.H.S. Stephens
177 Mrs Lee Keng Chye
178-179 Mrs Helen Bell
180 Lee Kip Lin
181 National Archives
182 Lee Kip Lin (plans)/photograph from *Twentieth Century Impressions*
183 National Archives
184 Lee Kip Lin
185 Lord Tedder of Glenquin
186 Lee Kip Lin
187-188 *Twentieth Century Impressions*
189 National Archives
190-191 Lee Kip Lin
192 National Archives (elevation)/Lee Kip Lin (floor plans)
193 Mrs Ivy Kwa
194 Lee Kip Lin
195 Lee Kip Lin (house)/Miss Pang Quek Cheng (portrait)
196-201 National Archives
202-204 Lee Kip Lin
205 National Archives (plans)/photographs courtesy of Hongkong and Shanghai Bank
206 Miss Chua Swee Neo
207 The Chia family
208 House from *One Hundred Years' History of the Chinese in Singapore*/National Archives (plans)
209 National Archives
210 Lee Kip Lin (photograph of house)/ portrait courtesy of J.W. Cashin/ National Archives (elevation)
211 National Archives (elevation)/Lee Kip Lin (floor plan)
212 Lee Kip Lin (houses)/*One Hundred Years' History of the Chinese in Singapore* (portrait)
213-214 Lee Kip Lin
215 *One Hundred Years' History of the Chinese in Singapore* (portrait)/National Archives (plan)/ Lee Kip Lin (photograph)
216-218 National Archives
219 Lee Kip Lin
220 National Archives (elevation)/*One Hundred Years of Singapore* (Galloway portrait)/*One Hundred Years' of the Chinese in Singapore* (S.Q. Wong)/Lee Kip Lin
221 National Archives
222 Lee Kip Lin
223 Lee Kip Lin/Ho Yue Weng (middle left and right)
224-225 Ho Yue Weng
226-227 Robert Hussey

ACKNOWLEDGEMENTS

A great many institutions and individuals have helped to make this book possible. The author would like to thank the following for their assistance and support.

Institutions

The National Archives
The National Library
The National Museum
The Land Office
The Registry of Land Titles and Deeds
The Royal Institute of British Architects, UK
The Nan Chiau High School
The Hokkien Huay Kuan
Hong Leong Holdings Limited
Hongkong & Shanghai Banking Corporation
Standard Chartered Bank
Schuet Mission

Individuals (in alphabetical order)

Mr Alwi Alkaff, Mr Mohd Alsagoff, Mrs Hedwig Anuar, Mr and Mrs M.B. Beal, Mrs Helen Bell, Mr James Bettley, Mr and Mrs D. Bloodworth, Mr and Mrs P.A. van Buuren, Mr W.M.H. Caldwell, Dr G.Y. Caldwell, Mr J.W. Cashin, Mr Henry Chen, Madam Chew Teck Neo, Miss Chia Boon Swee, Miss Chia Swee Neo, Miss Mildred Chiok, Associate Professor and Mrs Victor Choa, Miss Yu-Chee Chong, Mrs Choo Buan Hai, Dr David Chua, Mr Chua Teck Meng, Mr Chung Meng Ker, Mr Jimmy Chung Kum Chee, Father Frans De Ridder, Mr W. Dodwell, Mrs Marjorie Doggett, Mr and Mrs Henry Eng, members of the Eu family, Mrs Rosalind Foo, Mr A.M. Gareh, the late Dr. C.A. Gibson-Hill, Miss Angela Goh Beow Kheng, Mr Jean-Paul Guyere, Dr John Hall-Jones, Mrs Norma Handmer, Mr C.D. Harrison, Mr Ho Pak Toe, Mr Albert Hong, Mr Y.K. Hwang, Miss Mary Hui Bee Ngok, Mrs Mabel Hudson, Inche Jaafar bin Ahmad, Inche Suhaimi bin Haji Karim, Mrs Ivy Kwa, Miss Vivien Lai, Miss Lam Mo Lian, Mr Lee Fei Hoong, the late Mr Lee Keng Chye, Mr Lee Seng Gee, Mr Lee Wai Kok, Mr Leong Hong Toh, Miss Leong Wai Ying, Miss Adeline Lim Kim Swan, Mr Arthur Lim Beng Lock, Dr Connie Lim, Mr David Lim Joo Khoon, Dr Lim Joo Lee, Miss Joyce Lim, Mrs Joyce Liu, Miss Loh Heng Noi, Miss Jennifer Low, Mr and Mrs Ng Chong Lim, Mr Paul Notley, Miss Ong Chwee Lay, Miss Pang Quek Cheng, Madam Pang Siew Peck, Mr Gordon Peters, Mrs Rahmah binte Saini, Dr E. J. Seow, Mr John Shaw, Justice and Mrs S Sinnathuray, Mrs Marianne Soh, Dr D.H.S. Stephens, Mr Tan Choon Keng, Tan Jin Thong, Mr Tan Khiong Khoo, Mr Richard Tan Tiang Teck, Baron Tedder of Glenquin, Miss Irene Tay, Mr Tay Kheng Soon, Mr Thia Keng Phor, the late Mr R.K. Tyers, Mrs Tze Swee Ling, Mr William Irving Watson, Mr Wee Sip Chee, Mr Whang Tar Kway, Lady Sheila Whyte, Mr Bobby Wong, Mr Cecil V. Wong, Mrs Hazel Wong, Dr Wong Peng Onn, Mrs Yeo Bee Hong, Eugel Yeo.

I would like to especially thank the following for giving permission to reproduce artwork in their collections: Lord Tedder for the interior sketch of Inverturret by his father on page 185; Associate Professor and Mrs Victor Choa for the oil painting of the house of Choa Kim Keat by Low Kway Soo on pages 10-11; Dr Stephens for the painting of Magenta Cottage on page 176 and the National Museum for the painting of Mandalay Villa on page 124, both by A.L. Watson. And to the Tan family for permission to photograph and measure their house at 37 Kerbau Road and to Dr Lee Peng Hui for helping me to take measurements of the house.

My special thanks to Lily Tan and Connie Sheares for their assistance in obtaining materials and their continual support without which this book would not have seen the light of day.

Last but not least thanks to Gretchen Liu for her careful and conscientious editing and her infectious and encouraging enthusiasm.

Lee Kip Lin
October, 1988